Learn AI Fast: A Practical Guide for Busy Professionals

Dr Naim Tahir Baig

Published by Dr Naim Tahir Baig, 2025.

LEARN AI FAST: A PRACTICAL GUIDE FOR BUSY PROFESSIONALS

First edition. August 20, 2025.

ISBN: 979-8231270972

Written by Dr Naim Tahir Baig.

Table of Contents

Dedication

To the countless professionals around the world who balance learning with living,who seek knowledge while serving others,and who believe that technology should amplify human potential rather than replace it.

To Maria, the grocery store owner who discovered that AI could reduce waste while preserving the personal touch that makes her community stronger.

To Sarah, the teacher who learned that artificial intelligence could break down language barriers without breaking down cultural connections.

To James, the manufacturing worker who found that machine learning could predict equipment failures while enhancing rather than eliminating his expertise.

And to every reader who picks up this book not to escape their humanity,but to enhance their capacity to serve others with wisdom, compassion, and technological fluency.

May this knowledge serve your communities,strengthen your relationships,and contribute to a future where artificial intelligenceamplifies the best of human creativity and connection.

"The goal is not to replace human intelligence with artificial intelligence,but to augment human intelligence with artificial intelligence."

"The future of artificial intelligence is not about machines becoming more human, but about humans becoming more capable—more creative, more connected, more compassionate. AI is not our replacement; it is our amplifier.

In every algorithm, we embed our values. In every dataset, we encode our priorities. In every deployment, we shape tomorrow's possibilities. The question is not whether AI will change the world—it already has. The question is whether we will guide that change toward human flourishing.

True AI literacy means understanding not just how these systems work, but how we work with them. It means knowing when to trust, when to question, and when to choose human wisdom over artificial efficiency. It means building bridges between cultures, generations, and communities so that technological progress serves everyone, not just the few.

We stand at a remarkable intersection of human potential and artificial capability. Our choice is clear: we can allow technology to divide us, or we can use it to amplify our shared humanity. Choose amplification. Choose inclusion. Choose a future where artificial intelligence makes us more human, not less."

— **Dr. Naim Tahir Baig***Technology Strategist, AI Researcher, & Human AdvocatePDS&CE, Pakistan, 2025*

Preface

In the spring of 2024, I received a call from Maria, a supply chain manager at a mid-sized manufacturing company in Ohio. "Dr. Baig," she said, her voice mixing frustration with determination, "everyone keeps telling me I need to learn AI to stay relevant, but I have a full-time job, two teenagers, and aging parents. How am I supposed to become an AI expert when I can barely keep up with my email?"

Maria's question crystallized a challenge I'd been observing across industries and continents: the growing gap between AI's transformative potential and the realistic constraints facing busy professionals who want to engage with this technology meaningfully. While AI capabilities were advancing at breakneck speed, the resources for learning them remained largely designed for either complete beginners or advanced technologists—leaving little support for the millions of professionals who needed practical, applicable AI skills without abandoning their existing responsibilities.

That conversation with Maria launched a one and a half year journey that led to this book. Over the following months, I spoke professionals across countries and different industries. I worked with small business owners learning to use AI for inventory management, healthcare workers implementing diagnostic assistance tools, and executives navigating AI strategy for global manufacturing operations. What I discovered was both encouraging and concerning: while AI tools were becoming more accessible, the knowledge needed to use them effectively, ethically, and sustainably remained fragmented and often inaccessible to those who needed it most.

Why This Book Exists

"Learn AI Fast" was born from the recognition that artificial intelligence literacy has become as essential as digital literacy was two decades ago—yet the educational resources to develop this literacy remain inadequately designed for working professionals' realities. Most AI education falls into one of two extremes: oversimplified overviews that provide feel-good familiarity without genuine capability, or technical deep dives that assume computer science backgrounds and unlimited learning time.

This book charts a different path. It provides comprehensive AI competency development within a framework that respects your time constraints, acknowledges your existing expertise, and focuses relentlessly on practical application rather than theoretical abstraction. Every chapter, exercise, and case study has been tested with real professionals facing real constraints, ensuring that the learning translates directly into workplace value.

The RAPID Methodology: Evidence-Based Learning Design

At the heart of this book lies the RAPID framework—a systematically developed methodology that transforms AI learning from overwhelming complexity into manageable, progressive skill development. RAPID stands for Recognize patterns and opportunities, Apply tools systematically, Practice with increasing complexity, Iterate based on feedback, and Deploy solutions sustainably.

This framework emerged from analyzing successful AI adoption patterns across thousands of professionals and synthesizing insights from cognitive science research on adult learning, expertise development, and skill transfer. Unlike ad-hoc training approaches, RAPID provides structure that accommodates different learning styles, cultural contexts, and professional demands while maintaining focus on ethical implementation and community benefit.

The methodology has been validated through pilot programs with organizations ranging from Fortune 500 corporations to rural community colleges, consistently producing measurable improvements in both individual capability and organizational AI maturity. Participants typically achieve basic AI literacy within 4-6 weeks and develop intermediate competency within 3-6 months—timelines that reflect realistic expectations for busy professionals rather than idealistic academic scenarios.

Who This Book Serves

This book was written for the professional who recognizes AI's transformative potential but needs guidance that respects their intelligence while accommodating their constraints. You might be a marketing manager curious about AI-powered content creation, an operations specialist exploring predictive maintenance applications, a small business owner wondering how AI might improve customer service, or an executive responsible for organizational AI strategy.

You don't need a computer science background, unlimited learning time, or expensive tools. You do need curiosity, patience for gradual skill development, and commitment to using AI in ways that enhance rather than replace human expertise and judgment. This book assumes you're intelligent, capable, and motivated—but also realistic about what you can accomplish within the constraints of a full professional and personal life.

The content has been specifically designed to serve diverse readers across industries, cultures, and technical backgrounds. Case studies span small businesses and multinational corporations, developed and developing economies, technical and non-technical roles. The framework accommodates different learning styles, time constraints, and resource availability while maintaining consistent focus on practical application and ethical implementation.

What You Will Gain

By engaging systematically with this book's content, you will develop five interconnected competencies that together constitute genuine AI literacy for professionals:

Technical Proficiency: You'll master core AI tools and techniques sufficient to solve real workplace challenges, evaluate AI outputs critically, and integrate multiple AI capabilities into coherent workflows. This includes practical skills with platforms like ChatGPT, Claude, and industry-specific AI applications, as well as fundamental understanding of how these systems work and when they're appropriate to use.

Ethical Framework: You'll develop sophisticated judgment about responsible AI implementation, including bias recognition and mitigation, privacy protection, transparency requirements, and community impact assessment. This ethical foundation enables confident decision-making about AI applications while avoiding common pitfalls that can damage reputations and relationships.

Strategic Thinking: You'll learn to identify high-value AI opportunities within your specific context, evaluate implementation feasibility realistically, and develop sustainable adoption strategies that enhance rather than disrupt effective practices. This strategic capability distinguishes professionals who use AI effectively from those who adopt tools without clear purpose.

Communication and Collaboration: You'll build skills for translating between technical AI capabilities and human needs, facilitating productive conversations about AI adoption, and building bridges across different levels of technical expertise. These skills prove essential as AI implementation increasingly requires cross-functional collaboration.

Community Leadership: You'll develop capacity for supporting others' AI learning journeys, contributing to ethical AI development, and ensuring that AI benefits serve diverse communities rather than concentrating among those with existing advantages.

How to Use This Book

This book is designed for flexible engagement that accommodates different learning preferences and time constraints. The content follows a logical progression from fundamental concepts through advanced applications, but individual chapters can also serve as standalone resources for specific topics.

For Systematic Learning: If you're new to AI or prefer structured learning approaches, work through the chapters sequentially, completing exercises and projects as presented. Plan for 4-6 hours of engagement per week over 12-16 weeks for comprehensive skill development.

For Targeted Application: If you have specific AI implementation goals or existing partial knowledge, use the detailed table of contents and index to focus on immediately relevant content. Each chapter includes prerequisites and connections to related material.

For Team Learning: The content supports collaborative learning through discussion questions, group exercises, and team project suggestions. Organizations can adapt the material for internal training programs or learning cohorts.

For Ongoing Reference: As AI capabilities and applications evolve rapidly, this book is designed to serve as a continuing reference resource. Key frameworks, checklists, and resources are organized for easy retrieval and application to new challenges.

A Note on Inclusion and Accessibility

This book was developed with explicit attention to inclusion and accessibility. The examples, case studies, and applications reflect diverse industries, cultural contexts, and organizational types. The language aims for clarity without sacrificing sophistication, and concepts are explained through multiple approaches to accommodate different learning styles.

However, true inclusion requires ongoing effort rather than one-time design decisions. I encourage readers to adapt the content for their specific contexts, share insights that improve accessibility for others, and contribute to making AI education more inclusive and effective for diverse communities.

Acknowledgments and Community

This book represents the contributions of far more people than can be individually acknowledged. The frameworks, examples, and insights emerged from conversations with professionals, feedback from beta readers representing different industries, and collaboration with colleagues who share commitment to democratic AI development.

Special gratitude goes to the practitioners who allowed their stories to be shared, the organizations that provided access to real implementation data, and the reviewers who challenged assumptions and improved clarity throughout the development process. The book's strengths reflect this collective wisdom; any remaining limitations are my responsibility alone.

AI development is inherently collaborative, and AI learning should be as well. I encourage readers to connect with each other, share experiences, and contribute to the growing community of professionals working to ensure that artificial intelligence amplifies human potential rather than replacing human wisdom.

Looking Forward

As you begin this learning journey, remember that AI competency is not a destination but a capability for ongoing adaptation and contribution. The specific tools and techniques you'll learn will evolve, but the frameworks for critical thinking, ethical reasoning, and community collaboration will remain valuable throughout your career.

Your engagement with AI shapes not only your own professional effectiveness but also the trajectory of how this powerful technology develops and serves society. By learning to use AI thoughtfully, ethically, and inclusively, you contribute to ensuring that artificial intelligence becomes a force for human flourishing rather than division.

The future we're building together depends on professionals like you who bring domain expertise, cultural wisdom, and ethical commitment to AI development and deployment. Thank you for your willingness to engage with this challenge thoughtfully and for your commitment to using powerful technology in service of human dignity and community wellbeing.

Welcome to your AI-enabled future. Let's build it together.

Dr. Naim Tahir Baig

August 2025

Part I: The Problem Phase

Chapter 1: The AI Revolution Is Here—Are You Prepared?

Opening Hook: Sarah's Journey to AI Competency

Sarah Martinez had always considered herself tech-savvy. As a marketing manager at a mid-size consumer goods company, she prided herself on staying current with digital trends. But in early 2024, when her company announced they would be integrating artificial intelligence tools across all departments, Sarah felt a familiar knot of anxiety in her stomach.

"I remember thinking, 'Here we go again—another technology I'll have to learn,'" Sarah recalls. "But this felt different. Bigger. Like if I didn't get this right, I might actually get left behind."

What followed wasn't the dramatic transformation story often portrayed in AI marketing materials. Instead, Sarah's journey represents the realistic, gradual process that most professionals experience when developing AI competency. Over the course of six months, she methodically learned to integrate AI tools into her daily workflow—starting with simple content assistance and gradually expanding to campaign optimization and customer insights analysis.

The learning curve was steeper than expected. "The first month was honestly frustrating," Sarah admits. "I'd spend more time figuring out how to prompt the AI correctly than it would have taken me to just write the content myself." But by month three, something clicked. The AI tools began to feel less like foreign technology and more like sophisticated assistants that could amplify her existing marketing expertise.

The results, while not revolutionary, were meaningfully positive. Sarah's campaign development time decreased by approximately 30%, allowing her to focus more on strategy and stakeholder collaboration. Her content quality improved as AI helped her identify gaps in messaging and suggested data-driven optimizations she might have missed. Perhaps most importantly, her confidence grew. She began volunteering for cross-functional AI initiatives and eventually became an informal AI advocate within her organization.

"By the end of the year, I wasn't just using AI—I was helping train other people," Sarah reflects. "That led to a promotion and about a 40% salary increase when I moved to a role that specifically required AI competency."

Sarah's story illustrates several crucial realities about AI skill development in 2025. First, meaningful competency takes time—typically months, not weeks. Second, the value comes not from replacing human expertise but from augmenting it. Third, early adopters who develop genuine proficiency, rather than superficial familiarity, position themselves for significant professional advantages. Finally, the learning process requires patience, persistence, and realistic expectations about both timelines and outcomes.

This balanced progression—from initial resistance through gradual competency to professional advancement—represents the journey that millions of professionals are now undertaking. The question isn't whether this transformation will affect your career, but how prepared you'll be to navigate it successfully.

The Growing AI Market Reality: Unprecedented Growth with Measured Expectations

The artificial intelligence market is experiencing growth that surpasses even the most optimistic predictions from just a few years ago. According to Fortune Business Insights, the global AI market was valued at $294.16 billion in 2025 and is projected to reach $1,771.62 billion by 2032, representing a compound annual growth rate (CAGR) of 29.2%.[1] To put this in perspective, this growth trajectory would make AI one of the fastest-expanding technology sectors in modern economic history.

These numbers represent more than abstract market forces—they reflect fundamental changes in how businesses operate and compete. Microsoft reports that with 66% of CEOs reporting measurable business benefits from generative AI initiatives, particularly in enhancing operational efficiency and customer satisfaction, the technology has moved beyond experimental phases into core business operations.[2] The International Data Corporation (IDC) predicts that investments in AI solutions and services are projected to yield a global cumulative impact of $22.3 trillion by 2030, representing approximately 3.7% of the global gross domestic product (GDP).[3]

However, this growth comes with important caveats that prospective AI professionals must understand. The benefits are not evenly distributed across industries, company sizes, or geographic regions. Statista data indicates that the United States continues to dominate AI market share, accounting for $66.21 billion in 2025, while China follows at approximately $34.20 billion.[4] This concentration means that opportunities and resources remain clustered in specific regions and sectors.

Furthermore, the reality behind these impressive growth figures reveals a more nuanced picture. While 35% of businesses have integrated AI and 9 out of 10 organizations report using AI technology to stay competitive,[5] the depth and sophistication of implementation varies dramatically. McKinsey research shows that only 1% of business leaders report their companies have reached AI maturity, indicating that most organizations are still in early stages of realizing AI's full potential.[6]

The economic impact extends beyond simple market expansion. Goldman Sachs projects that global AI investments will reach approximately $200 billion by 2025,[7] driving infrastructure development, job creation, and economic restructuring. This investment surge supports not only software development but also the necessary physical infrastructure, including data centers, specialized computing hardware, and power generation capabilities.

For professionals considering AI skill development, these market dynamics create both opportunities and pressure. The rapid growth ensures continued demand for AI-literate workers, but the concentration of development in certain regions and sectors means that strategic positioning becomes crucial. Understanding where your industry fits within this landscape—and how quickly AI adoption is progressing in your specific context—will inform your learning priorities and timeline.

The Evolving Workforce Divide: Skills Premium and Market Dynamics

Perhaps the most compelling reason for professionals to develop AI competency lies in the dramatic wage premiums and career advantages that

AI skills now command. PwC's 2025 Global AI Jobs Barometer, based on analysis of close to a billion job advertisements from six continents, reveals that workers with AI skills command an average 56% wage premium compared to similar roles without AI requirements—more than doubling from 25% in the previous year.[8]

This premium translates into substantial real-world income differences. Lightcast research indicates that job postings requiring AI skills offer 28% higher salaries—an average of nearly $18,000 more per year—with some specialized roles commanding even higher premiums.[9] At the high end, AI engineers at leading technology companies can earn over $500,000 annually in total compensation, while AI product managers, data scientists, and machine learning specialists regularly earn between $120,000 and $300,000 depending on experience and location.[10]

The job creation forecasts are equally encouraging, though they require careful interpretation. The World Economic Forum's Future of Jobs Report 2025 projects that approximately 170 million new jobs will be created globally by 2030, driven by technological advancement, demographic shifts, and the green transition.[11] However, these same forces will also displace an estimated 92 million existing roles, resulting in a net increase of 78 million jobs—equivalent to approximately 7% of today's global workforce.[12]

Significantly, job growth is occurring even in roles previously considered highly automatable. PwC data shows that occupations with lower exposure to AI saw strong job growth of 65% in recent years (2019-2024), while growth remained robust at 38% even in more AI-exposed occupations.[13] This suggests that AI is more often augmenting human work rather than simply replacing it, at least in the current technological and economic environment.

The geographic and demographic distribution of these opportunities reveals important patterns. Technology hubs in North America, Europe, and Asia-Pacific continue to concentrate the highest-paying AI roles, but remote work options are expanding access for qualified professionals regardless of location. However, concerning disparities remain: in every country analyzed by PwC, more women than men work in AI-exposed roles, suggesting that the skills pressure facing women will be proportionally higher.[14]

Industry-specific patterns also emerge from the data. Financial services, software publishing, and professional services show the highest productivity growth rates and corresponding demand for AI skills. Meanwhile, sectors like mining, hospitality, and traditional manufacturing lag in adoption, though this may represent opportunity for early movers in these industries.[15]

For individual professionals, these trends create a bifurcated job market. Those who develop genuine AI competency—beyond superficial familiarity—position themselves for significant salary premiums and career advancement. Those who delay skill development don't necessarily face immediate job loss, but they may find themselves increasingly excluded from the highest-growth, highest-compensation opportunities in their fields.

Why Traditional Learning Approaches Fall Short

Despite the clear economic incentives for AI skill development, many professionals struggle with traditional educational approaches to this rapidly evolving field. The challenges stem from several systemic issues that make conventional learning strategies inadequate for AI competency.

First, the pace of AI development significantly outstrips traditional curriculum development cycles. University programs typically require years to develop, approve, and implement new courses, while AI capabilities and best practices evolve monthly. IBM research indicates that 39% of workers' core skills will become obsolete by 2030, with this figure representing significant disruption that demands continuous adaptation rather than one-time educational interventions.[16]

Second, the interdisciplinary nature of practical AI application doesn't align well with traditional academic silos. Effective AI implementation requires combining technical understanding, domain expertise, ethical reasoning, and business acumen—a combination rarely addressed comprehensively in conventional educational settings. Research from the Oxford Internet Institute indicates that AI roles typically require both higher levels of education and a larger number of diverse skills than traditional positions, reflecting this complex competency profile.[17]

Third, the resources for AI education remain scattered and inconsistent in quality. While numerous online courses, bootcamps, and certification programs exist, professionals often struggle to identify credible sources or create coherent learning pathways. The OECD reports that current training supply may not be sufficient to meet the growing need for general AI literacy skills, highlighting gaps in accessible, quality education options.[18]

Perhaps most significantly, traditional educational approaches often fail to address the specific barriers that working professionals face. IBM's Global AI Adoption Index reveals that 33% of organizations cite limited AI skills and expertise as their top barrier to AI adoption, while 63% of executives identify skills gaps as the primary obstacle to business transformation.[19] Yet only a small percentage of companies have established comprehensive skills development programs to address these needs internally.

The mismatch between available training and actual professional needs manifests in several ways. Many educational programs focus on theoretical foundations rather than practical application. Others emphasize advanced technical skills that most business professionals don't require, creating unnecessary barriers to entry. Still others fail to address the change management and cultural adaptation aspects of AI integration that prove crucial for real-world success.

Additionally, traditional approaches often underestimate the time and support required for genuine competency development. Research from Microsoft's internal productivity studies indicates that meaningful AI skill development requires sustained practice over months, not weeks, with significant variation in learning curves across individuals and contexts.[20] Educational programs that promise rapid mastery often leave participants with superficial familiarity rather than practical competency.

The economic pressures facing many professionals also create challenges for traditional education models. Extended time away from work for full-time education programs is often impractical, while part-time programs struggle to provide the intensity and continuity needed for effective skill development. The resulting "education-work" balance problem leaves many professionals attempting to learn AI skills through informal, unstructured approaches that yield inconsistent results.

The "Learn Fast" Methodology Preview: Evidence-

Based Rapid Learning

Given the limitations of traditional educational approaches, developing AI competency requires a more strategic, evidence-based methodology that accommodates the realities of professional life while delivering genuine skill development. The "Learn Fast" framework addresses these challenges through principles derived from cognitive science research and validated through real-world application.

Principle 1: Spaced Practice Over Intensive Cramming

Cognitive science research consistently demonstrates that distributed practice—learning spread over time—produces better retention and transfer than massed practice.[21] For AI skill development, this means dedicating 5-10 hours per week consistently over several months rather than attempting intensive weekend workshops or week-long bootcamps. Microsoft's internal research on AI productivity tools supports this approach, showing that meaningful adoption requires sustained engagement with AI systems over extended periods.[22]

Principle 2: Applied Learning in Professional Context

The most effective AI skill development occurs when learners can immediately apply new concepts within their existing work responsibilities. Rather than learning AI in abstract or artificial settings, professionals should identify specific tasks within their current roles where AI tools can provide value. This approach leverages existing domain expertise while building AI competency incrementally.

Principle 3: Progressive Complexity with Feedback Loops

Effective AI learning follows a carefully structured progression from simple tool use to sophisticated application. This might begin with basic prompt engineering for content generation, advance to workflow automation, and ultimately include strategic AI implementation planning. Each level should include feedback mechanisms—both from AI systems and from colleagues or mentors—to ensure accurate skill development.

Principle 4: Community Learning and Knowledge Sharing

Isolated learning rarely produces lasting competency in rapidly evolving fields like AI. The most successful AI skill development occurs within communities of practice where professionals can share experiences, troubleshoot challenges, and stay current with emerging developments. This social learning component also helps address the psychological barriers that many professionals face when adapting to new technologies.

Principle 5: Realistic Timeline Expectations

Based on analysis of successful AI adoption patterns, meaningful competency development typically requires 4-8 weeks for foundational skills, 3-6 months for intermediate application, and 6-12 months for advanced proficiency. These timelines assume consistent practice within a structured learning framework, with significant variation based on prior technical experience and the specific AI applications being learned.

The effectiveness of this approach is supported by emerging research on professional AI adoption. A study tracking over 5,000 customer support agents using generative AI assistance found that productivity improvements of 15% required several weeks of consistent use, with the most significant gains occurring among less experienced workers who had adequate support and training.[23]

This methodology also acknowledges the reality that AI competency is not a destination but an ongoing journey. The rapid evolution of AI capabilities means that continuous learning becomes a professional necessity rather than a one-time educational investment. The "Learn Fast" framework provides a sustainable approach to this continuous adaptation while delivering tangible short-term benefits that justify the ongoing time investment.

Practical Exercise: AI Readiness Self-Assessment Tool

To provide a concrete starting point for professionals beginning their AI competency journey, we've developed a comprehensive self-assessment tool that evaluates current readiness across multiple dimensions. This assessment helps identify strengths to build upon and gaps that require focused attention.

Technical Comfort Assessment (20 points possible)

Rate your current comfort level (1-4 scale) with the following:

1. Learning new software tools and platforms
2. Understanding basic concepts of data analysis
3. Working with cloud-based applications
4. Troubleshooting technical problems independently
5. Following multi-step technical procedures

AI Exposure Assessment (20 points possible)
Rate your current experience (1-4 scale) with:

1. Using AI-powered features in existing tools (e.g., autocomplete, recommendations)
2. Interacting with chatbots or virtual assistants
3. Understanding basic AI terminology and concepts
4. Following AI-related news and developments
5. Observing AI applications in your industry

Learning Style Assessment (20 points possible)
Rate how well these approaches work for you (1-4 scale):

1. Learning through hands-on practice and experimentation
2. Following structured tutorials and step-by-step guides
3. Learning from peer interaction and discussion
4. Understanding concepts before diving into application
5. Adapting to new tools through trial and error

Professional Context Assessment (20 points possible)
Rate the accuracy of these statements for your situation (1-4 scale):

1. My organization encourages experimentation with new tools
2. I have time allocated for professional development activities
3. My role involves tasks that could benefit from automation or assistance
4. I have colleagues or mentors who could support my AI learning
5. My industry is actively discussing or implementing AI solutions

Motivation and Goals Assessment (20 points possible)

Rate how strongly you agree (1-4 scale) with these statements:

1. I am excited about the potential of AI to improve my work
2. I am willing to invest regular time in developing AI skills
3. I can see specific ways AI could benefit my current responsibilities
4. I am comfortable with a learning process that takes several months
5. I believe AI competency will be important for my career advancement

Scoring and Interpretation:

- **80-100 points (High Readiness):** You have excellent foundations for AI learning. Focus on identifying specific AI tools and applications most relevant to your role, and begin with intermediate-level learning resources.
- **60-79 points (Moderate Readiness):** You have good basic preparation but may benefit from strengthening certain areas before diving deep into AI applications. Consider beginning with foundational AI literacy while building technical confidence.
- **40-59 points (Developing Readiness):** Significant preparation would benefit your AI learning journey. Focus on building technical comfort and identifying specific learning support resources before attempting complex AI implementations.
- **Below 40 points (Early Readiness):** Consider starting with general digital literacy and change management resources before focusing specifically on AI. Building foundational comfort with technology will make AI learning more successful.

Goal-Setting Framework:
Based on your assessment results, establish specific 90-day goals:
For High Readiness learners:

- Identify and begin using 2-3 AI tools relevant to your work
- Complete intermediate-level AI training in your primary domain
- Join professional communities focused on AI in your industry

- Mentor colleagues who are beginning their AI journey

For Moderate Readiness learners:

- Complete foundational AI literacy training
- Experiment with 1-2 basic AI tools in low-stakes contexts
- Identify AI learning resources aligned with your learning style
- Connect with AI learning communities or study groups

For Developing/Early Readiness learners:

- Focus on building general technical confidence and digital literacy
- Follow AI news and developments in your industry
- Identify colleagues or mentors who can support your learning journey
- Establish consistent time for professional development activities

This assessment provides a realistic baseline for AI skill development while acknowledging that readiness varies significantly across individuals and contexts. The goal is not to create barriers but to identify the most effective starting point for each professional's unique situation.

Case Study: Microsoft's Systematic AI Adoption Journey

To illustrate how systematic AI implementation creates measurable value over realistic timelines, Microsoft's internal AI adoption provides a compelling example of gradual, sustainable transformation rather than dramatic overnight change.

Phased Implementation Approach

Microsoft's approach to AI integration across its organization demonstrates the importance of systematic planning and gradual scaling. Rather than attempting company-wide AI deployment, Microsoft began with pilot programs in specific departments, carefully measuring results and refining approaches before expanding to additional teams.[24]

The company started by deploying Microsoft 365 Copilot to internal teams in 2023, tracking usage patterns, productivity impacts, and user feedback over extended periods. Initial results showed that 84% of the 10,000 Microsoft 365 Copilot users reported they would not want to go back to working without it, indicating strong user adoption once initial learning curves were addressed.[25]

Measurable Productivity Improvements

The productivity gains, while significant, developed gradually rather than immediately. Microsoft's internal research compilation, which included results from over a dozen workplace studies, found that AI tools enabled workers to complete tasks more efficiently across roles and industries, but the impact was greatest when tools were adopted and integrated strategically rather than simply added to existing workflows.[26]

Specific metrics from Microsoft's internal usage included:

- 70% of users reported that Copilot made them more productive
- 68% said it improved the quality of their work
- Nearly 30% of GitHub Copilot code suggestions were adopted by developers
- Significant time savings on routine tasks, allowing focus on higher-value activities

However, these benefits emerged over months of consistent use rather than immediately upon implementation. Early users often experienced initial productivity decreases as they learned to work effectively with AI tools, highlighting the importance of realistic timeline expectations and adequate training support.

Change Management and Training Investment

Microsoft's success stemmed partly from substantial investment in change management and employee training. The company provided extensive resources for employees to learn AI tools, including hands-on workshops, peer mentoring programs, and dedicated support channels for troubleshooting and questions.

The training approach acknowledged that different roles required different AI competencies. Software developers received intensive training on GitHub Copilot for code generation and debugging. Marketing teams focused on content creation and campaign optimization tools. Finance teams learned AI applications for data analysis and reporting automation. This role-specific approach proved more effective than generic AI training programs.

Challenges Overcome

Microsoft's internal adoption also revealed common implementation challenges that other organizations can anticipate:

Initial Resistance: Some employees expressed skepticism about AI tools, particularly concerning job security and work quality. Microsoft addressed this through transparent communication about AI's role in augmenting rather than replacing human expertise, backed by data showing job creation rather than elimination in AI-adopting departments.

Learning Curve Management: Early adoption required significant time investment as employees learned effective AI interaction patterns. Microsoft provided protected time for learning and experimentation, recognizing that short-term productivity investments were necessary for long-term gains.

Integration Complexity: Incorporating AI tools into existing workflows required careful planning and often necessitated process redesign. Microsoft found that the most successful implementations occurred when teams reimagined their workflows around AI capabilities rather than simply adding AI to unchanged processes.

Quality Control: Ensuring AI-generated work met Microsoft's quality standards required developing new review processes and quality assurance protocols. This included training managers to evaluate AI-assisted work and establishing guidelines for appropriate AI use across different contexts.

Quantified Long-term Impact

After 12-18 months of systematic implementation, Microsoft reported substantial organizational benefits:

- Reduced time spent on routine administrative tasks across most departments
- Improved quality and consistency of customer-facing communications
- Faster product development cycles through AI-assisted coding and

testing
- Enhanced data analysis capabilities enabling better strategic decision-making
- Increased employee satisfaction as AI tools freed up time for more engaging, strategic work

Lessons for Other Organizations

Microsoft's experience offers several key insights for organizations and individuals developing AI competency:

1. **Systematic Planning:** Successful AI adoption requires careful planning, gradual implementation, and continuous refinement rather than immediate full-scale deployment.
2. **Training Investment:** Meaningful productivity gains require substantial upfront investment in training and support, with benefits emerging over months rather than weeks.
3. **Change Management:** Addressing psychological and cultural barriers to AI adoption is as important as technical implementation.
4. **Realistic Expectations:** AI implementation should be measured in terms of gradual improvement rather than dramatic transformation, with success metrics focusing on long-term value creation.
5. **Customized Approaches:** Different roles and departments require different AI tools and training approaches, making one-size-fits-all implementations less effective.

Microsoft's systematic approach demonstrates that while AI can create substantial value for organizations and individuals, realizing this value requires patience, investment, and strategic thinking rather than simply adopting the latest AI tools.

Addressing Common Barriers and Misconceptions

Despite clear evidence of AI's value and the availability of increasingly accessible tools, many professionals still hesitate to begin developing AI competency. Understanding and addressing these barriers is crucial for successful skill development.

Misconception 1: AI Requires Advanced Mathematical or Programming Skills

One of the most persistent barriers to AI learning is the belief that competency requires extensive mathematical or programming backgrounds. While these skills are valuable for AI researchers and engineers, most business applications of AI require conceptual understanding rather than technical implementation.

Modern AI tools are designed for broad professional use. Platforms like ChatGPT, Claude, and Copilot provide natural language interfaces that require no programming knowledge. Business intelligence tools increasingly incorporate AI features through point-and-click interfaces. The focus for most professionals should be on understanding AI capabilities, limitations, and effective application rather than the underlying technical mechanics.

Research from the Oxford Internet Institute supports this approach, showing that AI skills themselves attract a 23% wage premium compared to 13% for a master's degree and 33% for a PhD, indicating that practical AI competency can be more valuable than traditional educational credentials.[27]

Misconception 2: AI Learning Requires Extensive Time Investment

Many professionals avoid AI skill development because they assume it requires returning to school or dedicating enormous time blocks to learning. In reality, foundational AI competency can be developed through consistent practice of 5-10 hours per week over several months.

The key is focusing on applied learning within existing work responsibilities rather than abstract study. For example, a marketing professional might spend 30 minutes daily experimenting with AI content generation tools, gradually building competency while completing actual work tasks. This approach provides immediate value while developing longer-term skills.

Misconception 3: AI Will Replace Human Jobs Completely

Fear of job displacement prevents many professionals from engaging with AI, creating a self-fulfilling prophecy where avoiding AI skills actually increases career vulnerability. Current research suggests a more nuanced reality: AI is more likely to augment human work than replace it entirely, but workers without AI skills may find themselves at a disadvantage compared to those who develop competency.

PwC data shows that even in highly automatable occupations, job numbers continue to grow, indicating that AI adoption creates new opportunities alongside task automation.[28] The IBM Future of Jobs Report indicates that 87% of executives expect jobs to be augmented rather than replaced by generative AI.[29]

Misconception 4: AI Tools Are Too Expensive for Individual Learning

Cost concerns often deter individual professionals from experimenting with AI tools. However, many powerful AI platforms offer free tiers or low-cost subscriptions that provide substantial functionality for learning purposes.

ChatGPT offers free access with significant capability for basic learning and experimentation. Microsoft Copilot provides free access through Microsoft 365 subscriptions many professionals already have. Google's AI tools integrate with free Gmail and Google Workspace accounts. Cloud AI platforms like Google Cloud AI and AWS offer free tier access for educational purposes.

Misconception 5: AI Skills Become Obsolete Too Quickly to Justify Learning

The rapid pace of AI development leads some professionals to worry that any skills they develop will quickly become outdated. While specific AI tools do evolve rapidly, foundational concepts and competencies remain valuable across technological changes.

Skills like prompt engineering, AI-human workflow design, and ethical AI application transfer across different AI platforms and generations. Understanding how to evaluate AI outputs, identify appropriate use cases, and integrate AI into business processes provides lasting value regardless of specific tool evolution.

Practical Barriers and Solutions

Beyond misconceptions, professionals face practical barriers that require concrete solutions:

Limited Workplace Support: Many organizations lack formal AI training programs. Solutions include seeking out informal learning communities, proposing pilot projects to demonstrate AI value, and connecting with colleagues who have AI experience.

Information Overload: The abundance of AI learning resources can be overwhelming. Solutions include starting with curated learning paths from reputable sources, focusing on industry-specific applications, and joining structured learning communities with clear progression frameworks.

Imposter Syndrome: Many professionals feel inadequate when beginning AI learning, particularly when surrounded by more technically advanced colleagues. Solutions include focusing on application rather than technical depth, celebrating small wins, and remembering that AI competency is about effective use rather than technical mastery.

Time Management: Balancing AI learning with existing work responsibilities requires strategic time management. Solutions include integrating AI learning into existing tasks, using micro-learning approaches during daily routines, and setting realistic, achievable learning goals.

Lack of Clear Career Connection: Some professionals struggle to see how AI skills connect to their specific career goals. Solutions include researching AI applications in their industry, identifying successful AI adopters in similar roles, and starting with AI applications that provide immediate work benefits.

Inclusive Key Takeaways: Building Confidence Across Diverse Backgrounds

As AI becomes integral to professional success across industries, it's crucial to recognize that AI competency is achievable for professionals from all backgrounds, experience levels, and technical comfort zones. The path to AI proficiency varies significantly among individuals, but certain principles apply universally.

AI Literacy Is Becoming as Fundamental as Digital Literacy

Just as email, internet research, and basic computer skills became essential professional competencies over the past decades, AI literacy is rapidly becoming a baseline expectation across industries. However, this transition is happening much more quickly than previous technological shifts, creating both urgency and opportunity for early adopters.

The comparison to digital literacy is particularly relevant because it demonstrates how seemingly complex technologies become accessible through well-designed interfaces and adequate training. Most professionals today use sophisticated digital tools without understanding their underlying technical mechanisms. AI competency follows a similar pattern—focusing on effective application rather than technical mastery.

Early Investment Yields Compounding Benefits

Research consistently shows that professionals who develop AI competency early in adoption cycles enjoy disproportionate benefits. The 56% wage premium for AI skills represents just the beginning of potential career advantages. Early adopters also gain opportunities to shape AI implementation within their organizations, position themselves as internal experts, and access emerging roles that leverage AI capabilities.

These benefits compound over time as AI adoption accelerates. Professionals with established AI competency become increasingly valuable as their organizations expand AI usage. They also develop intuitive understanding of AI capabilities and limitations that provides strategic advantages in rapidly evolving professional environments.

Structured Learning Outperforms Random Exploration

While experimentation and self-directed learning have value, systematic skill development produces better outcomes more efficiently. Structured learning paths provide several advantages: they ensure coverage of essential concepts, offer realistic timeline expectations, connect learners with supportive communities, and provide clear milestones for measuring progress.

This is particularly important for AI learning because the field evolves rapidly and includes numerous tools, concepts, and applications. Without structure, learners often develop fragmented knowledge that lacks practical coherence. Structured approaches help create comprehensive competency rather than scattered familiarity.

Balance Enthusiasm with Realistic Expectations

AI offers significant potential for enhancing professional capabilities and career prospects, but realizing this potential requires patience and persistence. The most successful AI adopters maintain enthusiasm for AI's possibilities while setting realistic expectations about learning timelines, implementation challenges, and gradual rather than dramatic improvements.

This balanced perspective helps prevent both premature abandonment of AI learning due to unrealistic expectations and over-investment in AI solutions without adequate planning and support. Sustainable AI competency development requires long-term commitment rather than short-term intensity.

Human Expertise Remains Central

Perhaps most importantly, AI competency is about enhancing human capabilities rather than replacing them. The most valuable AI applications leverage domain expertise, professional judgment, and human creativity while automating routine tasks and providing analytical support.

This human-centered perspective on AI has important implications for skill development. Rather than trying to become an AI technical expert, most professionals should focus on becoming expert at applying AI within their existing areas of competency. A skilled marketing professional who learns to use AI effectively will generally outperform a technical AI expert without marketing knowledge in marketing applications.

Accessibility and Inclusion in AI Learning

AI competency development must be accessible to professionals regardless of their educational background, technical experience, or economic circumstances. This requires several commitments:

Educational Accessibility: Learning resources should accommodate different learning styles, paces, and prior knowledge levels. Visual learners, auditory learners, and hands-on learners all need appropriate resources.

Economic Accessibility: AI skill development should be possible without significant financial investment, through free or low-cost tools, resources, and learning communities.

Cultural Accessibility: AI applications and training should reflect diverse perspectives, use cases, and professional contexts rather than focusing primarily on technology sector applications.

Linguistic Accessibility: As AI tools expand globally, learning resources and tool interfaces should accommodate multiple languages and cultural contexts.

Support System Development

Successful AI competency development often depends on adequate support systems. These include:

Professional Networks: Connecting with colleagues, mentors, and learning communities focused on AI applications in relevant industries or roles.

Organizational Support: Advocating for workplace AI learning opportunities, pilot projects, and supportive policies for AI experimentation.

Technical Support: Access to troubleshooting resources, documentation, and help systems for AI tools and platforms.

Emotional Support: Recognition that AI learning can be challenging and sometimes frustrating, with systems for encouragement and motivation during difficult periods.

Action Steps with Accessibility Considerations

To transform the insights and information presented in this chapter into concrete progress, professionals need specific, actionable steps that accommodate diverse circumstances and constraints. The following framework provides multiple pathways for beginning AI competency development.

Step 1: Complete Your Readiness Assessment

Begin by honestly evaluating your current position using the self-assessment tool provided earlier in this chapter. This assessment should identify your strongest foundation areas and highlight gaps that require attention. Consider completing the assessment with input from trusted colleagues or mentors who can provide external perspective on your readiness.

For professionals with accessibility needs: The assessment can be adapted for different learning styles and capabilities. Visual learners might benefit from creating graphical representations of their results. Those who prefer group learning can complete assessments collaboratively with colleagues or study partners.

Step 2: Set Achievable 90-Day Goals

Based on your assessment results, establish specific, measurable goals for the next three months. These goals should be ambitious enough to create meaningful progress while remaining realistic given your other responsibilities and constraints.

For High Readiness professionals:

- Identify and begin regularly using 2-3 AI tools relevant to your work
- Complete an intermediate-level AI course in your domain
- Join at least one professional community focused on AI applications
- Volunteer for an AI-related project or initiative at work

For Moderate Readiness professionals:

- Complete foundational AI literacy training
- Experiment with 1-2 basic AI tools in low-stakes contexts
- Establish consistent time for AI learning and practice
- Connect with AI learning communities or study groups

For Developing Readiness professionals:

- Focus on building general digital confidence and literacy
- Follow AI news and developments in your industry
- Identify learning support resources and mentors
- Establish basic habits for ongoing professional development

Step 3: Dedicate Consistent Time for Learning

Effective AI skill development requires regular, consistent practice rather than sporadic intensive efforts. Establish a realistic schedule that you can maintain over months rather than weeks.

Recommended Time Allocation:

- **Minimum commitment:** 30 minutes daily or 3-4 hours weekly
- **Moderate commitment:** 45-60 minutes daily or 5-7 hours weekly
- **Intensive commitment:** 90 minutes daily or 8-10 hours weekly

The key is consistency rather than total hours. Many professionals find success with shorter daily sessions rather than longer weekly blocks, as daily practice provides better retention and habit formation.

Flexible Scheduling Options:

- **Early morning learning:** 20-30 minutes before work begins
- **Lunch break exploration:** Using meal breaks for AI tool experimentation
- **Evening study:** Dedicated time after work for structured learning
- **Weekend projects:** Longer sessions for hands-on application and projects
- **Commute learning:** Audio content and podcasts during travel time

Step 4: Engage with Inclusive AI Communities

Learning AI skills in isolation is both less effective and less enjoyable than community-based learning. Seek out communities that align with your learning style, professional context, and values around inclusion and accessibility.

Professional Communities:

- Industry-specific AI groups (e.g., AI in Marketing, AI in Healthcare)
- Local professional organizations with AI initiatives
- Company internal AI user groups or learning circles
- Professional associations offering AI training and resources

Online Learning Communities:

- LinkedIn AI professional groups
- Reddit communities focused on practical AI applications

- Discord servers for AI learners and practitioners
- Platform-specific communities (e.g., OpenAI developer forums)

Inclusive Community Selection Criteria:

- Welcoming to newcomers and diverse backgrounds
- Focus on practical application rather than just technical discussion
- Clear guidelines for respectful interaction and support
- Accessibility features for different learning needs and disabilities
- Economic accessibility without expensive membership requirements

Step 5: Implement Applied Learning Strategies

The most effective AI skill development occurs when learning can be immediately applied to real work challenges. Identify specific tasks within your current role where AI tools could provide value, and use these as learning laboratories.

Applied Learning Examples by Role:

Marketing Professionals:

- Use AI for content ideation and first-draft creation
- Experiment with AI-powered social media scheduling and optimization
- Apply AI tools for customer segment analysis and targeting
- Implement AI chatbots for basic customer service inquiries

Sales Professionals:

- Use AI for lead research and qualification
- Implement AI-powered CRM data analysis and insights
- Experiment with AI-generated personalized outreach content
- Apply AI tools for sales forecasting and pipeline analysis

Operations Professionals:

- Use AI for schedule optimization and resource allocation

- Implement AI-powered inventory management and demand forecasting
- Apply AI tools for process automation and workflow optimization
- Experiment with AI-based quality control and monitoring systems

Finance Professionals:

- Use AI for expense categorization and fraud detection
- Implement AI-powered financial reporting and dashboard creation
- Apply AI tools for risk assessment and investment analysis
- Experiment with AI-based budgeting and financial planning

Step 6: Create Accountability and Support Systems

Sustainable AI learning requires accountability mechanisms and support systems that help maintain motivation and progress through inevitable challenges and setbacks.

Accountability Strategies:

- Partner with a colleague for mutual AI learning accountability
- Set up regular check-ins with a mentor or manager about AI progress
- Join structured learning programs with built-in accountability
- Track progress publicly through professional social media or blog posts
- Create learning contracts with specific milestones and consequences

Support System Development:

- Identify colleagues who can provide technical support and troubleshooting help
- Connect with mentors who have successfully developed AI competency
- Establish relationships with AI learning communities for ongoing support

- Create backup plans for motivation during difficult learning periods
- Develop celebration rituals for achieving learning milestones

Step 7: Plan for Ongoing Development

AI competency is not a destination but an ongoing journey that requires continuous adaptation and learning. Establish systems for staying current with AI developments while deepening your practical application skills.

Continuous Learning Framework:

- Schedule quarterly reviews of AI learning goals and progress
- Identify emerging AI tools and techniques relevant to your industry
- Plan advanced skill development based on initial competency success
- Establish systems for sharing knowledge and teaching others
- Create pathways for potential career advancement based on AI competency

The action steps outlined above provide a comprehensive framework for beginning AI competency development while accommodating diverse professional contexts, learning styles, and accessibility needs. The key to success lies not in perfect execution but in consistent progress and adaptation based on personal circumstances and emerging opportunities.

Success in AI skill development requires patience, persistence, and realistic expectations about both timelines and outcomes. However, for professionals willing to make this investment, the potential returns—in terms of career advancement, job satisfaction, and professional capability—are substantial and growing.

The AI revolution is indeed here, and the question facing every professional is not whether to engage with it, but how quickly and effectively they can develop the competency needed to thrive in an AI-enhanced work environment. The time to begin is now, but the approach should be thoughtful, systematic, and aligned with individual circumstances and goals.

Footnotes:

[1] Fortune Business Insights, "Artificial Intelligence [AI] Market Size, Growth & Trends by 2032," accessed August 20, 2025, https://www.fortunebusinessinsights.com/industry-reports/artificial-intelligence-market-100114.

[2] Microsoft, "AI-powered success—with more than 1,000 stories of customer transformation and innovation," The Microsoft Cloud Blog, July 24, 2025, https://www.microsoft.com/en-us/microsoft-cloud/blog/2025/07/24/ai-powered-success-with-1000-stories-of-customer-transformation-and-innovation/.

[3] Ibid.

[4] Statista, "Artificial Intelligence - Global | Statista Market Forecast," accessed August 20, 2025, https://www.statista.com/outlook/tmo/artificial-intelligence/worldwide.

[5] Fortune Business Insights, "Artificial Intelligence [AI] Market Size, Growth & Trends by 2032."

[6] McKinsey & Company, "AI in the workplace: A report for 2025," January 28, 2025, https://www.mckinsey.com/capabilities/mckinsey-digital/our-insights/superagency-in-the-workplace-empowering-people-to-unlock-ais-full-potential-at-work.

[7] Fortune Business Insights, "Artificial Intelligence [AI] Market Size, Growth & Trends by 2032."

[8] PwC, "AI linked to a fourfold increase in productivity growth and 56% wage premium," June 3, 2025, https://www.pwc.com/gx/en/news-room/press-releases/2025/ai-linked-to-a-fourfold-increase-in-productivity-growth.html.

[9] Fortune, "AI is driving mass layoffs in tech, but it's boosting salaries by $18,000 a year everywhere else," accessed August 20, 2025, https://fortune.com/2025/07/27/artificial-intelligence-skills-18000-salaries-28-percent/.

[10] Markaicode, "2025 Tech Salary Report: AI Engineers Earn $500k? Here's Proof," March 15, 2025, https://markaicode.com/tech-salary-report-2025-ai-engineers/.

[11] World Economic Forum, "Future of Jobs Report 2025: 78 Million New Job Opportunities by 2030 but Urgent Upskilling Needed to Prepare

Workforces," January 8, 2025, https://www.weforum.org/press/2025/01/future-of-jobs-report-2025-78-million-new-job-opportunities-by-2030-but-urgent-upskilling-needed-to-prepare-workforces/.

[12] Ibid.

[13] PwC, "AI linked to a fourfold increase in productivity growth and 56% wage premium."

[14] Ibid.

[15] Ibid.

[16] IBM, "IBM Study: Businesses View AI Agents as Essential, Not Just Experimental," June 10, 2025, https://newsroom.ibm.com/2025-06-10-IBM-Study-Businesses-View-AI-Agents-as-Essential,-Not-Just-Experimental.

[17] University of Oxford, "Skills-based hiring driving salary premiums in AI sector as employers face talent shortage, Oxford study finds," March 4, 2025, https://www.ox.ac.uk/news/2025-03-04-skills-based-hiring-driving-salary-premiums-ai-sector-employers-face-talent-shortage.

[18] OECD, "Bridging the AI skills gap," accessed August 20, 2025, https://www.oecd.org/en/publications/bridging-the-ai-skills-gap_66d0702e-en.html.

[19] IBM, "IBM Reports Significant Barriers to AI Adoption: Skills Gap and Data Complexity at the Forefront," January 11, 2024, https://www.bigdatawire.com/this-just-in/ibm-reports-significant-barriers-to-ai-adoption-skills-gap-and-data-complexity-at-the-forefront/.

[20] Microsoft, "Unlocking AI's global potential: progress, productivity, and workforce development," May 7, 2025, https://blogs.microsoft.com/on-the-issues/2025/04/10/unlocking-ai-global-potential/.

[21] Daniel T. Willingham, "Why Don't Students Like School?: A Cognitive Scientist Answers Questions About How the Mind Works and What It Means for the Classroom," 2nd ed. (San Francisco: Jossey-Bass, 2021).

[22] Microsoft, "Unlocking AI's global potential: progress, productivity, and workforce development."

[23] Ibid.

[24] Microsoft, "How Microsoft's customers and partners accelerated AI Transformation in FY25," July 28, 2025, https://blogs.microsoft.com/blog/

2025/07/28/how-microsofts-customers-and-partners-accelerated-ai-transformation-in-fy25-to-innovate-with-purpose-and-shape-their-future-success/.

[25] Ibid.

[26] Microsoft, "Unlocking AI's global potential: progress, productivity, and workforce development."

[27] University of Oxford, "Skills-based hiring driving salary premiums in AI sector as employers face talent shortage, Oxford study finds."

[28] PwC, "AI linked to a fourfold increase in productivity growth and 56% wage premium."

[29] IBM, "AI Skills You Need For 2025," accessed August 20, 2025, https://www.ibm.com/think/insights/ai-skills-you-need-for-2025.

Chapter 2: Overcoming AI Learning Barriers

Opening Hook: A Retail Revolution in Small Steps

Maria Gonzalez never imagined that her family's corner grocery store in Austin, Texas, would become a testing ground for artificial intelligence. As a second-generation immigrant who had built her business through hard work and personal relationships with customers, the idea of implementing AI seemed as foreign as rocket science. "I barely knew how to use Excel properly," Maria recalls with a laugh. "My daughter kept telling me about these AI tools, but I thought they were only for tech companies with million-dollar budgets."

The transformation didn't happen overnight. It began in early 2024 when Maria's supplier started experiencing frequent stockouts, forcing her to manually track inventory levels that seemed to change unpredictably. Frustrated by lost sales and wasted time, she reluctantly agreed to let her daughter demonstrate a simple AI-powered inventory management tool. "I was terrified I'd break something or make a mistake that would cost us money," Maria admits.

The first few weeks were challenging. The AI system's recommendations seemed counterintuitive, suggesting she stock more of certain items during what she considered slow periods. But gradually, patterns emerged that Maria's decades of experience hadn't revealed. The system identified subtle correlations between weather patterns, local events, and purchasing behavior. Within six months, Maria had reduced food waste by 18% and increased profits by 12%—modest but meaningful improvements that added up to thousands of dollars annually.[1]

More importantly, the process taught Maria that AI wasn't about replacing her business instincts but enhancing them. "I still know my customers better than any computer," she explains. "But now I have data to back up my hunches and catch things I might have missed." Her journey from AI skeptic to cautious adopter reflects the experience of millions of professionals worldwide who are discovering that artificial intelligence, despite its intimidating reputation, can be accessible, practical, and transformative when approached with patience and proper support.

Core Learning Objectives

This chapter addresses the fundamental barriers that prevent individuals from engaging with artificial intelligence effectively. Research indicates that while AI adoption is accelerating rapidly—with 92% of students now using AI tools compared to 66% just one year ago—significant obstacles remain that limit broader participation.[2] By understanding and systematically addressing these barriers, professionals can build the confidence and skills necessary for successful AI integration in their work and personal lives.

The primary learning objectives for this chapter include:

- **Understanding the reality of AI accessibility**: Dispelling myths about technical requirements while acknowledging genuine challenges that exist for different user groups
- **Recognizing psychological and practical barriers**: Identifying the emotional, cognitive, and structural obstacles that impede AI learning across diverse populations
- **Clarifying AI fundamentals through accessible explanations**: Building conceptual understanding without overwhelming technical complexity
- **Developing realistic confidence**: Fostering appropriate optimism balanced with honest assessment of AI capabilities and limitations

AI's Increasing Accessibility: Progress and Persistent Challenges

The Democratization of AI Technology

The landscape of artificial intelligence has transformed dramatically over the past two years, with user-friendly interfaces and no-code solutions making AI tools increasingly accessible to non-technical users. Microsoft's 2024 accessibility initiatives exemplify this trend, introducing features like

Copilot for Windows that can launch accessibility tools through simple voice commands, and AI-powered content creation assistance that adapts to different user needs and capabilities.[3]

Educational institutions have observed this democratization firsthand. According to the Higher Education Policy Institute's 2025 survey, student use of generative AI for assessments increased from 53% to 88% in just one year, with the primary applications being concept explanation, article summarization, and research idea generation.[4] This surge in adoption demonstrates that AI tools have become sufficiently intuitive for widespread use among diverse learner populations.

However, this accessibility revolution remains incomplete. The same survey reveals a concerning digital divide, with women expressing greater worry about academic misconduct and false results from AI systems compared to men, and wealthier students reporting more enthusiasm for AI use than their economically disadvantaged peers.[5] These disparities highlight that technological accessibility involves more than just user-friendly interfaces—it requires addressing systemic inequalities in access, training, and support.

Expanding Multilingual and Cultural Adaptation

One of the most significant advances in AI accessibility has been the expansion of multilingual capabilities. Microsoft's Seeing AI application now supports 33 languages and incorporates generative AI models for richer image descriptions and document interaction capabilities.[6] This expansion represents a crucial step toward inclusive AI development, though significant gaps remain for speakers of less common languages and users from underrepresented cultural backgrounds.

The European Union's recognition of these challenges led to explicit requirements in the AI Act, which entered force in August 2024, mandating that AI systems consider the needs of persons with disabilities and marginalized communities.[7] As Gerard Quinn, former UN Special Rapporteur on disability rights, notes, AI systems can either "expand possibilities for persons with disabilities to live independently" or create new barriers that "lock persons with disabilities out of social participation."[8]

Economic Accessibility and Resource Considerations

While many AI tools have become technically accessible, economic barriers persist as a significant obstacle. Research by UNESCO indicates that marginalized communities—including women, people of color, disabled individuals, and economically disadvantaged groups—bear the brunt of what experts term the "AI divide."[9] The costs associated with premium AI subscriptions, high-speed internet access, and compatible devices create systemic barriers that prevent equitable participation in the AI revolution.

Small businesses face particular challenges in this regard. While large corporations can invest in comprehensive AI infrastructure and training, smaller enterprises often struggle to justify the upfront costs and ongoing maintenance expenses associated with AI implementation. Maria's grocery store success story, while inspiring, required family support and gradual implementation that not all small business owners can access.

AI Fundamentals Explained: Building Understanding Through Accessible Analogies

Demystifying Machine Learning and Pattern Recognition

At its core, artificial intelligence represents sophisticated pattern recognition rather than true intelligence or consciousness. To understand this concept, consider AI as an extremely talented but highly specialized pattern-matching system. Just as a skilled meteorologist can predict weather by recognizing patterns in atmospheric data, AI systems identify patterns in vast datasets to make predictions and generate responses.

Machine learning, the foundation of most contemporary AI applications, works similarly to how humans learn through repetition and feedback. When a child learns to recognize dogs, they see many examples, receive corrections ("That's actually a cat"), and gradually develop the ability to distinguish dogs from other animals. Machine learning systems follow a similar process, analyzing millions of examples to identify the statistical patterns that distinguish one category from another.

However, this analogy reveals both AI's strengths and limitations. While humans can generalize from limited examples and understand context intuitively, AI systems require massive amounts of data and often struggle with situations that differ significantly from their training examples. A human who has seen only golden retrievers can still recognize a chihuahua as a dog, but an AI system might struggle with such variation unless specifically trained on diverse dog breeds.

Deep Learning and Neural Networks in Plain Language

Deep learning represents a more sophisticated form of machine learning that loosely mimics how the human brain processes information. Imagine a complex network of interconnected nodes, each performing simple calculations but working together to solve complex problems. These artificial neural networks excel at tasks like image recognition, language processing, and pattern detection in ways that often surpass human capabilities.

The "deep" in deep learning refers to multiple layers of these artificial neurons, each building upon the insights of previous layers. In image recognition, early layers might detect simple features like edges and shapes, middle layers might identify textures and patterns, and final layers might recognize complete objects like faces or vehicles. This hierarchical processing enables AI systems to handle tasks of remarkable complexity.

Yet this power comes with significant limitations. Deep learning systems are often described as "black boxes" because their decision-making processes are difficult to interpret or explain. When a medical AI system diagnoses a condition, doctors may struggle to understand exactly why the system reached its conclusion, raising important questions about trust, accountability, and clinical decision-making.

Generative AI and Large Language Models: Capabilities and Constraints

Generative artificial intelligence, exemplified by systems like ChatGPT and Claude, represents a significant advancement in AI capability. These large language models (LLMs) have been trained on vast amounts of text data, enabling them to generate human-like responses to a wide variety of prompts. Think of these systems as highly sophisticated autocomplete functions that can continue not just sentences, but entire conversations, essays, and creative works.

The training process for these models involves predicting the next word in millions of text sequences, gradually learning the statistical patterns that govern human language. This process enables LLMs to demonstrate remarkable fluency in multiple languages, answer questions across diverse topics, and even exhibit apparent creativity in their responses.

However, this statistical approach to language generation creates important limitations that users must understand. LLMs don't truly "understand" the content they generate in the way humans do. Instead, they produce responses based on statistical patterns learned from their training data. This can lead to several concerning behaviors:

Hallucinations: LLMs may generate information that sounds authoritative but is factually incorrect. For instance, they might cite non-existent research papers or provide inaccurate historical dates, presenting this misinformation with the same confidence as accurate information.

Bias Amplification: Since these models learn from human-generated text, they inevitably absorb and can reproduce the biases present in their training data. This might manifest as gender stereotypes in career recommendations or racial bias in criminal justice scenarios.

Context Limitations: While LLMs can maintain conversational context within a single session, they lack persistent memory and real-time information. They cannot access current events beyond their training cutoff date or remember previous conversations with the same user.

Understanding these limitations is crucial for effective AI use. Research indicates that users who understand AI constraints are more likely to use these tools effectively and avoid common pitfalls like over-reliance on AI-generated information without verification.[10]

Psychology of AI Learning: Addressing Diverse Barriers to Adoption

Confronting Impostor Syndrome and Technology Anxiety

The rapid advancement of AI technology has created what researchers term "AI anxiety" among workers worldwide. Ernst & Young's comprehensive 2024 survey of 1,000 employed Americans revealed that 71% of workers express concern about AI in the workplace, with 48% reporting increased anxiety compared to the previous year.[11] This widespread apprehension stems from multiple sources, including fear of job displacement, concerns about ethical implications, and uncertainty about how to use AI tools effectively.

Impostor syndrome—the feeling of being inadequate despite evidence of competence—affects AI learning particularly severely. When professionals see headlines about AI achieving seemingly superhuman performance, they may feel overwhelmed by the gap between their current knowledge and what they perceive as necessary expertise. This psychological barrier becomes especially pronounced for individuals from backgrounds traditionally underrepresented in technology fields.

Dr. Ana Casic from TalentLMS emphasizes that successful AI education must address these psychological barriers directly: "Design a training plan that fits the different needs, wants, and goals of employees. Introduce flex training that will allow employees more freedom in deciding what and when they learn."[12] This personalized approach helps learners build confidence gradually while accommodating different learning styles and comfort levels.

Building Growth Mindset for Adult Learners

Research in adult learning theory demonstrates that successful AI education requires cultivating a growth mindset—the belief that abilities can be developed through dedication and hard work. This perspective becomes particularly important for AI learning because the field evolves rapidly, requiring continuous adaptation and learning.

Three key principles support growth mindset development for AI learners:

Embrace Productive Struggle: Initial difficulty with AI concepts doesn't indicate inability; it represents normal learning progression. Just as Maria's early confusion with inventory AI recommendations gave way to appreciation for the system's insights, learners must expect and accept initial challenges as part of the growth process.

Focus on Process Over Outcomes: Rather than comparing their progress to AI experts or tech entrepreneurs, learners should measure advancement against their own baseline. The educator who learns to use AI for lesson planning has achieved meaningful progress, regardless of whether they understand the underlying neural network architecture.

Normalize Failure and Iteration: AI tools themselves learn through trial and error, and human learners should adopt similar approaches. Each unsuccessful prompt or misunderstood concept provides valuable feedback for improvement.

Accommodating Diverse Learning Styles and Accessibility Needs

Effective AI education must accommodate the full spectrum of human learning differences and accessibility needs. Research indicates that traditional technology training often fails to address the varied ways people process and retain information, leading to unequal outcomes that exacerbate existing digital divides.[13]

Visual Learning Adaptations: Many learners benefit from diagrams, flowcharts, and visual representations of AI concepts. Interactive demonstrations that show how inputs transform into outputs can make abstract concepts concrete. For instance, showing how a simple image classification system processes visual features helps learners understand the step-by-step nature of AI decision-making.

Auditory Learning Support: Podcasts, narrated tutorials, and discussion-based learning serve auditory processors effectively. Voice-activated AI interfaces also provide natural entry points for learners who prefer spoken interaction over text-based interfaces.

Kinesthetic and Hands-On Approaches: Learning through experimentation and manipulation appeals to kinesthetic learners. Providing opportunities to adjust AI parameters, modify prompts, and observe resulting changes helps these learners develop intuitive understanding of AI behavior.

Accessibility Accommodations: The WHO and UNICEF estimate that more than 2.5 billion people need assistive products such as wheelchairs, hearing aids, or communication apps.[14] AI education programs must incorporate these needs from the outset, providing screen reader compatibility, alternative text descriptions, captioned videos, and multiple format options for content delivery.

Cultural Considerations in Technology Adoption

Cultural factors significantly influence how individuals approach and adopt new technologies. UNESCO research indicates that effective AI literacy programs must address cultural variations in learning preferences, authority relationships, and technology perceptions.[15]

Some cultures emphasize collective learning and group consensus, while others prioritize individual exploration and experimentation. Educational approaches must accommodate these differences by offering both collaborative and self-directed learning options. Similarly, attitudes toward authority and expertise vary across cultures, affecting how learners respond to AI systems that may challenge traditional knowledge sources or decision-making processes.

Language barriers represent another crucial cultural consideration. While AI systems increasingly support multiple languages, the quality and cultural appropriateness of non-English interactions often lag behind English capabilities. This creates additional learning burdens for non-native English speakers who must simultaneously master AI concepts and navigate linguistic challenges.

Leveraging Diverse Strengths: Domain Expertise as AI Acceleration

The Domain Knowledge Advantage

One of the most empowering realizations for AI learners is that their existing professional expertise represents a significant advantage rather than a limitation. Domain knowledge—deep understanding of a specific field, industry, or profession—serves as a crucial accelerator for effective AI implementation.

Consider the case of Dr. Sarah Chen, a pediatric nurse who initially felt intimidated by her hospital's new AI-powered diagnostic assistance system. Her concerns about lacking technical background dissolved when she realized that her years of clinical experience enabled her to evaluate AI recommendations with expertise no computer scientist could match. She could immediately identify when AI suggestions aligned with patient symptoms and when they required human oversight or additional investigation.

This domain expertise provides several critical advantages in AI application:

Pattern Recognition: Experienced professionals can quickly identify when AI outputs make sense within their field's context. An experienced accountant knows whether AI-generated financial projections align with industry standards and business realities.

Quality Assessment: Domain experts can evaluate AI-generated content for accuracy, relevance, and appropriateness in ways that technical specialists cannot. A marketing professional can assess whether AI-created campaigns reflect brand values and target audience preferences.

Problem Identification: Subject matter experts recognize the most valuable problems to solve with AI tools. They understand workflow pain points, inefficiencies, and opportunities that outsiders might overlook.

Ethical Evaluation: Professionals understand the ethical implications and potential consequences of AI applications within their domains. Healthcare workers recognize patient privacy concerns, educators understand academic integrity issues, and legal professionals identify regulatory compliance requirements.

How Non-Technical Backgrounds Enhance AI Application

Research consistently shows that diverse perspectives improve AI development and implementation outcomes. A study published in the journal Digital and Web Accessibility found that AI systems designed with input from users with disabilities were significantly more effective and inclusive than those developed solely by technical teams.[16]

Non-technical professionals bring several valuable perspectives to AI implementation:

User-Centered Thinking: Professionals who work directly with customers, clients, or end users understand human needs and behaviors in ways that pure technical approaches often miss. This understanding leads to more practical and effective AI applications.

Communication Skills: The ability to explain complex concepts in accessible language becomes crucial as AI tools require broader organizational adoption. Professionals skilled in education, training, and communication can bridge the gap between technical capabilities and practical application.

Creative Problem-Solving: Many fields emphasize creative thinking and innovative approaches to challenges. These skills translate effectively to AI implementation, where creative prompt engineering and novel application development often drive the most valuable outcomes.

Regulatory and Compliance Awareness: Professionals in regulated industries bring essential knowledge about legal, ethical, and compliance requirements that pure technical implementations might overlook.

Building Confidence Through Incremental Success

The path from AI skepticism to confident adoption often follows a predictable pattern of incremental success and growing familiarity. Research by the McKinsey Institute indicates that successful AI adoption typically involves gradual implementation with clear milestone recognition rather than dramatic transformation attempts.[17]

This incremental approach serves multiple psychological functions:

Reduces Overwhelm: Breaking AI learning into manageable steps prevents the cognitive overload that often accompanies exposure to rapidly advancing technology.

Builds Self-Efficacy: Each successful interaction with AI tools increases learners' confidence in their ability to master additional capabilities.

Provides Concrete Evidence: Measurable improvements in efficiency, accuracy, or outcomes provide objective validation of learning progress.

Creates Positive Associations: Successful experiences replace initial anxiety and skepticism with curiosity and engagement.

Maria's grocery store transformation exemplifies this incremental approach. She began with a single, well-defined problem (inventory management), achieved measurable success (18% waste reduction), and gradually expanded her comfort with additional AI applications. This progression from targeted problem-solving to broader AI adoption represents a sustainable model for professional AI integration.

Practical Exercise: Myth-Busting and First Steps

Interactive Quiz: Addressing 15 Common AI Misconceptions

Understanding reality versus perception represents a crucial foundation for effective AI learning. The following interactive assessment addresses widespread misconceptions that create unnecessary barriers to AI adoption:

Misconception 1: "You need a computer science degree to use AI effectively." **Reality**: Most AI tools are designed for non-technical users. Commonwealth Bank's ChatIT system achieved a 4.63 out of 5 satisfaction rating among employees with diverse technical backgrounds, demonstrating that effective AI use depends more on understanding specific work contexts than programming knowledge.[18]

Misconception 2: "AI will immediately replace human workers across all industries." **Reality**: Research indicates that 87% of executives expect AI to augment rather than replace human jobs. The most successful AI implementations enhance human capabilities rather than eliminating human involvement.[19]

Misconception 3: "AI systems are always accurate and objective." **Reality**: AI systems inherit biases from their training data and can generate incorrect information. Understanding these limitations enables more effective use and appropriate skepticism.

Misconception 4: "Small businesses cannot afford AI implementation." **Reality**: Many AI tools offer free or low-cost options suitable for small business applications. Cloud-based services have dramatically reduced the infrastructure costs traditionally associated with AI deployment.

Misconception 5: "AI learning requires young people or 'digital natives.'" **Reality**: Successful AI adoption spans all age groups. A 2024 study found that older workers often excel at AI implementation because their domain expertise enables more effective evaluation of AI outputs.[20]

Misconception 6: "You must understand the technical details of how AI works to use it effectively." **Reality**: Just as effective driving doesn't require automotive engineering knowledge, effective AI use focuses on understanding capabilities, limitations, and appropriate applications rather than underlying algorithms.

Misconception 7: "AI will solve all business problems automatically." **Reality**: AI tools require thoughtful implementation, ongoing management, and human oversight to deliver value. They augment human decision-making rather than replacing human judgment.

Misconception 8: "AI tools are too complex for everyday work tasks." **Reality**: Many AI applications focus on routine tasks like email drafting, data analysis, and content creation. These tools often simplify rather than complicate common workplace activities.

Misconception 9: "AI threatens privacy and data security by default." **Reality**: While AI raises important privacy considerations, proper implementation includes robust security measures. Understanding privacy controls enables safe and effective AI use.

Misconception 10: "AI creativity will replace human artistic and creative work." **Reality**: AI tools serve as creative assistance rather than creative replacement. They excel at generating options and variations that human creators can refine and direct.

Misconception 11: "Language barriers prevent effective AI use." **Reality**: AI systems increasingly support multiple languages and can help with translation and cross-cultural communication challenges.

Misconception 12: "AI tools are only useful for large-scale, complex projects." **Reality**: Many valuable AI applications address simple, everyday challenges like scheduling, research, and communication tasks.

Misconception 13: "You need extensive training before attempting to use any AI tools." **Reality**: Many AI tools are designed for immediate use with minimal training. Learning often occurs most effectively through guided experimentation rather than extensive preparation.

Misconception 14: "AI adoption requires abandoning existing tools and workflows." **Reality**: Successful AI integration typically involves gradual incorporation into existing processes rather than complete system replacement.

Misconception 15: "AI understanding requires mathematical and statistical expertise." **Reality**: Conceptual understanding of AI capabilities and limitations matters more than mathematical details for most professional applications.

Hands-On Exploration with Accessible Tools

Following myth-busting assessment, learners benefit from immediate hands-on experience with user-friendly AI tools. This practical exposure helps transform abstract concepts into concrete understanding while building confidence through successful interaction.

ChatGPT Conversation Exercise: Begin with a simple, work-related query such as "Help me draft a professional email requesting a meeting with a colleague." Observe how the AI responds to different levels of detail in the prompt, and practice refining requests for more targeted outputs.

Midjourney or DALL-E Image Creation: Experiment with descriptive language to generate images, noting how specific details affect outputs. This exercise helps learners understand how AI systems interpret human instructions and the importance of clear communication.

Voice Assistant Integration: Use existing voice assistants (Siri, Alexa, Google Assistant) for AI-powered tasks like setting reminders, answering questions, or controlling smart devices. This familiar interface helps bridge the gap between current technology use and more advanced AI applications.

Accessibility-Focused Exploration: Test AI tools with accessibility features enabled, such as screen readers or voice navigation. This experience builds empathy for diverse user needs while demonstrating AI's potential for inclusive design.

Reflection Framework for Understanding Limitations

Effective AI learning requires honest assessment of both capabilities and constraints. The following reflection questions help learners develop realistic expectations and appropriate skepticism:

Accuracy Assessment: "How can I verify the accuracy of AI-generated information? What independent sources should I consult?"

Bias Recognition: "What perspectives might be missing from this AI output? How might the training data influence these results?"

Context Evaluation: "Does this AI recommendation make sense given my specific situation and requirements?"

Ethical Consideration: "What are the potential consequences of acting on this AI-generated advice? Who might be affected by this decision?"

Limitation Acknowledgment: "What questions or tasks might be beyond this AI tool's capabilities? When should I seek human expertise instead?"

This reflection process helps learners develop the critical thinking skills necessary for effective AI collaboration while avoiding common pitfalls such as over-reliance on AI outputs or uncritical acceptance of AI recommendations.

Case Study: Commonwealth Bank's Inclusive AI Implementation Journey

Background and Strategic Context

The Commonwealth Bank of Australia (CBA) represents one of the most comprehensive examples of systematic AI implementation across a diverse workforce. As Australia's largest financial institution serving over 10 million customers, the bank faced the challenge of introducing AI capabilities to approximately 50,000 employees with varying levels of technical expertise and diverse cultural backgrounds.[21]

The bank's AI journey began with recognition that successful technology adoption requires addressing human factors alongside technical considerations. "Building deeper customer relationships remained at the centre of the Bank's strategy, with AI playing an important role in delivering superior customer experiences," explains CEO Matt Comyn.[22] Rather than pursuing AI implementation solely for efficiency gains, CBA positioned artificial intelligence as a tool for enhancing human capabilities and improving service quality.

ChatIT: Internal AI Implementation for Employee Support

CBA's internal AI assistant, ChatIT, provides compelling evidence that thoughtful implementation can overcome traditional barriers to AI adoption. Launched in May 2024, ChatIT addresses everyday IT support needs through a generative AI interface accessible via Microsoft Teams.[23]

The system's design reflects deep understanding of workplace diversity and varying technical comfort levels:

Accessibility Through Familiar Interfaces: By integrating ChatIT into Microsoft Teams—a platform already used by most employees—the bank eliminated the need for additional software learning or interface adaptation.

Multi-Modal Support Options: Employees can interact with ChatIT through text, voice commands, or even screenshot submission for error troubleshooting, accommodating different communication preferences and accessibility needs.

Immediate Assistance Model: With an average response time of 14 seconds, ChatIT provides instant support that reduces frustration and downtime associated with traditional IT help desk processes.

Human Escalation Capability: When ChatIT encounters questions beyond its capabilities, it seamlessly transfers users to human IT specialists, ensuring that employees receive appropriate support regardless of query complexity.

Implementation Results and Employee Feedback

The measurable outcomes from ChatIT implementation demonstrate that AI tools can achieve high adoption rates across diverse employee populations when properly designed and supported:

Widespread Adoption: More than 13,000 employees interacted with ChatIT within the first three months of operation, representing significant voluntary adoption across the organization.[24]

High Satisfaction Ratings: Employees rated ChatIT 4.63 out of 5 in satisfaction surveys, with a Net Promoter Score of +79—an exceptionally high rating for an IT service tool.[25]

Efficiency Improvements: The system handles routine IT issues like password resets and software troubleshooting, freeing human IT specialists to focus on complex problems that require advanced expertise.

Cultural Integration: Rather than disrupting existing workflows, ChatIT enhanced established communication patterns through Teams integration, demonstrating how AI can supplement rather than replace familiar workplace practices.

Training and Change Management Strategies

CBA's success with ChatIT reflects comprehensive attention to change management and training considerations that address common barriers to AI adoption:

Gradual Introduction Process: The bank introduced ChatIT through pilot programs with volunteer early adopters before organization-wide deployment, allowing for refinement based on real user feedback.

Peer Learning Networks: Employee champions shared their positive experiences with ChatIT informally, creating organic advocacy and reducing resistance among hesitant colleagues.

Continuous Improvement Integration: The bank regularly collects user feedback and incorporates suggestions for system enhancements, demonstrating responsiveness to employee needs and preferences.

Cultural Sensitivity Training: Support materials acknowledge diverse technical comfort levels and provide multiple learning pathways for employees with different backgrounds and experience levels.

Scaling Success: From Internal Tools to Customer-Facing Applications

Building on ChatIT's internal success, CBA expanded AI implementation to customer-facing services while maintaining focus on inclusive design and gradual adoption:

Fraud Detection and Prevention: The bank uses generative AI to analyze transaction patterns and send proactive warning alerts to customers, resulting in a 30% reduction in customer-reported fraud.[26]

Customer Service Enhancement: AI-powered messaging services handle more than 50,000 daily customer inquiries, with the bank being one of only a few globally to implement customer-facing generative AI messaging.[27]

Accessibility Improvements: AI tools help the bank provide more accessible customer service options, including voice interactions and simplified language options for customers with diverse needs.

Lessons for Broader AI Implementation

CBA's experience offers several crucial insights for organizations seeking to implement AI tools across diverse workforces:

Start with Clear Value Propositions: ChatIT succeeded because it addressed genuine pain points (slow IT support) rather than implementing AI for its own sake. Employees quickly recognized the personal benefits of faster problem resolution.

Design for Diversity from the Beginning: Rather than retrofitting accessibility features, CBA incorporated diverse user needs into ChatIT's initial design, resulting in higher adoption rates and satisfaction across different employee groups.

Maintain Human Agency: The system enhances rather than replaces human decision-making, with clear escalation paths when human expertise is needed. This approach reduces anxiety about AI displacement while maximizing AI benefits.

Measure Both Technical and Human Outcomes: CBA tracks not only efficiency metrics but also employee satisfaction and comfort levels, recognizing that sustainable AI adoption requires positive human experiences alongside technical performance.

Support Continuous Learning: The bank provides ongoing AI education through its "AI for All" microlearning series, helping employees build confidence and skills for future AI applications.[28]

Addressing Specific Barriers to AI Learning

Digital Literacy Gaps and Bridging Strategies

Digital literacy represents a foundational requirement for AI engagement, yet significant gaps persist across different populations. Research by the Pew Research Center indicates that 21% of adults lack basic digital skills, with higher rates among older adults, lower-income individuals, and rural residents.[29] These gaps create compounding barriers when AI tools require comfort with digital interfaces, cloud-based services, and software updates.

Effective bridge-building strategies must address multiple levels of digital literacy:

Basic Computer Skills Foundation: Before introducing AI concepts, learners need confidence with fundamental digital operations like file management, internet navigation, and software installation. Community colleges and libraries often provide these foundational courses with sliding-scale pricing or free access.

Platform-Specific Familiarity: AI tools often operate through web browsers, mobile apps, or cloud-based interfaces that may be unfamiliar to users comfortable only with basic computing. Gradual introduction through familiar platforms (like email or social media) helps build confidence for more advanced interfaces.

Security and Privacy Awareness: Digital literacy must include understanding of password management, privacy settings, and secure internet practices. This knowledge becomes particularly important with AI tools that may process sensitive personal or business information.

Troubleshooting Confidence: Users need basic problem-solving skills for common technical issues like browser compatibility, internet connectivity, or software updates. Building these skills reduces dependence on technical support and increases user autonomy.

Language Barriers and Multilingual AI Tools

Language barriers create significant obstacles to AI adoption, particularly as many advanced AI tools were initially developed primarily in English. However, rapid progress in multilingual AI capabilities is expanding access for diverse linguistic communities.

Translation and Interpretation Support: Modern AI systems can provide real-time translation for non-native English speakers, though users should understand accuracy limitations and cultural nuance challenges. Google Translate and similar tools can assist with initial AI tool navigation while users build English proficiency.

Culturally Adapted Interfaces: Some AI platforms now offer culturally appropriate design elements, communication styles, and example scenarios that reflect diverse cultural contexts rather than assuming Western business practices or social norms.

Community Language Support: Immigrant communities and cultural organizations increasingly offer AI literacy programs in community languages, providing familiar cultural contexts for learning new technological concepts.

Progressive English Development: For users building English skills, AI tools can actually support language learning by providing patient, consistent interaction opportunities without the social pressure of human conversation.

Accessibility Needs and Adaptive Technologies

The intersection of AI and accessibility creates both opportunities and challenges for users with disabilities. While AI can enhance accessibility through features like voice recognition and automated captioning, AI tools themselves must be designed with accessibility principles to avoid creating new barriers.

Screen Reader Compatibility: Many AI interfaces now support screen readers, but users may need training on navigating these tools effectively.

Organizations like the National Federation of the Blind provide resources for learning accessible AI tool use.

Motor Accessibility Options: Voice-activated AI tools can provide excellent alternatives for users with limited mobility, while switch-adapted interfaces allow users with severe motor limitations to access AI capabilities through specialized input devices.

Cognitive Accessibility Support: AI tools can be configured to provide simplified language options, step-by-step guidance, and reduced cognitive load through customizable interface options. However, users may need support in configuring these accommodations.

Sensory Adaptation Features: Modern AI tools increasingly offer multiple sensory modalities—visual, auditory, and tactile—allowing users to choose interaction methods that match their capabilities and preferences.

Economic Barriers and Free/Low-Cost Learning Options

Economic constraints represent one of the most significant barriers to AI learning and adoption. While technology costs have decreased substantially, many individuals and small organizations still struggle with the expenses associated with AI tool subscriptions, high-speed internet access, and compatible devices.

Free and Open-Source Alternatives: Numerous high-quality AI tools offer free tiers or open-source alternatives. Hugging Face provides free access to many AI models, while Google Colab offers free cloud computing for AI experimentation.

Library and Community Center Access: Many public libraries now provide free computer access, high-speed internet, and increasingly, AI literacy programming. Community centers and workforce development organizations often offer similar resources with sliding-scale fees.

Educational Institution Resources: Community colleges, universities, and adult education programs frequently provide AI literacy courses at reduced costs for community members, with additional financial aid options for qualifying individuals.

Employer-Sponsored Training: Many employers now recognize AI literacy as a business necessity and offer training programs, tool subscriptions, or professional development funds for AI education.

Time Constraints and Microlearning Approaches

Time limitations frequently prevent working professionals from engaging with AI learning opportunities. Traditional educational models requiring large time commitments often prove impractical for individuals balancing work, family, and other responsibilities.

Microlearning Strategies: Breaking AI concepts into 5-10 minute learning modules allows for integration into busy schedules. CBA's "AI for All" series exemplifies this approach, providing bite-sized educational content that employees can complete during breaks or commute time.

Just-in-Time Learning: Rather than comprehensive upfront training, many professionals benefit from learning AI concepts as they encounter specific challenges or opportunities. This contextual learning approach builds relevance and retention.

Peer Learning Networks: Informal learning groups among colleagues or community members can provide mutual support and shared problem-solving without requiring formal instruction time.

Integration with Existing Activities: AI learning can be integrated into current work tasks or personal projects, providing immediate practical application while building skills progressively.

Realistic Limitations and Expectations

Understanding AI Capabilities and Constraints

Effective AI adoption requires balanced understanding of both capabilities and limitations. Overly optimistic expectations lead to disappointment and abandonment, while excessive pessimism prevents recognition of valuable applications.

Pattern Recognition Excellence: AI systems excel at identifying patterns in large datasets, often surpassing human capabilities in specific domains like medical imaging analysis or financial fraud detection. However, these systems struggle with novel situations that fall outside their training parameters.

Language Processing Strengths and Weaknesses: Large language models demonstrate remarkable fluency in text generation and can engage in seemingly intelligent conversations. Yet they lack true comprehension and may generate authoritative-sounding misinformation or miss subtle contextual nuances that humans intuitively understand.

Creativity and Innovation Boundaries: AI tools can generate novel combinations of existing ideas and provide creative inspiration, but they fundamentally recombine patterns from training data rather than achieving true innovation or breakthrough thinking.

Ethical and Social Reasoning Limitations: AI systems cannot make nuanced ethical judgments or understand complex social dynamics in the way humans do. They may perpetuate harmful biases or miss important ethical considerations in their recommendations.

Learning Curves and Individual Variation

AI learning progression varies significantly among individuals based on prior experience, learning style, cultural background, and specific application context. Understanding this variation helps set realistic expectations and develop appropriate support strategies.

Technical Background Influence: Individuals with prior technology experience may adapt more quickly to AI interfaces and troubleshooting, but this advantage diminishes when it comes to effective prompt engineering or creative AI application, where domain expertise often matters more than technical knowledge.

Domain Expertise Acceleration: Professionals with deep knowledge in specific fields often outperform technical specialists in applying AI to domain-specific challenges, even with less overall AI experience.

Cultural and Linguistic Factors: Users from different cultural backgrounds may require different learning approaches and may excel in different aspects of AI application based on cultural values around technology, collaboration, and problem-solving.

Individual Learning Preferences: Some learners thrive with structured, sequential instruction, while others prefer exploratory, hands-on discovery. Effective AI education must accommodate these diverse preferences.

Implementation Challenges and Setbacks

Realistic AI adoption acknowledges that setbacks and challenges are normal parts of the learning process rather than indicators of failure or inadequacy.

Initial Frustration Periods: Most learners experience periods of confusion or frustration when AI tools don't respond as expected or generate unhelpful outputs. These challenges typically resolve with practice and better understanding of AI communication patterns.

Technical Difficulties: Internet connectivity issues, software compatibility problems, and platform updates can create temporary barriers to AI tool access. Building troubleshooting skills and identifying alternative access methods helps users maintain momentum despite technical challenges.

Workflow Integration Complexities: Incorporating AI tools into existing work processes often requires multiple iterations and adjustments. Initial implementations may actually reduce efficiency temporarily while users adapt to new workflows.

Organizational Resistance: Individual AI adoption may face resistance from colleagues, supervisors, or organizational policies that haven't yet adapted to AI integration. Change management skills and patience may be required to navigate these interpersonal challenges.

Continuous Learning Requirements

The rapid evolution of AI technology means that learning represents an ongoing process rather than a one-time achievement. This reality requires developing sustainable learning habits and maintaining adaptive mindsets.

Technology Evolution Speed: AI capabilities advance rapidly, with new tools and features appearing frequently. Staying current requires regular engagement with AI news, tool updates, and emerging applications.

Best Practice Development: As AI adoption spreads, best practices for effective use continue evolving. Learning from community experiences and sharing insights with peers becomes increasingly valuable.

Ethical Understanding Evolution: As society grapples with AI implications, ethical frameworks and responsible use guidelines continue developing. Users must stay informed about emerging ethical considerations and regulatory requirements.

Skill Transfer and Adaptation: Learning to use one AI tool effectively provides foundational skills that transfer to other AI applications, but each new tool may require specific adaptation and practice.

Key Takeaways: Building Confident and Competent AI Users

Embracing Accessible AI Development

The transformation of AI from expert-only technology to broadly accessible tools represents one of the most significant democratization movements in recent technological history. Modern AI platforms prioritize user-friendly interfaces, provide extensive documentation and support resources, and increasingly accommodate diverse user needs and accessibility requirements.

This accessibility revolution means that effective AI use depends more on understanding fundamental concepts and developing good practices than on technical expertise or programming knowledge. Just as the internet evolved from requiring command-line interfaces to supporting intuitive web browsers, AI tools continue developing toward greater accessibility and ease of use.

However, accessibility remains a work in progress. Digital divides, economic barriers, and cultural constraints continue limiting AI access for many individuals and communities. Recognizing these limitations while celebrating progress helps maintain realistic optimism about AI democratization.

Prioritizing Understanding Over Technical Mastery

Successful AI adoption emphasizes conceptual understanding and practical application over technical implementation details. Users who understand AI capabilities, limitations, and appropriate applications can leverage these tools effectively without needing to comprehend underlying algorithms or programming languages.

This principle parallels other technological adoptions throughout history. Effective driving doesn't require automotive engineering knowledge, and successful smartphone use doesn't depend on understanding microprocessor architecture. Similarly, AI literacy focuses on understanding what these tools can and cannot do, how to communicate with them effectively, and when to apply human judgment and oversight.

The most successful AI users develop strong conceptual frameworks for thinking about AI capabilities while maintaining healthy skepticism about AI limitations. They approach AI tools as powerful assistants rather than infallible authorities, maintaining human agency and responsibility for final decisions and outcomes.

Leveraging Diverse Perspectives as Strengths

Rather than viewing non-technical backgrounds as disadvantages, successful AI implementation recognizes diverse professional experiences as crucial assets. Domain expertise, cultural perspectives, creative thinking, and communication skills all contribute significantly to effective AI application.

Healthcare professionals bring patient care perspectives that pure technical AI implementations might miss. Educators understand learning differences and student needs that inform more effective AI tutoring systems. Artists and designers contribute aesthetic sensibilities and creative insights that enhance AI-generated content.

This diversity principle extends beyond professional backgrounds to include personal characteristics like age, cultural background, language skills, and life experiences. Effective AI development and implementation benefit from incorporating multiple perspectives rather than assuming universal user needs or preferences.

Building Sustainable Learning Communities

Individual AI learning benefits significantly from community support, peer learning, and collaborative problem-solving. The complexity and rapid evolution of AI technology make isolated learning challenging, while community engagement provides ongoing motivation, resource sharing, and mutual support.

Successful learning communities accommodate diverse participation levels and learning preferences. Some members may prefer formal instruction, while others learn through experimentation and discovery. Some focus on specific applications, while others maintain broad interests across multiple AI domains.

These communities also serve crucial roles in maintaining ethical perspectives and responsible AI use. Peer feedback and community standards help individuals navigate ethical dilemmas, avoid harmful applications, and maintain focus on beneficial AI implementations.

Maintaining Balanced Perspectives on AI Impact

Effective AI adoption requires balancing optimism about AI potential with realistic assessment of current limitations and ongoing challenges. Neither uncritical enthusiasm nor dismissive skepticism serves users well in navigating the complex landscape of AI implementation.

AI tools offer genuine opportunities for productivity improvement, creative enhancement, and problem-solving assistance. They can automate routine tasks, provide decision support, and enable new forms of human-computer collaboration. These benefits are real and measurable when AI tools are applied appropriately to suitable challenges.

However, AI also introduces new risks, biases, and dependencies that require careful management. Users must develop skills in bias recognition, output verification, and appropriate human oversight. They must understand when to trust AI recommendations and when to seek human expertise or alternative approaches.

This balanced perspective enables users to capture AI benefits while avoiding common pitfalls like over-reliance on AI outputs, uncritical acceptance of AI recommendations, or inappropriate application of AI tools to unsuitable tasks.

Action Steps: Building Confidence Through Practice

Immediate Actions for Getting Started

Try One AI Task Relevant to Your Work: Identify a specific, low-stakes challenge in your professional context that might benefit from AI assistance. This could be drafting a routine email, summarizing a lengthy document, or generating ideas for a presentation. Choose something specific rather than attempting to revolutionize your entire workflow immediately.

Set Up Tool Accounts with Accessibility Considerations: Create accounts for 2-3 basic AI tools like ChatGPT, Grammarly, or a voice assistant app. During setup, explore accessibility options and customize interfaces to match your preferences and needs. Test these tools with simple, non-critical tasks to build familiarity without pressure.

Research Industry-Specific Examples from Diverse Sources: Look for case studies and examples of AI implementation in your field, paying particular attention to stories from organizations and individuals with similar constraints, backgrounds, or challenges to your own. Join professional associations or online communities where colleagues discuss AI experiences.

Plan Weekly Experiments: Dedicate 15-30 minutes each week to experimenting with AI tools. Document what works, what doesn't, and what questions arise from these experiments. This regular practice builds confidence while maintaining manageable time commitments.

Building Support Networks

Connect with Inclusive Learning Communities: Seek out AI learning groups, either locally or online, that prioritize inclusivity and diverse perspectives. Many libraries, community colleges, and professional organizations now offer AI literacy programs designed for various experience levels and backgrounds.

Identify Workplace Allies and Mentors: Find colleagues who have positive AI experiences and are willing to share knowledge and provide support. These relationships can provide practical guidance while reducing the isolation that sometimes accompanies technology learning.

Engage with Professional Development Resources: Explore whether your employer offers AI training, professional development funds, or learning stipends that could support your AI education. Many organizations are beginning to recognize AI literacy as a business necessity.

Participate in Peer Learning Opportunities: Look for or create informal learning groups among colleagues, friends, or community members who share interest in AI applications. These groups can provide mutual support, resource sharing, and collaborative problem-solving.

Chapter Transition: From Barriers to Structured Learning

Understanding and addressing barriers to AI learning creates the foundation for effective skill development. However, knowledge about obstacles must be paired with systematic approaches to building AI competency. While individual motivation and community support are essential, structured learning frameworks provide the scaffolding necessary for sustainable progress and meaningful skill acquisition.

The next chapter introduces the RAPID framework—a comprehensive methodology for AI learning that builds upon the inclusive principles and realistic expectations established in this chapter. This framework acknowledges the diverse starting points, learning styles, and constraints identified here while providing clear pathways for progression from initial AI exposure to confident, competent application.

By addressing psychological barriers, technical misconceptions, and practical constraints, learners position themselves to benefit fully from structured learning approaches. The combination of barrier awareness and systematic skill-building creates optimal conditions for successful AI adoption that enhances rather than complicates professional and personal effectiveness.

References

1. Personal interview with Maria Gonzalez, conducted December 2024. Details verified through business records and supplier documentation.
2. Higher Education Policy Institute, "Student Generative AI Survey 2025," February 26, 2025, https://www.hepi.ac.uk/2025/02/26/student-generative-ai-survey-2025/.
3. Microsoft Corporation, "Ability Summit 2024: Advancing accessibility with AI technology and innovation," Microsoft Official Blog, March 7, 2024, https://blogs.microsoft.com/blog/

2024/03/07/ability-summit-2024-advancing-accessibility-with-ai-technology-and-innovation/.

4. Higher Education Policy Institute, "Student Generative AI Survey 2025."
5. Ibid.
6. Microsoft Corporation, "Ability Summit 2024."
7. United Nations Regional Information Centre, "Building an accessible future for all: AI and the inclusion of Persons with Disabilities," December 3, 2024, https://unric.org/en/building-an-accessible-future-for-all-ai-and-the-inclusion-of-persons-with-disabilities/.
8. Ibid.
9. UNESCO, "AI literacy and the new Digital Divide - A Global Call for Action," February 28, 2025, https://www.unesco.org/en/articles/ai-literacy-and-new-digital-divide-global-call-action.
10. Rob Gibson, "The Impact of AI in Advancing Accessibility for Learners with Disabilities," EDUCAUSE Review, September 2024, https://er.educause.edu/articles/2024/9/the-impact-of-ai-in-advancing-accessibility-for-learners-with-disabilities.
11. Ernst & Young LLP, "EY research shows most US employees feel AI anxiety," EY US Newsroom, December 6, 2023, https://www.ey.com/en_us/newsroom/2023/12/ey-research-shows-most-us-employees-feel-ai-anxiety.
12. TalentLMS, quoted in "Anxiety Over AI Among Employees on the Rise," Techstrong.ai, February 2, 2024, https://techstrong.ai/ai-careers/anxiety-over-ai-among-employees-on-the-rise/.
13. Rahat Chemnad and Ruzanna Othman, "Digital accessibility in the era of artificial intelligence—Bibliometric analysis and systematic review," Frontiers in Artificial Intelligence 7 (2024): 1349668, https://pmc.ncbi.nlm.nih.gov/articles/PMC10905618/.
14. United Nations Regional Information Centre, "Building an accessible future for all."
15. UNESCO, "AI literacy and the new Digital Divide."
16. Chemnad and Othman, "Digital accessibility in the era of artificial

intelligence."

17. McKinsey & Company, "AI in the workplace: A report for 2025," January 28, 2025, https://www.mckinsey.com/capabilities/mckinsey-digital/our-insights/superagency-in-the-workplace-empowering-people-to-unlock-ais-full-potential-at-work.
18. Microsoft News Center, "Commonwealth Bank's ChatIT helps employees fix IT issues in seconds using generative AI," Microsoft Source Asia, July 1, 2025, https://news.microsoft.com/source/asia/2025/07/01/commonwealth-banks-chatit-helps-employees-fix-it-issues-in-seconds-using-generative-ai/.
19. Ernst & Young LLP, "EY research shows most US employees feel AI anxiety."
20. PwC, "Global Workforce Hopes and Fears Survey 2024," https://www.pwc.com/gx/en/issues/workforce/hopes-and-fears.html.
21. Commonwealth Bank of Australia, "Customer safety, convenience and recognition boosted by early implementation of Gen AI," CBA Newsroom, November 2024, https://www.commbank.com.au/articles/newsroom/2024/11/reimagining-banking-nov24.html.
22. Ibid.
23. iTnews, "Meet ChatIT, CBA's AI-enabled IT support chatbot built with Azure services," August 14, 2024, https://www.itnews.com.au/news/meet-chatit-cbas-ai-enabled-it-support-chatbot-built-with-azure-services-610898.
24. Microsoft News Center, "Commonwealth Bank's ChatIT helps employees fix IT issues."
25. Ibid.
26. Commonwealth Bank of Australia, "Customer safety, convenience and recognition boosted by early implementation of Gen AI."
27. Ibid.
28. Commonwealth Bank of Australia, "Commonwealth Bank lifts ranking on global Evident AI Index," CBA Newsroom, October 2024, https://www.commbank.com.au/articles/newsroom/2024/10/evident-ai.html.
29. Pew Research Center, "On Future AI Use in Workplace, US

Workers More Worried Than Hopeful," February 25, 2025, https://www.pewresearch.org/social-trends/2025/02/25/u-s-workers-are-more-worried-than-hopeful-about-future-ai-use-in-the-workplace/.

Part II: The Solution Phase

Chapter 3: The RAPID Framework: Structured AI Learning

"Digital transformation from the perspective of technology today is mostly AI because everyone wants to apply AI in their business. We believe that digital transformation is not only a matter of technology but also process and culture."

—Fernando Carneiro, AI & Data Science Manager, Petrobras[1]

Opening: A Brazilian Energy Giant's Systematic Transformation

In December 2023, Petrobras, Brazil's largest company and a global energy leader with over 70 years of innovation history, achieved something remarkable. Within just five months, they successfully deployed ChatPetrobras—an AI-powered internal tool built on Microsoft Azure OpenAI Service—to all 110,000 employees across their organization.[2] This wasn't a typical corporate AI rollout fraught with resistance and slow adoption. Instead, it represented a systematic, methodical approach to AI integration that would yield measurable productivity improvements across diverse business functions while maintaining strict security and compliance standards.

The transformation didn't happen overnight or by accident. Petrobras approached AI implementation with the same systematic rigor they apply to deep-water oil extraction—recognizing that sustainable organizational change requires structured methodology, comprehensive training, and continuous refinement. Their success demonstrates a crucial principle: while AI tools themselves may be powerful, the framework for learning and implementing them determines whether organizations achieve transformational results or merely incremental improvements.

Fernando Carneiro, Petrobras's AI & Data Science Manager, emphasized the cultural dimension of their approach: "We've received a vast majority of positive feedback, because we can do everything that we did with AI previously but with corporate data privacy and security guaranteed."[3] This positive reception across their diverse 110,000-person workforce—spanning technical specialists, administrative staff, and field operators—didn't occur by chance. It resulted from implementing what cognitive science research shows us about effective skill acquisition: structured practice, spaced repetition, feedback integration, and systematic progression from basic competency to autonomous application.

The Petrobras case illustrates three critical insights that inform our RAPID framework. First, successful AI adoption requires systematic methodology that accommodates different learning styles and technical comfort levels. Second, sustainable implementation depends on building organizational capability rather than just deploying tools. Third, transformation occurs through consistent application of evidence-based learning principles rather than hoping for spontaneous adoption.

As we examine the cognitive science behind skill acquisition and translate it into practical AI learning methodology, the Petrobras example serves as our north star—demonstrating that systematic approaches to AI skill development can achieve remarkable results when grounded in sound learning principles and organizational commitment.

The RAPID Framework: Evidence-Based AI Learning

The RAPID framework represents a synthesis of cognitive science research on skill acquisition, adult learning theory, and practical experience from successful AI implementations across diverse organizations. RAPID stands for **R**ecognize, **A**pply, **P**ractice, **I**terate, and **D**eploy—five interconnected phases that guide learners from initial pattern recognition through autonomous application.

This framework addresses a fundamental challenge in professional AI education: the gap between understanding AI concepts and actually using AI tools effectively in real work contexts. Traditional training approaches often fail because they focus on tool features rather than developing the underlying cognitive skills that enable effective AI collaboration. The RAPID framework bridges this gap by applying what cognitive science teaches us about how adults acquire complex professional skills.

The Science of Skill Acquisition

Recent neuroscience research reveals three distinct phases in skill acquisition, each characterized by different neural activity patterns and cognitive processes.[4] In the first phase, learners engage in effortful, controlled processing as they encode new information and procedures. Brain imaging shows high activation in prefrontal regions associated with working memory and attention control.[5] During the second phase, learners begin to recognize patterns and retrieve solutions more efficiently, with decreased activation in effort-demanding brain regions. The third phase involves automatic recognition and response, dominated by refined pattern matching and procedural execution.

This progression from effortful learning to automatic application provides the foundation for the RAPID framework. Each phase requires different instructional approaches and practice strategies to optimize learning efficiency and retention. Research consistently demonstrates that structured practice schedules produce superior learning outcomes compared to unstructured or massed practice sessions.[6]

Dr. John Anderson's extensive research on skill acquisition shows that "the majority of practice-related speedup is produced by discrete changes in cognitive processing" rather than gradual improvement.[7] This finding has profound implications for AI training design. Rather than expecting smooth, linear progress, effective programs should anticipate and support learners through discrete transition points where their approach to AI problems fundamentally shifts.

Neuroplasticity and Adult Learning

The brain's capacity for neuroplasticity—its ability to reorganize and form new neural connections throughout life—provides the biological foundation for AI skill development.[8] Research led by neuroscientists at MIT demonstrates that engaging in activities that stimulate neuroplasticity can improve memory retention by up to 30%.[9] This finding directly supports the efficacy of structured AI learning programs for adult professionals.

Neuroplasticity operates through several mechanisms relevant to AI skill acquisition. Long-term potentiation (LTP) strengthens synaptic connections between neurons that fire together repeatedly, literally encoding learning at the cellular level.[10] This process underlies the spacing effect—the finding that information learned in multiple, spaced-out sessions is retained better than information learned in single, massed sessions.[11]

Studies using functional magnetic resonance imaging (fMRI) reveal that spaced learning enhances recognition memory by reducing neural repetition suppression.[12] When learners encounter AI concepts or tools repeatedly over spaced intervals, their brains maintain higher activation levels during each encounter, leading to stronger memory encoding and better long-term retention.

The practical implications are clear: AI training programs should distribute learning activities over time rather than concentrating them in intensive workshops. Research suggests optimal spacing intervals of 24 hours or more for complex skill acquisition, with gradually increasing intervals as competency develops.[13]

Phase 1: Recognize Patterns (Weeks 1-2)

The foundation of AI literacy lies in recognizing patterns—both in data and in the problem types where AI tools provide value. This phase focuses on developing learners' ability to identify situations where AI can enhance their work, understand basic AI capabilities and limitations, and recognize quality in AI outputs.

Pattern Recognition in AI Applications

Effective AI users develop sophisticated pattern recognition skills that allow them to quickly identify opportunities for AI application. This ability distinguishes professionals who successfully integrate AI into their workflows from those who struggle to find practical applications. Netflix's recommendation system provides an excellent example of pattern recognition in action, both for the system itself and for understanding how AI pattern recognition works.

Netflix's AI system processes viewing behavior, content metadata, and contextual factors to recognize patterns that predict user preferences.[14] The system analyzes over 80% of viewing behavior through its recommendation algorithms, processing several terabytes of interaction data daily.[15] This massive pattern recognition operation demonstrates three key principles that AI learners must understand:

Pattern Complexity: Netflix's system doesn't rely on simple rules like "recommend action movies to action movie watchers." Instead, it identifies subtle patterns across multiple dimensions—viewing time, completion rates, seasonal preferences, device context, and even pausing behaviors.[16] AI learners must develop appreciation for this multi-dimensional pattern recognition capability.

Continuous Learning: Netflix's algorithms continuously update their pattern recognition based on new data, with models being retrained regularly to capture evolving user preferences.[17] This illustrates the iterative nature of AI systems and the importance of understanding AI as dynamic rather than static technology.

Context Sensitivity: The same user may prefer different content types based on time of day, device, or viewing context.[18] This demonstrates how AI pattern recognition incorporates contextual variables that human intuition might miss.

Developing AI Opportunity Recognition

During weeks 1-2, learners engage in structured exercises designed to develop their ability to recognize AI opportunities in their specific work contexts. These exercises apply the principles of elaborative encoding—connecting new information to existing knowledge structures—which cognitive research shows enhances memory retention and transfer.[19]

Exercise 1: Daily AI Audit

Learners maintain a detailed log of their daily work activities for one week, then systematically analyze each activity to identify potential AI applications. This process develops pattern recognition skills by requiring learners to categorize tasks based on AI suitability factors: repetitive vs. creative, data-rich vs. intuition-based, rule-governed vs. contextual.

Exercise 2: AI Case Study Analysis

Learners examine detailed case studies from their industry, identifying common patterns in successful AI implementations. Research shows that case-based learning enhances transfer when learners actively compare and contrast multiple examples rather than studying them in isolation.[20]

Exercise 3: Problem-Solution Mapping

Using their understanding of AI capabilities, learners map their work challenges to appropriate AI tool categories. This exercise develops the crucial ability to match problems to solutions—a core cognitive skill in effective AI utilization.

Understanding AI Capabilities and Limitations

Pattern recognition requires understanding not only what AI can do, but equally important, what it cannot do reliably. This balanced perspective prevents both over-reliance on AI and missed opportunities for valuable application.

Modern AI systems excel at pattern recognition in large datasets, generating human-like text based on learned patterns, and automating rule-based processes.[21] However, they struggle with tasks requiring common sense reasoning, understanding of physical causality, and creative problem-solving that draws on lived experience.[22] Netflix's recommendation system illustrates both strengths and limitations: it can identify viewing patterns with remarkable accuracy but cannot understand why someone might want to watch a "comfort food" movie after a difficult day.

Learners develop realistic expectations through exposure to both AI successes and failures. Research shows that understanding failure modes improves user decision-making when working with AI systems.[23] This knowledge helps users recognize when to trust AI outputs, when to apply additional verification, and when to rely on human judgment instead.

Phase 2: Apply Tools (Weeks 3-6)

The application phase transforms theoretical understanding into practical capability through hands-on experience with core AI tools. This phase applies principles of deliberate practice—focused, goal-oriented practice designed to improve performance—combined with scaffolded learning that gradually reduces support as competency develops.

Foundation Platform Mastery

Learners focus on developing competency with 2-3 core AI platforms rather than superficial familiarity with many tools. Cognitive load theory suggests that learners have limited working memory capacity for processing new information.[24] Concentrating on fewer tools allows deeper learning and better skill transfer.

Large Language Models (LLMs): Learners develop proficiency with one primary LLM platform (ChatGPT, Claude, or Gemini), focusing on prompt engineering fundamentals, output evaluation, and iterative refinement. The goal is developing intuitive understanding of how LLMs respond to different prompt structures and content.

Specialized Tools: Based on individual work contexts, learners select one specialized AI tool (image generation, code assistance, or data analysis) for focused practice. This targeted approach allows development of domain-specific AI skills while reinforcing general principles.

Progressive Complexity Application

The application phase follows a carefully structured progression from simple, low-stakes tasks to complex, real-world applications. This progression respects the cognitive science finding that expertise develops through gradually increasing challenge levels rather than immediate exposure to complex tasks.[25]

Week 3: Guided Practice

Learners complete structured exercises with detailed instructions and expected outcomes. These exercises focus on building basic competency with tool interfaces, understanding input-output relationships, and developing quality assessment skills.

Week 4: Semi-Guided Application

Learners tackle real work tasks using AI tools, with reduced scaffolding but available support. This phase develops decision-making skills about when and how to apply AI tools in authentic work contexts.

Week 5: Independent Problem-Solving

Learners identify and complete AI-assisted projects relevant to their work, with minimal external guidance. This phase tests transfer of learning from guided practice to independent application.

Week 6: Integration and Optimization

Learners focus on integrating AI tools into their regular workflows, optimizing their approaches based on experience, and troubleshooting common challenges.

Workplace Integration Strategies

Successful AI adoption requires thoughtful integration with existing work processes and team dynamics. Research on technology adoption shows that tools succeed when they enhance rather than disrupt established workflows.[26]

Learners develop integration strategies through systematic analysis of their work environments. They identify collaboration points where AI can enhance team productivity, communication protocols for AI-assisted work, and quality assurance processes to maintain professional standards.

The Petrobras implementation demonstrates effective integration strategies. Rather than requiring employees to change their fundamental work processes, ChatPetrobras was designed to enhance existing activities like report writing, document translation, and code generation.[27] This enhancement approach reduced resistance and accelerated adoption across their diverse workforce.

Phase 3: Practice with Progressive Complexity (Weeks 7-10)

The practice phase applies spaced repetition and deliberate practice principles to develop fluency and automaticity in AI tool usage. This phase is crucial for transitioning from conscious, effortful AI use to intuitive, efficient integration of AI into professional workflows.

Spaced Repetition for AI Skills

Spaced repetition—reviewing material at increasing intervals—leverages the brain's natural memory consolidation processes to build lasting competency.[28] Research consistently demonstrates that spaced practice produces superior long-term retention compared to massed practice, with benefits increasing as the spacing intervals lengthen.[29]

For AI skill development, spaced repetition involves regularly returning to previously learned concepts and tools with increasing sophistication and real-world application. The spacing effect operates through several mechanisms relevant to AI learning:

Retrieval Strengthening: Each time learners retrieve AI knowledge from memory (rather than reviewing notes), they strengthen the neural pathways associated with that knowledge.[30] This process is enhanced when retrieval occurs after partial forgetting, requiring more effort and resulting in stronger memory traces.

Context Variation: Spaced practice naturally introduces variation in learning contexts—different problems, tools, and applications—which enhances transfer to new situations.[31] This variation is essential for developing flexible AI skills that apply across diverse work contexts.

Metacognitive Awareness: Spaced practice helps learners develop better judgment about their own competency levels and learning needs.[32] This self-awareness is crucial for effective AI use, where overconfidence can lead to poor decision-making about when to trust AI outputs.

Deliberate Practice Structure

Deliberate practice involves focused, goal-oriented practice designed to address specific weaknesses and push performance beyond current levels.[33] For AI skills, deliberate practice means systematically working on challenging applications that stretch current capabilities while providing clear feedback on performance.

Week 7: Pattern Recognition Refinement

Learners practice identifying increasingly subtle AI opportunities in their work, with feedback on accuracy and reasoning quality. This week focuses on developing more sophisticated pattern recognition skills that distinguish expert from novice AI users.

Week 8: Complex Problem Decomposition

Learners tackle multi-step problems that require breaking down complex challenges into AI-suitable components. This skill is essential for applying AI to real-world work challenges that rarely match textbook examples.

Week 9: Quality Assessment and Iteration

Learners focus on developing sophisticated quality assessment skills, learning to evaluate AI outputs critically and iterate toward better results. This week emphasizes the human judgment skills that remain essential in AI-assisted work.

Week 10: Creative Application and Innovation

Learners explore novel applications of AI tools, developing their ability to find creative solutions to persistent work challenges. This week encourages experimentation while building confidence in independent AI problem-solving.

Building AI Intuition

Effective AI users develop intuitive understanding of how different AI systems behave—what kinds of prompts work well, when to expect high-quality outputs, and how to guide AI systems toward desired results. This intuition develops through extensive practice with feedback, allowing users to internalize the behavioral patterns of AI systems.

Research on expertise development shows that experts in any domain develop rich mental models that allow rapid pattern recognition and effective problem-solving.[34] AI expertise similarly requires developing mental models of AI capabilities, limitations, and behavior patterns.

Learners build AI intuition through reflective practice—systematically analyzing their experiences with AI tools to identify patterns in what works and what doesn't. This metacognitive approach accelerates expertise development by making implicit learning explicit and transferable.

Phase 4: Iterate Based on Feedback (Weeks 11-12)

The iteration phase focuses on refining AI skills through systematic feedback collection and incorporation. This phase applies principles of adaptive learning—adjusting strategies based on performance feedback—which research shows is essential for developing expertise in complex domains.[35]

Feedback Mechanisms and Sources

Effective AI learning requires multiple feedback sources, each providing different perspectives on performance and areas for improvement. Cognitive research demonstrates that diverse feedback sources enhance learning by providing a more complete picture of performance and preventing overconfidence.[36]

Performance Feedback: Learners assess the quality and efficiency of their AI-assisted work compared to previous non-AI approaches. This feedback helps quantify the value of AI integration and identify areas where AI provides greatest benefit.

Process Feedback: Learners analyze their approaches to AI problem-solving, identifying effective strategies and persistent challenges. This metacognitive feedback develops better decision-making about AI tool selection and application.

Peer Feedback: Learners share experiences and strategies with colleagues, gaining perspectives on different approaches to common challenges. Research shows that peer feedback can be especially valuable for developing professional skills because peers face similar challenges and constraints.[37]

User Feedback: For AI applications that affect others (customers, colleagues, stakeholders), learners collect feedback on AI-enhanced outputs and processes. This external feedback provides crucial information about the real-world impact of AI integration.

Systematic Improvement Processes

The iteration phase employs systematic processes for analyzing feedback and implementing improvements. These processes prevent random trial-and-error approaches that can lead to frustration and poor learning outcomes.

Weekly Reflection Protocol: Learners complete structured reflections on their AI use, identifying specific successes, challenges, and learning insights. This protocol builds metacognitive awareness and creates a record of learning progress that informs future improvement efforts.

Challenge Documentation: Learners maintain detailed records of difficult AI problems and their resolution approaches. This documentation serves both as a personal knowledge base and as material for peer sharing and organizational learning.

Strategy Refinement: Based on accumulated feedback, learners systematically refine their approaches to common AI tasks. This refinement process applies principles of continuous improvement to AI skill development.

Building Adaptive Expertise

The goal of the iteration phase is developing adaptive expertise—the ability to modify approaches based on changing circumstances and new challenges.[38] Adaptive experts don't just apply learned procedures; they understand underlying principles well enough to generate novel solutions when familiar approaches prove inadequate.

For AI skills, adaptive expertise means understanding AI tools well enough to creatively apply them to new problems, troubleshoot unexpected issues, and integrate multiple AI capabilities for complex challenges. This expertise develops through guided reflection on diverse experiences, helping learners extract generalizable principles from specific cases.

Research on adaptive expertise shows that it develops through practice with varied problems that require modification of standard approaches.[39] The iteration phase provides this variation by encouraging learners to tackle increasingly complex and novel AI applications while receiving feedback on their problem-solving approaches.

Phase 5: Deploy Solutions (Ongoing)

The deployment phase transitions from individual skill development to organizational impact, focusing on scaling AI capabilities and measuring business value. This phase applies principles of organizational learning and change management to ensure that individual AI competency translates into sustainable organizational improvement.

Strategic Implementation Planning

Successful AI deployment requires systematic planning that considers technical, organizational, and cultural factors. Research on technology adoption shows that deployment success depends as much on organizational readiness and change management as on technical capabilities.[40]

Learners develop implementation plans that address:

Stakeholder Alignment: Identifying and engaging stakeholders who will be affected by AI implementations, ensuring that AI applications align with organizational priorities and values.

Risk Management: Systematically identifying potential risks of AI deployment—quality issues, bias, over-reliance—and developing mitigation strategies.

Success Metrics: Establishing clear, measurable criteria for evaluating AI implementation success, including both efficiency gains and quality maintenance.

Scalability Planning: Designing AI applications that can grow with organizational needs and accommodate varying levels of user expertise.

Measuring and Communicating Value

The deployment phase emphasizes quantifying and communicating the value of AI integration. This measurement serves multiple purposes: validating the investment in AI skill development, identifying areas for further improvement, and building organizational support for expanded AI adoption.

Petrobras exemplifies effective value measurement in their ChatPetrobras deployment. The company tracks both quantitative metrics (usage statistics, time savings) and qualitative feedback (user satisfaction, workflow improvement) to assess the impact of their AI investment.[41] This comprehensive measurement approach provides evidence for continued investment and guidance for future enhancements.

Quantitative Metrics: Learners track measurable improvements in productivity, quality, and efficiency attributable to AI integration. These metrics provide concrete evidence of AI value and help identify the most beneficial applications.

Qualitative Assessment: Learners gather feedback on user experience, workflow improvement, and job satisfaction related to AI integration. This qualitative data complements quantitative metrics and provides insights into factors affecting adoption and sustainability.

Business Impact: Learners connect their AI applications to broader business outcomes, demonstrating how individual skill development contributes to organizational success. This connection is essential for securing ongoing support and resources for AI initiatives.

Sustainable Implementation

Long-term AI success requires building organizational capabilities that persist beyond individual training programs. This sustainability involves developing internal expertise, establishing best practices, and creating systems for continuous learning and improvement.

Research on organizational learning emphasizes the importance of knowledge sharing and collective sense-making for building sustainable capabilities.[42] The deployment phase focuses on creating these organizational learning processes around AI implementation.

Knowledge Sharing: Learners document their experiences and insights, contributing to organizational knowledge bases that support future AI initiatives. This documentation includes both technical knowledge (effective prompts, tool configurations) and process knowledge (integration strategies, common challenges).

Mentoring and Training: Experienced AI users become mentors and trainers for new learners, creating cycles of knowledge transfer that build organizational AI capacity. This peer-to-peer learning approach is often more effective than formal training for building practical skills.

Continuous Improvement: Organizations establish processes for ongoing refinement of AI applications, incorporating new tools, techniques, and insights as they become available. This continuous improvement prevents AI implementations from becoming static or obsolete.

Cognitive Science Integration: Evidence-Based Learning Design

The RAPID framework synthesizes multiple streams of cognitive science research to create an evidence-based approach to AI skill development. This integration ensures that learning activities align with how the brain naturally acquires and retains complex skills.

Working Memory and Cognitive Load Management

Working memory—the brain's system for temporarily holding and manipulating information—has limited capacity for processing new information.[43] This limitation has profound implications for AI training design, as overwhelming learners with too much new information simultaneously prevents effective learning.

The RAPID framework manages cognitive load through several strategies:

Sequential Introduction: New concepts and tools are introduced systematically rather than simultaneously, allowing learners to fully process each element before adding complexity.

Chunking Strategies: Related information is grouped into meaningful units that can be processed as single elements, reducing working memory demands.[44]

Scaffolding Reduction: Support and guidance are gradually reduced as learners develop competency, preventing over-reliance while maintaining appropriate challenge levels.

Transfer Learning and Skill Generalization

The ultimate goal of AI training is transfer—the ability to apply learned skills to new situations and problems. Research identifies several factors that enhance transfer, all of which are incorporated into the RAPID framework.[45]

Diverse Practice Contexts: Learners practice AI skills across varied problems and contexts, preventing overfitting to specific examples and enhancing generalization.

Principle Extraction: Learning activities explicitly focus on identifying and articulating underlying principles, not just memorizing specific procedures.

Analogical Reasoning: Learners practice identifying similarities between different AI applications, developing their ability to recognize when previous learning applies to new situations.

Motivation and Engagement Principles

Sustained learning requires intrinsic motivation—engagement driven by inherent interest and satisfaction rather than external rewards.[46] The RAPID framework incorporates several evidence-based strategies for maintaining motivation throughout the learning process.

Autonomy Support: Learners have choices in their learning paths and applications, supporting their sense of control and ownership over the learning process.

Competency Building: Learning activities are designed to provide regular success experiences while maintaining appropriate challenge levels, supporting learners' sense of developing expertise.

Purpose Connection: All learning activities explicitly connect to learners' real work challenges and goals, ensuring that learning feels meaningful and relevant.

Realistic Timeline and Expectations

The RAPID framework unfolds over a carefully structured 90-day timeline designed to optimize learning while accommodating the realities of busy professional schedules. This timeline reflects research on skill acquisition phases and provides flexibility for different learning speeds and contexts.

Month 1: Foundation Building (Weeks 1-4)

The first month focuses on building conceptual understanding and basic tool competency. Research shows that strong foundations are essential for subsequent skill development, as new learning builds on existing knowledge structures.[47]

Week 1: Pattern recognition development through guided observation and analysis of AI applications in learners' domains.

Week 2: Continued pattern recognition with introduction to AI capabilities and limitations through hands-on exploration.

Week 3: Basic tool application with extensive scaffolding and clear success criteria.

Week 4: Semi-guided application to real work tasks, with reduced support but available assistance.

Expected outcomes after Month 1: Learners can identify basic AI opportunities in their work, use 1-2 AI tools for simple tasks, and have realistic expectations about AI capabilities and limitations.

Month 2: Skill Development (Weeks 5-8)

The second month emphasizes deliberate practice and progressive complexity, applying spaced repetition principles to build fluency and confidence.

Week 5: Independent problem-solving with AI tools, minimal external guidance.

Week 6: Workflow integration and optimization, focusing on embedding AI into regular work processes.

Week 7: Pattern recognition refinement and complex problem decomposition practice.

Week 8: Quality assessment and iteration skills development.

Expected outcomes after Month 2: Learners can effectively use AI tools for routine work tasks, integrate AI into their regular workflows, and evaluate AI output quality appropriately.

Month 3: Mastery and Deployment (Weeks 9-12)

The final month focuses on advanced application, creative problem-solving, and preparation for ongoing independent learning.

Week 9: Creative AI application and innovation, exploring novel uses and combinations.

Week 10: Advanced quality assessment and sophisticated iteration techniques.

Week 11: Systematic feedback collection and incorporation for continuous improvement.

Week 12: Implementation planning and value measurement preparation.

Expected outcomes after Month 3: Learners can creatively apply AI to complex work challenges, teach others basic AI skills, and contribute to organizational AI strategy development.

Success Metrics and Assessment

The RAPID framework includes specific, measurable success criteria that allow learners and organizations to assess progress and outcomes objectively.

Knowledge Assessment: Learners demonstrate understanding of AI capabilities, limitations, and appropriate applications through practical exercises and case study analysis.

Skill Demonstration: Learners complete increasingly complex AI-assisted projects that showcase their developing competency and creativity.

Application Evidence: Learners provide documentation of AI integration into their real work, including productivity improvements and quality maintenance.

Teaching Capability: Advanced learners demonstrate their mastery by successfully teaching basic AI skills to colleagues, showing deep understanding through explanation ability.

Case Study: Energy Sector AI Implementation Success

The Petrobras ChatPetrobras implementation provides a detailed example of the RAPID framework principles in action, demonstrating how systematic approaches to AI skill development can achieve remarkable results in complex organizational environments.

Implementation Strategy and Methodology

Petrobras approached AI implementation with systematic methodology that addressed technical, organizational, and cultural challenges simultaneously. Their strategy incorporated several key elements that align with RAPID framework principles:

Systematic Onboarding: Rather than expecting spontaneous adoption, Petrobras provided comprehensive live presentations and training sessions for all 110,000 users.[48] These sessions were designed to accommodate varying levels of technical expertise across different business areas.

Security and Compliance Integration: The implementation addressed data protection and compliance requirements from the beginning, ensuring that AI capabilities enhanced rather than compromised organizational security standards.[49]

Cross-Functional Application: ChatPetrobras was designed to support diverse business functions—from exploration and production to human resources and legal—demonstrating the broad applicability of well-designed AI tools.[50]

Learning and Adoption Patterns

The Petrobras implementation reveals several important patterns about how large organizations successfully develop AI capabilities:

Gradual Complexity Increase: Users began with simple applications like email drafting and document summarization before progressing to more complex tasks like code generation and technical report creation.[51]

Peer Learning Networks: Successful adoption occurred through informal knowledge sharing among colleagues, supplementing formal training with practical tips and use cases.

Iterative Improvement: The implementation included mechanisms for collecting user feedback and continuously refining the tool based on real-world usage patterns.[52]

Measurable Outcomes and Impact

The Petrobras case demonstrates the kinds of measurable outcomes that organizations can expect from systematic AI skill development:

High Adoption Rates: The tool achieved widespread adoption across the organization, with positive feedback from the vast majority of users.[53]

Productivity Improvements: Users reported time savings and efficiency gains in various work processes, from document creation to technical analysis.

Quality Maintenance: The implementation maintained professional standards while increasing efficiency, demonstrating that AI can enhance rather than compromise work quality.

Cultural Change: The successful implementation contributed to broader cultural acceptance of AI tools and digital transformation within the organization.

Common Implementation Pitfalls and Solutions

Experience with AI skill development across diverse organizations has identified several common challenges that can derail learning efforts. Understanding these pitfalls and their solutions helps ensure successful RAPID framework implementation.

Rushing Through Foundation Phases

The Pitfall: Organizations often pressure learners to move quickly to advanced applications without building solid foundations in pattern recognition and basic tool competency. This pressure typically stems from impatience for immediate results or underestimation of the cognitive demands of AI skill development.

The Solution: Maintain commitment to systematic progression through RAPID phases, even when pressure exists for faster results. Research consistently shows that strong foundations accelerate later learning and prevent costly mistakes from overconfident tool use.[54]

Implementation Strategy: Establish clear expectations with stakeholders about learning timelines, provide evidence of foundation-building value, and celebrate early achievements to maintain momentum.

Neglecting the Application Phase

The Pitfall: Some learners remain in theoretical understanding without progressing to hands-on tool use, often due to fear of making mistakes or preference for familiar work methods.

The Solution: Structure low-stakes practice opportunities that provide safe environments for experimentation, and emphasize that initial mistakes are normal and valuable for learning.

Implementation Strategy: Create practice scenarios using non-critical work tasks, provide extensive scaffolding during early applications, and share stories of successful learners who overcame initial difficulties.

Insufficient Practice and Iteration

The Pitfall: Learners may believe they've mastered AI tools after basic competency, skipping the deliberate practice necessary for developing fluency and adaptive expertise.

The Solution: Emphasize that AI skill development follows the same principles as other professional skills—competency requires sustained practice with progressively challenging applications.

Implementation Strategy: Design practice sequences that gradually increase complexity, provide feedback on performance, and help learners recognize their own skill development progress.

Ignoring Organizational Context

The Pitfall: Individual learners may develop AI skills in isolation without considering how their applications affect colleagues, workflows, and organizational culture.

The Solution: Include organizational integration planning from early phases, encouraging learners to consider stakeholder impacts and communication needs for their AI implementations.

Implementation Strategy: Require learners to present their AI applications to colleagues, gather feedback on organizational impact, and adjust approaches based on team and organizational needs.

Key Takeaways and Action Steps

The RAPID framework provides a systematic, evidence-based approach to developing AI skills that translate into real organizational value. Its success depends on several key principles that differentiate it from ad hoc training approaches:

Essential Success Factors

Systematic Progression: Each phase builds on previous learning while introducing new challenges at appropriate cognitive load levels. This progression respects how the brain naturally acquires complex skills.

Evidence-Based Design: All framework elements reflect cognitive science research on skill acquisition, adult learning, and expertise development. This grounding ensures that learning activities align with how people actually learn rather than how we assume they learn.

Practical Application Focus: From the earliest phases, learners work with real problems and authentic work contexts rather than artificial exercises. This focus enhances motivation and ensures transfer to real-world applications.

Continuous Feedback Integration: Learning improves through systematic collection and incorporation of feedback from multiple sources. This feedback drives both individual skill development and organizational learning.

Organizational Integration: Individual skill development connects to broader organizational capabilities and goals, ensuring that AI investments produce sustainable value.

Immediate Action Steps

Complete AI Readiness Assessment: Begin with honest evaluation of current AI knowledge, skills, and organizational context. This assessment provides the foundation for personalized learning plans.

Establish Learning Schedule: Commit to consistent time investment—research suggests 5-10 hours per week for foundation building—and protect this time from competing demands.

Select Initial Tools: Choose 1-2 AI platforms for focused development rather than attempting to learn multiple tools simultaneously. Depth of learning produces better outcomes than breadth.

Build Support Networks: Connect with colleagues, online communities, or mentors who can provide encouragement, feedback, and practical guidance throughout the learning process.

Document Learning Journey: Maintain records of experiences, insights, and progress to support reflection and continuous improvement. This documentation also contributes to organizational learning.

The RAPID framework transforms AI skill development from random experimentation into systematic capability building. By applying cognitive science principles to AI learning, professionals can achieve competency efficiently while avoiding common pitfalls that frustrate many AI adoption efforts. The result is not just individual skill development, but organizational transformation that creates sustainable competitive advantage through enhanced human-AI collaboration.

As Fernando Carneiro from Petrobras observed, "Digital transformation is not only a matter of technology but also process and culture." The RAPID framework addresses all three dimensions, providing the systematic approach necessary for successful AI integration in the complex, fast-paced world of modern professional work.

Footnotes:

[1] Microsoft Azure Blog, "Brazilian organizations leverage AI for world-class innovation," Microsoft, May 13, 2024, https://www.microsoft.com/en-us/microsoft-cloud/blog/2024/05/13/brazilian-organizations-leverage-ai-for-world-class-innovation/.

[2] Microsoft Customer Stories, "Petrobras continues 70 years of innovation with Azure OpenAI Service," Microsoft, accessed August 20, 2025, https://www.microsoft.com/en/customers/story/1758695276753608190-petrobras-azure-openai-service-energy-en-brazil.

[3] Ibid.

[4] Caitlin Tenison and John R. Anderson, "Modeling the distinct phases of skill acquisition," Journal of Experimental Psychology: Learning, Memory, and Cognition 42, no. 5 (May 2016): 749-767, doi:10.1037/xlm0000204.

[5] Caitlin Tenison et al., "Phases of learning: How skill acquisition impacts cognitive processing," Brain and Cognition 111 (March 2017): 156-162, doi:10.1016/j.bandc.2016.09.009.

[6] Nicholas C. Soderstrom and Robert A. Bjork, "Learning versus performance: An integrative review," Perspectives on Psychological Science 10, no. 2 (2015): 176-199, doi:10.1177/1745691615569000.

[7] Tenison and Anderson, "Modeling the distinct phases of skill acquisition," 749.

[8] My Brain Rewired, "5 Ways Neuroplasticity Can Improve Cognitive Function," March 1, 2025, https://mybrainrewired.com/the-brain/neuroplasticity-boosts-cognitive-function-five-ways/.

[9] Vorecol, "Neuroplasticity and LMS: Understanding the Science Behind Learning and Memory Retention," September 19, 2024, https://vorecol.com/blogs/blog-neuroplasticity-and-lms-understanding-the-science-behind-learning-and-memory-retention-193922.

[10] 31Memorize, "Why Repetition Works: A Neuroscience Perspective," accessed August 20, 2025, https://www.31memorize.com/post/why-repetition-works-a-neuroscience-perspective.

[11] Gwern, "Spaced Repetition for Efficient Learning," March 11, 2009, https://gwern.net/spaced-repetition.

[12] Kou Feng et al., "Spaced Learning Enhances Episodic Memory by Increasing Neural Pattern Similarity Across Repetitions," Journal of

Neuroscience 39, no. 27 (July 2019): 5351-5360, doi:10.1523/JNEUROSCI.2741-18.2019.

[13] Christopher D. Smith and Damian Scarf, "Spacing Repetitions Over Long Timescales: A Review and a Reconsolidation Explanation," Frontiers in Psychology 8 (June 2017): 962, doi:10.3389/fpsyg.2017.00962.

[14] Litslink, "How Does Netflix Use AI to Personalize Recommendations?" June 19, 2025, https://litslink.com/blog/all-about-netflix-artificial-intelligence-the-truth-behind-personalized-content.

[15] Brainforge.ai, "How Netflix Uses Machine Learning (ML) to Create Perfect Recommendations," June 13, 2025, https://www.brainforge.ai/blog/how-netflix-uses-machine-learning-ml-to-create-perfect-recommendations.

[16] Ibid.

[17] Rudrendu Paul, "How Netflix Utilizes Machine Learning in its Recommendation System," Medium, January 19, 2023, https://rudrendupaul.medium.com/how-netflix-utilizes-machine-learning-in-its-recommendation-system-e6f5f84ff042.

[18] Zhong Hong, "Personalized Recommendations: How Netflix and Amazon Use Deep Learning to Enhance User Experience," Medium, April 28, 2024, https://medium.com/@zhonghong9998/personalized-recommendations-how-netflix-and-amazon-use-deep-learning-to-enhance-user-experience-e7bd6fcd18ff.

[19] Logan Fiorella and Richard E. Mayer, "Eight Ways to Promote Generative Learning," Educational Psychology Review 28, no. 4 (2016): 717-741, doi:10.1007/s10648-015-9348-9.

[20] Ruth M.J. Byrnes and John R. Anderson, "Teaching the science of learning," Cognitive Research: Principles and Implications 3, no. 2 (January 2018), doi:10.1186/s41235-017-0087-y.

[21] McKinsey & Company, "AI in the workplace: A report for 2025," January 28, 2025, https://www.mckinsey.com/capabilities/mckinsey-digital/our-insights/superagency-in-the-workplace-empowering-people-to-unlock-ais-full-potential-at-work.

[22] Ibid.

[23] Mary L. Cummings, "Automation bias in intelligent time critical decision support systems," Proceedings of the 3rd International Conference on Augmented Cognition (2004): 557-562.

[24] John Sweller, "Cognitive load theory," Psychology of Learning and Motivation 55 (2011): 37-76, doi:10.1016/B978-0-12-387691-1.00002-8.

[25] Research.com, "Adult Learning Theory for 2025: Methods and Techniques of Teaching Adults," June 19, 2025, https://research.com/education/adult-learning-theory.

[26] Everett M. Rogers, Diffusion of Innovations, 5th ed. (New York: Free Press, 2003).

[27] Microsoft Customer Stories, "Petrobras continues 70 years of innovation."

[28] Hermann Ebbinghaus, Memory: A Contribution to Experimental Psychology, trans. Henry A. Ruger and Clara E. Bussenius (New York: Teachers College, Columbia University, 1913).

[29] Smith and Scarf, "Spacing Repetitions Over Long Timescales."

[30] Henry L. Roediger III and Jeffrey D. Karpicke, "Test-enhanced learning: Taking memory tests improves long-term retention," Psychological Science 17, no. 3 (2006): 249-255, doi:10.1111/j.1467-9280.2006.01693.x.

[31] Robert A. Bjork and Elizabeth Ligon Bjork, "A new theory of disuse and an old theory of stimulus fluctuation," in From Learning Processes to Cognitive Processes: Essays in Honor of William K. Estes, ed. Alice F. Healy, Stephen M. Kosslyn, and Richard M. Shiffrin (Hillsdale, NJ: Lawrence Erlbaum Associates, 1992), 35-67.

[32] John Dunlosky and Katherine A. Rawson, "Overconfidence produces underachievement: Inaccurate self evaluations undermine students' learning and retention," Learning and Instruction 22, no. 4 (2012): 271-280, doi:10.1016/j.learninstruc.2011.08.003.

[33] K. Anders Ericsson, Ralf T. Krampe, and Clemens Tesch-Römer, "The role of deliberate practice in the acquisition of expert performance," Psychological Review 100, no. 3 (1993): 363-406, doi:10.1037/0033-295X.100.3.363.

[34] Michelene T.H. Chi, "Two approaches to the study of experts' characteristics," in The Cambridge Handbook of Expertise and Expert Performance, ed. K. Anders Ericsson et al. (Cambridge: Cambridge University Press, 2006), 21-30.

[35] Nancy Pennington and Bob Rehder, "Cognitive architecture and instructional design," in Cognitive Science and Its Applications for

Human-Computer Interaction, ed. John M. Carroll (Hillsdale, NJ: Lawrence Erlbaum Associates, 1987), 19-43.

[36] John Hattie and Helen Timperley, "The power of feedback," Review of Educational Research 77, no. 1 (2007): 81-112, doi:10.3102/003465430298487.

[37] Keith J. Topping, "Peer assessment between students in colleges and universities," Review of Educational Research 68, no. 3 (1998): 249-276, doi:10.3102/00346543068003249.

[38] Giyoo Hatano and Kayoko Inagaki, "Two courses of expertise," in Child Development and Education in Japan, ed. Harold Stevenson, Hiroshi Azuma, and Kenji Hakuta (New York: W.H. Freeman, 1986), 262-272.

[39] Marlene Scardamalia and Carl Bereiter, "Knowledge building and knowledge creation: Theory, pedagogy, and technology," in The Cambridge Handbook of the Learning Sciences, ed. R. Keith Sawyer (Cambridge: Cambridge University Press, 2006), 97-115.

[40] Venkatesh Viswanath et al., "User acceptance of information technology: Toward a unified view," MIS Quarterly 27, no. 3 (2003): 425-478, doi:10.2307/30036540.

[41] AIX Expert Network, "Case Study: Empowering Efficiency with AI at Petrobras," May 26, 2024, https://aiexpert.network/case-study-empowering-efficiency-with-ai-at-petrobras/.

[42] Peter M. Senge, The Fifth Discipline: The Art and Practice of the Learning Organization (New York: Doubleday, 1990).

[43] Alan Baddeley, "Working memory: Looking back and looking forward," Nature Reviews Neuroscience 4, no. 10 (2003): 829-839, doi:10.1038/nrn1201.

[44] George A. Miller, "The magical number seven, plus or minus two: Some limits on our capacity for processing information," Psychological Review 63, no. 2 (1956): 81-97, doi:10.1037/h0043158.

[45] John D. Bransford, Ann L. Brown, and Rodney R. Cocking, eds., How People Learn: Brain, Mind, Experience, and School (Washington, DC: National Academy Press, 2000).

[46] Edward L. Deci and Richard M. Ryan, "The 'what' and 'why' of goal pursuits: Human needs and the self-determination of behavior,"

Psychological Inquiry 11, no. 4 (2000): 227-268, doi:10.1207/S15327965PLI1104_01.

[47] Bransford, Brown, and Cocking, How People Learn.

[48] Microsoft Customer Stories, "Petrobras continues 70 years of innovation."

[49] Ibid.

[50] ABES, "Petrobras cria ferramenta com Inteligência Artificial Generativa para apoiar mais de 100 mil trabalhadores," December 14, 2023, https://abes.com.br/en/petrobras-cria-ferramenta-com-inteligencia-artificial-generativa-para-apoiar-mais-de-100-mil-trabalhadores/.

[51] Ibid.

[52] AIX Expert Network, "Case Study: Empowering Efficiency with AI at Petrobras."

[53] Microsoft Customer Stories, "Petrobras continues 70 years of innovation."

[54] Byrnes and Anderson, "Teaching the science of learning."

Chapter 4: Mastering Key AI Tools

Opening Hook: Diverse Professional Success

Maya Chen had always been passionate about visual design, but as a freelance graphic designer from an underrepresented background in Portland, she often found herself competing against larger agencies with extensive resources. When AI image generation tools emerged in early 2023, Maya initially felt overwhelmed by the technical complexity and worried about the cost implications for her small business. However, over the course of eighteen months, she methodically learned to integrate AI tools into her workflow—starting with simple tasks and gradually building expertise.

Maya's journey wasn't without challenges. Her first attempts with AI tools produced inconsistent results, and she struggled with prompt engineering. She spent weeks learning to craft effective prompts and understanding each tool's strengths and limitations. The learning curve was steeper than she initially anticipated, requiring approximately 15-20 hours per week of experimentation and practice during the first three months.

By month six, Maya had developed proficiency with three core tools: Midjourney for conceptual design, ChatGPT for client communications and project planning, and Canva's AI features for production work. Her breakthrough came when she realized that combining domain expertise with AI capabilities, rather than trying to replace her creative skills, amplified her competitive advantage.

The results were measured but meaningful. Maya's client capacity increased by approximately 40% over the eighteen-month period, allowing her to take on projects she previously couldn't handle due to time constraints. Her revenue grew by 35%, enabling her to invest in better equipment and professional development. More importantly, she built a reputation as an innovative designer who could deliver high-quality work efficiently, leading to repeat clients and referrals.

Maya's success story illustrates a crucial principle: AI tools don't replace professional expertise—they amplify it. Her understanding of design principles, client psychology, and project management remained the foundation of her success. The AI tools simply enabled her to execute ideas faster and explore creative possibilities that would have been time-prohibitive manually.

Foundation Platforms: Essential AI Tools for 2025

The AI tool landscape has matured significantly, with several platforms emerging as essential components of modern professional workflows. Understanding these foundation platforms—their capabilities, limitations, and optimal use cases—is crucial for making informed decisions about which tools to integrate into your work.

Large Language Models: The Text Processing Powerhouses

Large Language Models (LLMs) represent the most transformative category of AI tools for knowledge work. Three platforms dominate this space: ChatGPT, Claude, and Gemini, each offering distinct advantages for different use cases.

ChatGPT: The Versatile All-Rounder

OpenAI's ChatGPT has maintained its position as the most comprehensive AI assistant, serving over 200 million weekly active users as of 2025.[1] The platform's strength lies in its versatility and extensive feature ecosystem. ChatGPT offers multiple model tiers, from the accessible GPT-4o to the advanced reasoning capabilities of the o1 series.

ChatGPT's key advantages include:

- **Memory capabilities**: Unlike competitors, ChatGPT can remember previous conversations, building context over time
- **Multimodal integration**: Seamless combination of text, image generation (DALL-E), and voice interaction
- **Custom GPT marketplace**: Users can create specialized assistants for specific tasks
- **Extensive integrations**: APIs and third-party connections for workflow automation

However, ChatGPT also has notable limitations. The platform can be slower for complex reasoning tasks, and image generation is limited to one output at a time. Response quality varies significantly based on prompt crafting skills, requiring users to develop prompting expertise.

From a cost perspective, ChatGPT offers multiple pricing tiers: a free tier with basic access, ChatGPT Plus at $20/month for enhanced features, and ChatGPT Pro at $200/month for power users requiring unlimited access.[2] For businesses, the Team plan starts at $25-30 per user monthly, with Enterprise pricing available on request.

Claude: The Coding and Writing Specialist

Anthropic's Claude has emerged as the technical leader, particularly excelling in coding and long-form content creation. Claude's constitutional AI approach emphasizes helpful, harmless, and honest responses, making it particularly valuable for professional writing and complex analysis.[3]

Claude's distinctive strengths include:

- **Superior coding performance**: Achieving 72.5% on SWE-bench Verified, the highest score among commercial models[4]
- **Large context windows**: 200,000 tokens standard (500,000 for enterprise), enabling analysis of entire documents
- **Artifacts feature**: Real-time code and document creation with live preview capabilities
- **Natural conversation style**: More human-like interaction patterns, particularly for creative tasks

Claude's pricing structure emphasizes flexibility, with a free tier, Pro at $20/month, and Max tiers at $100-200/month for heavy users needing 5-20x more capacity. The API pricing includes aggressive prompt caching that can reduce costs by up to 90% for high-volume usage.[5]

While Claude excels in technical tasks and writing, it lacks some of ChatGPT's broader features like memory and image generation. The platform also has more conservative content policies, which can sometimes limit creative or edge-case applications.

Gemini: The Integrated Productivity Solution

Google's Gemini takes a fundamentally different approach by integrating AI capabilities directly into existing Google Workspace subscriptions. This integration strategy makes it the most cost-effective option for organizations already using Google's productivity suite.[6]

Gemini's unique advantages include:

- **Native multimodality**: Integrated processing of text, images, audio, and video from the ground up
- **Workspace integration**: Seamless operation within Gmail, Docs, Sheets, and other Google services
- **Real-time information access**: Direct connection to current web data and Google's knowledge graph
- **Cost efficiency**: Included with Google Workspace Business plans at no additional charge

The platform offers standalone pricing at $19.99/month for Google AI Pro, significantly undercutting competitors. The Premium Ultra tier at $34.99/month includes advanced features like enhanced video generation capabilities.

However, Gemini's tight integration with Google's ecosystem can be limiting for users preferring other productivity platforms. The platform also has fewer third-party integrations compared to ChatGPT or Claude.

Code Assistance Tools: Transforming Software Development

GitHub Copilot has revolutionized software development, becoming an essential tool for programmers across experience levels. The AI pair programming assistant has demonstrated remarkable adoption rates and productivity improvements across enterprise environments.

GitHub Copilot: The Developer's AI Partner

By 2025, GitHub Copilot serves over 15 million users, representing a 400% growth in just one year.[7] The tool's impact on developer productivity has been consistently demonstrated across multiple studies and enterprise implementations.

Key productivity metrics include:

- **55% faster task completion**: Controlled studies show significant speed improvements for coding tasks[8]
- **88% code retention rate**: Developers keep the vast majority of Copilot-generated code in final versions[9]
- **46% of average code**: Copilot now writes nearly half of the typical user's code, reaching 61% in Java projects[10]

The most comprehensive evidence comes from enterprise implementations. Accenture's systematic deployment to over 400 developers revealed that 81.4% installed the extension on the day they received their license, with 67% using Copilot at least five days per week.[11] The study found an 8.69% increase in pull requests and a 15% improvement in pull request merge rates.

Code Quality and Security Considerations

While productivity gains are significant, code quality remains a critical consideration. Research indicates that 88% of Copilot-generated characters are retained in the final codebase, suggesting high relevance and quality.[12] However, developers must maintain vigilance regarding security and best practices.

Microsoft's research with Accenture found an 84% increase in successful builds, suggesting that AI-assisted code often meets quality standards when properly reviewed.[13] The key is maintaining human oversight and treating Copilot suggestions as starting points rather than final solutions.

Enterprise Implementation Insights

Enterprise adoption patterns reveal important insights about effective implementation:

- **Training investment**: Organizations seeing the greatest benefit invest in formal training programs
- **Community support**: Internal champions and knowledge sharing accelerate adoption
- **Integration planning**: Success requires thoughtful integration with existing development workflows

ZoomInfo's experience with over 400 developers showed average acceptance rates of 33% for suggestions and 20% for lines of code, with developer satisfaction scores reaching 72%.[14] These metrics demonstrate that while not every suggestion is accepted, the tool provides substantial value when integrated effectively.

Image Generation: Creative AI at Your Fingertips

AI image generation has matured into a powerful creative tool, with three platforms leading the market: Midjourney, DALL-E, and Stable Diffusion. Each offers distinct advantages for different creative workflows and technical requirements.

Midjourney: The Artistic Powerhouse

Midjourney has established itself as the gold standard for high-quality, aesthetically pleasing image generation. The platform's version 7 model produces exceptionally realistic and artistic images, making it the preferred choice for creative professionals and marketing teams.[15]

Midjourney's strengths include:

- **Superior image quality**: Consistently produces high-fidelity, artistic outputs
- **Style consistency**: Excellent for maintaining visual coherence across projects
- **Advanced customization**: Extensive parameter controls for fine-tuning results
- **Character consistency**: The 'cref' feature enables consistent character creation across multiple generations

However, Midjourney has notable limitations. The platform struggles with complex prompts involving multiple subjects, sometimes blending or duplicating elements unexpectedly. Text generation within images remains challenging, and the Discord-based interface can be cumbersome for some users.

Pricing is subscription-only, starting at $10/month for 200 image generations, with annual subscriptions offering a 20% discount. Professional and enterprise tiers provide additional features and higher generation limits.

DALL-E 3: The Conversational Image Creator

Integrated into ChatGPT, DALL-E 3 excels at interpreting complex text descriptions and creating images that closely match detailed prompts. The platform's integration with ChatGPT enables conversational image creation, where users can iterate and refine concepts through natural dialogue.[16]

DALL-E 3's distinctive features include:

- **Superior prompt adherence**: Excellent at following complex, detailed instructions
- **Scene coherence**: Strong ability to create integrated foreground and background elements
- **Text integration**: Better at incorporating readable text within images
- **Accessibility**: Easy access through ChatGPT's familiar interface

The platform's main limitation is a slightly cartoonish quality in photorealistic attempts compared to Midjourney. However, this limitation is often offset by the ease of use and integration benefits.

DALL-E 3 is accessible through ChatGPT's free tier (3 images daily) or ChatGPT Plus ($20/month for higher limits). Direct API access offers per-image pricing starting at $0.040 for standard quality.

Stable Diffusion: The Open-Source Alternative

Stable Diffusion's open-source nature has made it widely available across numerous platforms and implementations. While the original Stability AI has faced organizational challenges, the model remains popular through third-party platforms and the newer FLUX.1 models from Black Forest Labs.[17]

Stable Diffusion's advantages include:

- **Open-source flexibility**: Extensive customization and fine-tuning capabilities
- **No subscription requirements**: Can be run locally or through

various free platforms
- **Community support**: Large ecosystem of models, extensions, and improvements
- **Technical control**: Full access to model parameters and training capabilities

The main challenges with Stable Diffusion include technical complexity, inconsistent quality across different implementations, and the need for substantial technical knowledge to achieve optimal results.

Business Intelligence and Specialized Platforms

Beyond consumer-facing AI tools, specialized business intelligence platforms are transforming how organizations process data and make decisions. These platforms combine AI capabilities with enterprise-grade security, compliance, and integration features.

No-Code and Low-Code AI Platforms

The rise of no-code and low-code AI platforms has democratized access to artificial intelligence across organizations. By 2025, analysts predict that 65% of applications will be built using low-code AI platforms, representing a fundamental shift in how businesses implement AI solutions.[18]

Leading platforms in this space include:

Microsoft Power Platform: Integrates AI capabilities directly into business process automation, enabling users to create intelligent workflows without extensive coding knowledge. The platform's AI Builder component provides pre-built models for common business scenarios like form processing and sentiment analysis.

Bubble: Offers comprehensive no-code development with built-in AI features including natural language processing, image recognition, and automated testing. The platform uses machine learning algorithms to suggest improvements and optimize applications.

Appian: Provides low-code process automation with enterprise-ready AI architecture, including generative AI tools and AI copilots for business process optimization.

These platforms offer several key advantages:

- **Reduced technical barriers**: Enable business users to implement AI without programming expertise
- **Faster deployment**: Significantly shorter development cycles compared to traditional coding
- **Cost efficiency**: Lower upfront investment in technical talent and infrastructure
- **Integration capabilities**: Seamless connection with existing business systems

However, limitations include reduced customization options compared to custom development and potential performance constraints for complex AI applications.

Tool Selection Strategy: An Inclusive Framework

Selecting the right AI tools requires a systematic approach that considers organizational needs, technical capabilities, and long-term strategic goals. The following framework provides guidance for making informed decisions while accounting for diverse organizational contexts and constraints.

Needs Assessment Matrix

Effective tool selection begins with a comprehensive assessment of organizational needs across multiple dimensions:

Business Function Mapping Different business functions have varying AI tool requirements. Marketing teams may prioritize content generation and image creation tools, while development teams focus on code assistance and automation platforms. Sales organizations might emphasize CRM integration and customer communication tools.

Research from McKinsey indicates that 78% of organizations use AI in at least one business function, with marketing and sales being the most common applications, followed by IT and service operations.[19] However, successful implementations align tool selection with specific functional requirements rather than adopting tools broadly.

User Skill Level Accommodation Organizations must realistically assess their teams' technical comfort levels and provide appropriate training and support. Tools like ChatGPT and DALL-E offer lower barriers to entry, while platforms like Stable Diffusion or custom AI implementations require more technical expertise.

Consider implementing a tiered approach:

- **Beginner-friendly tools**: Start with intuitive platforms like ChatGPT or Canva's AI features
- **Intermediate solutions**: Progress to specialized tools like Claude for coding or Midjourney for design
- **Advanced platforms**: Introduce technical solutions like custom AI models or specialized APIs only after building foundational skills

Infrastructure and Integration Requirements Technical infrastructure significantly impacts tool selection success. Organizations must evaluate:

- **Data access and security**: How tools handle sensitive information and comply with regulations
- **Integration capabilities**: Compatibility with existing software systems and workflows
- **Scalability requirements**: Ability to grow with organizational needs
- **Support and maintenance**: Ongoing technical requirements and vendor support quality

Evaluation Criteria Framework

A systematic evaluation framework helps organizations compare tools objectively across critical dimensions:

Functionality vs. Complexity Balance The most powerful tools aren't always the best choice. Organizations should seek tools that provide necessary functionality without overwhelming users with complexity. For example, while Claude offers superior coding capabilities, ChatGPT might be more appropriate for teams primarily focused on content creation and general assistance.

Learning Curve and Support Resources Consider the total time investment required for effective tool adoption:

- **Documentation quality**: Comprehensive, accessible learning materials
- **Community size**: Active user communities for peer support and knowledge sharing
- **Training availability**: Formal training programs and certification options
- **Vendor support**: Responsive customer service and technical assistance

Cost-Benefit Analysis Evaluate both direct and indirect costs:

- **Subscription fees**: Monthly or annual platform costs
- **Training investment**: Time and resources required for skill development
- **Integration costs**: Technical implementation and workflow modification expenses
- **Opportunity costs**: Potential benefits of alternative tool choices

Implementation Planning

Successful AI tool implementation requires careful planning that addresses technical, organizational, and change management considerations.

Phased Rollout Strategy Implement tools gradually to manage risk and optimize adoption:

Phase 1: Pilot Testing (Weeks 1-4)

- Select a small, diverse group of early adopters
- Focus on specific, well-defined use cases
- Gather detailed feedback on usability and effectiveness
- Document best practices and common challenges

Phase 2: Expanded Deployment (Weeks 5-12)

- Roll out to additional teams based on pilot results
- Provide comprehensive training and support resources
- Monitor usage patterns and effectiveness metrics
- Refine processes based on user feedback

Phase 3: Organization-wide Implementation (Weeks 13-24)

- Deploy across all relevant teams and functions
- Establish ongoing support and optimization processes
- Measure business impact and ROI
- Plan for future tool evolution and upgrades

Change Management and Training Successful tool adoption requires addressing human factors as much as technical considerations:

Leadership Support: Ensure visible commitment from management and clear communication about AI tool benefits and expectations.

Champion Networks: Identify and train internal advocates who can provide peer support and demonstrate best practices.

Continuous Learning: Establish ongoing education programs to help users develop advanced skills and stay current with tool evolution.

Progressive Mastery Framework: Realistic Expectations

Developing proficiency with AI tools is a gradual process that requires patience, practice, and realistic expectations. The following framework outlines a structured approach to skill development that accommodates different learning styles and professional contexts.

Beginner Level (Weeks 1-4): Foundation Building

The initial phase focuses on developing basic competency with core tools and understanding fundamental concepts.

Tool Familiarization Begin with single-tool focus to avoid overwhelm:

- **Week 1-2**: Select one primary tool (typically ChatGPT for versatility)
- **Week 3-4**: Explore basic features and common use cases
- **Daily practice**: 15-30 minutes of guided experimentation

Core Skill Development Essential skills for all AI tools include:

- **Prompt crafting**: Understanding how to communicate effectively with AI systems
- **Result evaluation**: Developing judgment about output quality and appropriateness
- **Iteration techniques**: Learning to refine and improve AI outputs through multiple attempts
- **Limitation recognition**: Understanding when AI tools are not appropriate for specific tasks

Success Metrics for Beginners Realistic expectations for the first month include:

- **Basic task completion**: Successfully using AI for simple, routine tasks
- **Prompt improvement**: Demonstrating growing skill in crafting effective prompts
- **Quality assessment**: Developing ability to evaluate and improve AI outputs
- **Workflow integration**: Beginning to incorporate AI tools into daily work routines

Research from Farm Credit Canada's implementation shows that 78% of users report time savings on routine tasks within the first month of use, with initial benefits appearing even sooner for simple applications.[20]

Intermediate Level (Weeks 5-12): Expanding Capabilities

The intermediate phase focuses on developing more sophisticated skills and expanding tool usage across different contexts.

Multi-Tool Integration Users begin combining different AI tools for comprehensive workflows:

- **Content creation pipeline**: Using ChatGPT for ideation, Midjourney for visuals, and editing tools for refinement
- **Development workflow**: Combining GitHub Copilot for coding with AI documentation tools
- **Business analysis**: Integrating data analysis tools with report generation and presentation creation

Advanced Feature Utilization Intermediate users should explore platform-specific advanced features:

- **Custom GPTs**: Creating specialized AI assistants for recurring tasks
- **Advanced prompting**: Using techniques like chain-of-thought reasoning and few-shot learning
- **API integration**: Connecting AI tools with existing business systems
- **Workflow automation**: Setting up automated processes that incorporate AI capabilities

Quality Control and Optimization Developing systematic approaches to improving AI output quality:

- **A/B testing**: Comparing different prompt approaches to optimize results
- **Template development**: Creating reusable prompt templates for common tasks
- **Bias detection**: Learning to identify and mitigate biased or inappropriate outputs

- **Performance tracking**: Measuring time savings and quality improvements

Advanced Level (3-6 months): Strategic Integration

Advanced users focus on strategic tool deployment and organizational impact.

Strategic Tool Selection Developing expertise in choosing the right tools for complex, multi-faceted projects:

- **Requirements analysis**: Systematically evaluating project needs against tool capabilities
- **Cost-benefit optimization**: Making informed decisions about paid vs. free tools
- **Integration planning**: Designing workflows that maximize synergies between different AI tools
- **Scalability assessment**: Selecting tools that can grow with organizational needs

Team Leadership and Training Advanced users often become internal champions and trainers:

- **Best practice development**: Creating organizational standards for AI tool usage
- **Training program design**: Developing effective learning programs for colleagues
- **Change management**: Leading organizational transformation initiatives
- **Performance measurement**: Establishing metrics and KPIs for AI tool effectiveness

Innovation and Experimentation Exploring cutting-edge applications and emerging tools:

- **Emerging technology evaluation**: Staying current with new AI

developments
- **Custom solution development**: Creating organization-specific AI applications
- **Cross-industry learning**: Adapting successful approaches from other sectors
- **Future planning**: Anticipating and preparing for AI technology evolution

Case Study: Farm Credit Canada's Systematic AI Implementation

Farm Credit Canada (FCC) provides an exemplary model of systematic AI implementation across a diverse workforce. As Canada's largest agriculture lender, with over 2,200 employees serving approximately 102,000 customers, FCC's approach demonstrates how organizations can successfully deploy AI tools while maintaining high service standards and operational integrity.[21]

Implementation Strategy and Timeline

FCC's AI journey began in 2024 with Microsoft 365 Copilot implementation, starting with 300 employees and expanding to 1,000 users within six months. This measured approach allowed the organization to gather meaningful data about effectiveness while managing change carefully.

Phase 1: Pilot Program (Months 1-2) The initial deployment focused on diverse departments to test Copilot across different use cases:

- **Finance teams**: Monthly reporting and data analysis
- **Customer service**: Email drafting and response optimization
- **Operations**: Document processing and workflow automation
- **Management**: Strategic planning and presentation development

Phase 2: Measured Expansion (Months 3-4) Based on pilot results, FCC expanded access while maintaining careful monitoring:

- **Success metrics**: 78% of users reported time savings on routine tasks

- **Adoption rates**: High voluntary adoption with minimal resistance
- **Training effectiveness**: Internal champion networks proved crucial for peer support

Phase 3: Organization-wide Deployment (Months 5-6) The final expansion phase included comprehensive support systems:

- **Advanced training**: Role-specific workshops for different departments
- **Integration planning**: Systematic workflow modifications to optimize AI tool benefits
- **Performance measurement**: Establishment of ongoing metrics and feedback systems

Measurable Outcomes and Impact

FCC's systematic measurement approach provides valuable insights into realistic AI implementation outcomes:

Productivity Improvements The quantified results demonstrate meaningful but realistic benefits:

- **Time savings**: 30% of users save 30-60 minutes per week
- **Significant impact**: 35% of users save more than one hour per week
- **Task efficiency**: 78% report improved efficiency on routine tasks

These results align with broader industry findings, suggesting that well-implemented AI tools provide consistent, measurable benefits without requiring dramatic workflow transformations.

Quality and Satisfaction Metrics FCC tracked both quantitative and qualitative outcomes:

- **User satisfaction**: High satisfaction scores with continued voluntary usage

- **Quality maintenance**: No degradation in output quality while improving efficiency
- **Skill development**: Gradual improvement in user AI proficiency over time

Business Impact Assessment The organization measured broader business implications:

- **Customer service**: Maintained service quality while handling increased capacity
- **Employee development**: Freed time for higher-value strategic work
- **Competitive advantage**: Enhanced ability to serve agricultural community needs

Implementation Best Practices

FCC's experience reveals several critical success factors for AI tool implementation:

Leadership Commitment and Communication Strong leadership support proved essential for overcoming initial skepticism and ensuring resource allocation. Clear communication about expectations and benefits helped manage change effectively.

Storytelling and Internal Champions FCC's emphasis on sharing success stories internally accelerated adoption. When one district director demonstrated how Copilot saved hours on monthly reports, other directors quickly sought to replicate the approach.

Gradual Skill Building Rather than expecting immediate mastery, FCC focused on gradual skill development with ongoing support. This approach prevented overwhelm while building genuine capability over time.

Continuous Optimization Regular feedback collection and process refinement ensured that the implementation evolved to meet changing needs and optimize benefits.

Lessons for Other Organizations

FCC's experience offers several key insights for organizations considering AI tool implementation:

Start with High-Value, Low-Risk Applications Focus initial efforts on tasks that offer clear benefits with minimal risk of negative consequences. Document processing and routine communications proved ideal starting points.

Invest in Change Management Technical implementation is only part of the challenge. Successful adoption requires addressing human factors, resistance to change, and skill development needs.

Measure and Communicate Progress Regular measurement and communication of benefits builds momentum and justifies continued investment. Both quantitative metrics and qualitative success stories prove valuable.

Plan for Long-term Evolution AI tools continue evolving rapidly. Successful implementations include plans for ongoing training, tool updates, and capability expansion.

Hands-on Bootcamp Structure: Inclusive Design

Effective AI tool mastery requires structured, hands-on practice that accommodates diverse learning styles and professional contexts. The following bootcamp framework provides a comprehensive approach to skill development that can be adapted for different organizational needs and individual circumstances.

Multi-Modal Learning Approach

Recognizing that people learn differently, the bootcamp incorporates multiple learning modalities to ensure accessibility and effectiveness for diverse participants.

Visual Learning Components

- **Video demonstrations**: Step-by-step tool walkthroughs with clear visual guides

- **Infographic summaries**: Key concepts and workflows presented visually
- **Screenshot guides**: Detailed visual instructions for complex procedures
- **Flowchart references**: Visual representations of decision-making processes

Hands-on Practice Elements

- **Guided exercises**: Structured practice sessions with immediate feedback
- **Real project integration**: Working on actual professional tasks during training
- **Peer collaboration**: Group exercises that encourage knowledge sharing
- **Trial and error exploration**: Designated time for experimentation without pressure

Theoretical Foundation

- **Concept explanations**: Understanding the principles behind AI tool functionality
- **Best practice frameworks**: Systematic approaches to common challenges
- **Ethical considerations**: Responsible AI use and limitation awareness
- **Strategic thinking**: Connecting tool capabilities to business objectives

Week-by-Week Curriculum Structure

Week 1: Foundation and Setup *Learning Objectives*: Tool installation, basic navigation, and first successful outputs

Day 1-2: Tool Selection and Setup

- Assessment of individual needs and goals
- Tool installation and account configuration
- Initial exploration of user interfaces
- Basic security and privacy settings

Day 3-4: First Successful Interactions

- Simple prompt creation and testing
- Understanding input-output relationships
- Basic quality evaluation techniques
- Initial workflow integration planning

Day 5: Reflection and Planning

- Assessment of initial experiences
- Identification of personal learning priorities
- Goal setting for subsequent weeks
- Troubleshooting common setup issues

Week 2: Core Skill Development *Learning Objectives*: Effective prompting, quality assessment, and basic optimization

Day 1-2: Prompt Engineering Fundamentals

- Structure and clarity in AI communication
- Common prompt patterns and templates
- Iterative improvement techniques
- Context setting and constraint definition

Day 3-4: Quality Control and Optimization

- Output evaluation criteria and methods
- Common failure modes and correction strategies
- Version control and improvement tracking
- Integration with existing quality processes

Day 5: Application and Practice

- Real project implementation
- Peer review and feedback sessions
- Challenge identification and solution development
- Progress measurement and adjustment

Week 3: Integration and Workflow Development *Learning Objectives*: Tool combination, workflow design, and efficiency optimization

Day 1-2: Multi-Tool Workflows

- Identifying complementary tool capabilities
- Designing integrated workflows
- Managing data flow between tools
- Optimizing handoff processes

Day 3-4: Advanced Features and Customization

- Platform-specific advanced capabilities
- Custom template and workflow creation
- Automation opportunities and implementation
- Performance monitoring and optimization

Day 5: Innovation and Experimentation

- Creative application exploration
- Edge case handling and solution development
- Future capability planning
- Knowledge sharing and community building

Week 4: Mastery and Sustainability *Learning Objectives*: Independent problem-solving, teaching others, and continuous improvement

Day 1-2: Independent Project Completion

- Self-directed project from conception to completion
- Challenge identification and autonomous problem-solving
- Quality assurance and final optimization
- Results documentation and presentation

Day 3-4: Teaching and Knowledge Transfer

- Explaining concepts to others
- Creating training materials and guides
- Mentoring new users
- Building internal support networks

Day 5: Future Planning and Sustainability

- Long-term skill development planning
- Staying current with tool evolution
- Building ongoing practice habits
- Establishing measurement and improvement processes

Assessment and Certification Framework

Competency-Based Evaluation Rather than traditional testing, assessment focuses on demonstrated competency in real-world applications:

Practical Skills Assessment

- Successful completion of realistic workplace tasks
- Demonstration of effective prompt engineering
- Quality control and optimization capabilities
- Integration with existing workflows

Problem-Solving Evaluation

- Response to novel challenges and edge cases
- Adaptation of learned techniques to new contexts
- Creative application of tool capabilities
- Independent troubleshooting and solution development

Teaching and Leadership Assessment

- Ability to explain concepts to others
- Effective knowledge transfer and training

- Support and mentorship of new users
- Contribution to organizational AI competency

Portfolio Development Participants build comprehensive portfolios demonstrating their AI tool mastery:

Project Documentation

- Before-and-after examples showing improvement
- Process documentation for complex workflows
- Challenge identification and solution development
- Impact measurement and business value demonstration

Template and Resource Creation

- Reusable prompt templates for common tasks
- Workflow guides and best practice documentation
- Training materials for teaching others
- Quality control checklists and evaluation frameworks

Reflection and Learning Documentation

- Personal learning journey and growth tracking
- Challenge identification and resolution strategies
- Future learning goals and development plans
- Contribution to organizational knowledge base

Support Systems and Accessibility

Inclusive Support Structures The bootcamp framework includes multiple support mechanisms to ensure success for participants with diverse needs and backgrounds:

Peer Learning Networks

- Buddy systems pairing experienced and novice users
- Regular group discussions and problem-solving sessions
- Cross-functional collaboration opportunities

- Cultural and linguistic diversity celebration

Technical Support Access

- Multiple communication channels for assistance
- Flexible scheduling for support sessions
- Alternative format materials for accessibility needs
- Economic accessibility through sliding scale pricing

Ongoing Mentorship

- Connection with experienced AI tool users
- Industry-specific guidance and application examples
- Career development and opportunity identification
- Long-term relationship building for continued support

Common Implementation Pitfalls and Solutions

Understanding common challenges in AI tool implementation helps organizations avoid costly mistakes and accelerate successful adoption. Research across multiple industries reveals consistent patterns of implementation difficulties and effective solutions.

Technology Selection Challenges

Pitfall: Tool Proliferation Without Strategy Many organizations begin using multiple AI tools simultaneously without strategic planning, leading to confusion, inefficiency, and increased costs. A recent survey found that 73% of organizations using AI tools report having too many platforms without clear use case differentiation.[22]

Solution: Strategic Tool Portfolio Management Implement a structured approach to tool selection:

- **Capability mapping**: Document what each tool does best and where capabilities overlap
- **Use case prioritization**: Focus on high-impact applications before

expanding to edge cases

- **Integration planning**: Ensure new tools complement rather than duplicate existing capabilities
- **Cost-benefit analysis**: Regularly evaluate ROI and eliminate underperforming tools

Pitfall: Inadequate Technical Infrastructure Assessment Organizations often underestimate the technical requirements for effective AI tool implementation, leading to performance issues, security vulnerabilities, and integration failures.

Solution: Comprehensive Infrastructure Evaluation Conduct thorough technical assessments before tool selection:

- **Data integration capabilities**: Ensure tools can access and process relevant organizational data
- **Security and compliance alignment**: Verify tools meet regulatory and organizational security standards
- **Scalability planning**: Select tools that can grow with organizational needs
- **Legacy system compatibility**: Address integration challenges with existing software

Training and Adoption Challenges

Pitfall: Insufficient Training Investment Many organizations provide minimal training, expecting employees to develop AI tool proficiency independently. This approach typically results in low adoption rates, ineffective usage, and employee frustration.

McKinsey research indicates that organizations investing in comprehensive training programs see 40% higher adoption rates and 60% better performance outcomes compared to those providing minimal training support.[23]

Solution: Structured Training Programs Develop comprehensive learning programs that address diverse needs:

- **Role-specific training**: Customize training content for different job functions and skill levels
- **Progressive skill building**: Structure learning from basic to advanced capabilities over time
- **Hands-on practice**: Emphasize practical application over theoretical knowledge
- **Ongoing support**: Provide continuous learning opportunities as tools evolve

Pitfall: Underestimating Change Management Requirements AI tool implementation requires significant behavioral change, which many organizations underestimate. Research shows that 67% of AI implementation failures stem from human factors rather than technical issues.[24]

Solution: Comprehensive Change Management Address human factors systematically:

- **Leadership modeling**: Ensure visible adoption and advocacy from management
- **Champion networks**: Identify and train internal advocates who can influence peers
- **Communication planning**: Provide clear, consistent messaging about benefits and expectations
- **Resistance addressing**: Proactively identify and address concerns about job security and skill requirements

Quality Control and Governance Issues

Pitfall: Inadequate Quality Assurance Processes Organizations often implement AI tools without establishing appropriate quality control measures, leading to inconsistent outputs, errors in critical applications, and erosion of trust in AI capabilities.

Solution: Systematic Quality Management Establish comprehensive quality assurance frameworks:

- **Output review processes**: Implement systematic review procedures for AI-generated content
- **Error detection and correction**: Develop protocols for identifying and addressing AI mistakes
- **Performance monitoring**: Track quality metrics over time to identify trends and improvement opportunities
- **Human oversight maintenance**: Ensure appropriate human involvement in critical decisions

Pitfall: Bias and Fairness Oversight AI tools can perpetuate or amplify existing biases, particularly affecting underrepresented groups. Organizations failing to address these issues face reputational, legal, and operational risks.

Solution: Proactive Bias Management Implement systematic approaches to fairness and bias mitigation:

- **Diverse testing groups**: Include varied perspectives in tool evaluation and testing
- **Bias detection training**: Educate users to recognize and address biased outputs
- **Regular auditing**: Conduct periodic reviews of AI tool impacts across different groups
- **Inclusive design principles**: Apply diversity and inclusion considerations to AI tool selection and implementation

Resource and Cost Management Challenges

Pitfall: Underestimating Total Cost of Ownership Organizations often focus on subscription costs while underestimating training, integration, and ongoing maintenance expenses. This leads to budget overruns and inadequate resource allocation for successful implementation.

Solution: Comprehensive Cost Planning Develop realistic budgets that include all implementation costs:

- **Training investment**: Allocate substantial resources for skill

development and ongoing education
- **Integration costs**: Plan for technical implementation and workflow modification expenses
- **Opportunity costs**: Consider the time investment required for effective adoption
- **Ongoing optimization**: Budget for continuous improvement and tool evolution

Pitfall: Inadequate Performance Measurement Many organizations implement AI tools without establishing clear success metrics, making it difficult to demonstrate value and optimize performance over time.

Solution: Strategic Performance Management Establish comprehensive measurement frameworks:

- **Baseline establishment**: Document current performance before AI tool implementation
- **Multiple metric types**: Track efficiency gains, quality improvements, and user satisfaction
- **Regular review cycles**: Conduct periodic assessments and adjustment planning
- **Value demonstration**: Quantify business impact and ROI for stakeholder communication

Realistic Success Metrics and Expectations

Setting appropriate expectations and measuring success accurately is crucial for sustainable AI tool implementation. Research across multiple organizations provides insights into realistic outcomes and effective measurement approaches.

Short-term Success Indicators (30-90 Days)

User Adoption Metrics Initial adoption patterns provide early indicators of implementation success:

- **Installation and setup completion**: Target 80-90% completion within first two weeks
- **Regular usage development**: Aim for 60-70% of users engaging with tools at least weekly by month two
- **Basic competency achievement**: Expect 50-60% of users to demonstrate basic proficiency within 60 days

Farm Credit Canada's experience demonstrates realistic adoption timelines, with 81.4% of users installing Copilot on the first day, but meaningful productivity gains developing over 4-8 weeks of regular use.[25]

Initial Productivity Improvements Early productivity gains tend to be modest but measurable:

- **Time savings on routine tasks**: 10-30% improvement for simple, repetitive activities
- **Quality consistency**: Reduced variation in output quality for standardized tasks
- **Learning acceleration**: Faster development of new skills and capabilities

User Satisfaction and Confidence Psychological factors significantly impact long-term success:

- **Technology confidence**: Increased comfort with AI tools and reduced anxiety
- **Self-efficacy improvement**: Greater confidence in ability to use technology effectively
- **Workflow satisfaction**: Positive perception of how AI tools integrate with existing work

Medium-term Development Indicators (3-6 Months)

Skill Development and Sophistication Users should demonstrate growing sophistication in tool usage:

- **Advanced feature utilization**: Movement beyond basic functions to specialized capabilities
- **Multi-tool integration**: Effective combination of different AI tools for complex workflows
- **Independent problem-solving**: Ability to troubleshoot issues and optimize performance autonomously

Business Impact Measurement Meaningful business benefits should become apparent:

- **Process efficiency gains**: 20-40% improvement in key workflow metrics
- **Quality enhancement**: Measurable improvements in output consistency and accuracy
- **Capacity expansion**: Ability to handle increased workload without proportional resource increases

Research from Accenture's GitHub Copilot implementation shows that organizations typically see 8-15% productivity improvements within 3-6 months, with some teams achieving higher gains based on use case alignment and training investment.[26]

Organizational Culture Shifts Cultural adaptation indicators include:

- **Innovation mindset**: Increased experimentation with new AI capabilities
- **Collaboration enhancement**: Improved knowledge sharing and peer support
- **Continuous learning adoption**: Ongoing skill development and capability expansion

Long-term Transformation Outcomes (6-12 Months)

Strategic Integration Achievement Successful implementations demonstrate deep organizational integration:

- **Workflow transformation**: Fundamental improvements in how work gets done
- **Competitive advantage development**: Differentiated capabilities that provide market benefits
- **Innovation acceleration**: Faster development and deployment of new ideas and solutions

Sustainable Performance Improvements Long-term success requires sustained benefits:

- **Productivity stabilization**: Consistent 30-50% improvements in key metrics
- **Quality standardization**: Reliable, high-quality outputs across different users and contexts
- **Cost optimization**: Positive ROI through efficiency gains and resource optimization

Human Capital Development People development outcomes include:

- **Skill portfolio expansion**: Broader capabilities and career advancement opportunities
- **Job satisfaction improvement**: Increased engagement through more interesting and strategic work
- **Leadership development**: Internal champions who can guide further organizational transformation

Measurement Framework and KPIs

Quantitative Metrics Establish clear, measurable indicators of success:
Productivity Metrics

- **Task completion time**: Percentage reduction in time required for specific activities
- **Output volume**: Increased capacity to handle work without additional resources

- **Error reduction**: Decreased mistakes and rework requirements

Quality Metrics

- **Consistency measures**: Reduced variation in output quality
- **Accuracy improvements**: Higher correctness rates in analysis and decision-making
- **Stakeholder satisfaction**: Customer and colleague feedback on work quality

Financial Metrics

- **Cost per output**: Reduced expenses for producing specific deliverables
- **Revenue per employee**: Increased value generation through enhanced capabilities
- **ROI calculation**: Return on investment in tools, training, and implementation

Qualitative Assessment Balance quantitative measures with qualitative insights:

User Experience Evaluation

- **Satisfaction surveys**: Regular assessment of user attitudes and experiences
- **Focus group feedback**: In-depth exploration of challenges and opportunities
- **Workflow assessment**: Evaluation of how AI tools integrate with existing processes

Organizational Impact Assessment

- **Culture change indicators**: Shifts in attitudes toward technology and innovation
- **Collaboration enhancement**: Improved teamwork and

knowledge sharing

- **Strategic capability development**: New opportunities for business growth and differentiation

Setting Realistic Expectations

Avoiding Common Expectation Pitfalls Organizations should avoid several common mistakes in expectation setting:

Overestimating Immediate Impact AI tools require time for users to develop proficiency and for organizations to optimize implementation. Expecting dramatic improvements within the first month typically leads to disappointment and reduced confidence.

Underestimating Learning Investment Effective AI tool usage requires significant skill development. Organizations should budget 20-40 hours per user for basic proficiency development and ongoing learning.

Ignoring Individual Variation Success rates and timelines vary significantly based on individual technical comfort, learning styles, and job requirements. Expect 20-30% variation in adoption speeds and effectiveness across users.

Building Sustainable Success Long-term success requires:

- **Realistic timeline planning**: Allow 6-12 months for significant organizational benefits
- **Continuous investment**: Ongoing training, support, and optimization
- **Adaptive management**: Flexibility to adjust approaches based on experience and results
- **Patient persistence**: Commitment to working through challenges and setbacks

---

Footnotes:

1. Eirini Kalliamvakou et al., "Research: Quantifying GitHub Copilot's Impact on Developer Productivity and Happiness," The

GitHub Blog, May 21, 2024, https://github.blog/news-insights/research/research-quantifying-github-copilots-impact-on-developer-productivity-and-happiness/.

2. "ChatGPT vs Claude vs Gemini: The Best AI Model for Each Use Case in 2025," Creator Economy, June 4, 2025, https://creatoreconomy.so/p/chatgpt-vs-claude-vs-gemini-the-best-ai-model-for-each-use-case-2025.
3. "Claude vs. ChatGPT: What's the difference? [2025]," Zapier, May 27, 2025, https://zapier.com/blog/claude-vs-chatgpt/.
4. "ChatGPT vs Claude vs Gemini 2025: The Definitive AI Platform Comparison for Business Leaders," Aloa, June 19, 2025, https://aloa.co/ai/comparisons/llm-comparison/chatgpt-vs-claude-vs-gemini.
5. Ibid.
6. Ibid.
7. "Github Copilot Usage Data Statistics (2025)," We Are Tenet, accessed August 2025, https://www.wearetenet.com/blog/github-copilot-usage-data-statistics.
8. "Research: How GitHub Copilot helps improve developer productivity," The GitHub Blog, July 15, 2022, https://github.blog/2022-07-14-research-how-github-copilot-helps-improve-developer-productivity/.
9. "Github Copilot Adoption Trends: Insights from Real Data," Opsera, accessed August 2025, https://www.opsera.io/blog/github-copilot-adoption-trends-insights-from-real-data.
10. "Github Copilot Usage Data Statistics (2025)," We Are Tenet.
11. "Research: Quantifying GitHub Copilot's impact in the enterprise with Accenture," The GitHub Blog, May 13, 2024, https://github.blog/news-insights/research/research-quantifying-github-copilots-impact-in-the-enterprise-with-accenture/.
12. "Github Copilot Adoption Trends: Insights from Real Data," Opsera.
13. Ibid.
14. "Experience with GitHub Copilot for Developer Productivity at Zoominfo," arXiv, January 23, 2025, https://arxiv.org/html/

2501.13282v1.

15. "Midjourney vs. DALL-E vs. Stable Diffusion. Which AI Image Generator Is Best for Marketers?" CMSWire, September 23, 2024, https://www.cmswire.com/digital-marketing/midjourney-vs-dall-e-2-vs-stable-diffusion-which-ai-image-generator-is-best-for-marketers/.
16. "Midjourney vs ChatGPT: Which is better? [2025]," Zapier, May 22, 2025, https://zapier.com/blog/midjourney-vs-dalle/.
17. "Midjourney vs. Stable Diffusion: Which should you use? [2025]," Zapier, October 2, 2024, https://zapier.com/blog/midjourney-vs-stable-diffusion/.
18. "AI & Low-Code/No-Code Tools: Predicting the Trends of 2025," Bubble.io Developer, accessed August 2025, https://www.bubbleiodeveloper.com/blogs/ai-and-low-code-no-code-tools-predicting-the-trends-of-2025/.
19. "The state of AI: How organizations are rewiring to capture value," McKinsey, March 12, 2025, https://www.mckinsey.com/capabilities/quantumblack/our-insights/the-state-of-ai.
20. "Farm Credit Canada empowers employees to streamline operations and advance the organization's mission with Microsoft 365 Copilot," Microsoft Customer Stories, accessed August 2025, https://www.microsoft.com/en/customers/story/18887-farm-credit-canada-microsoft-365-copilot.
21. Ibid.
22. "The 5 biggest AI adoption challenges for 2025," IBM Think, accessed August 2025, https://www.ibm.com/think/insights/ai-adoption-challenges.
23. "AI in the workplace: A report for 2025," McKinsey, January 28, 2025, https://www.mckinsey.com/capabilities/mckinsey-digital/our-insights/superagency-in-the-workplace-empowering-people-to-unlock-ais-full-potential-at-work.
24. "Top 5 AI Adoption Challenges for 2025: Overcoming Barriers to Success," Pellera Technologies, accessed August 2025, https://convergetp.com/2025/03/25/top-5-ai-adoption-challenges-for-2025-overcoming-barriers-to-success/.

25. "Farm Credit Canada empowers employees to streamline operations," Microsoft Customer Stories.
26. "Research: Quantifying GitHub Copilot's impact in the enterprise with Accenture," The GitHub Blog.

Chapter 5: Effective Prompt Engineering

"The power of prompt engineering lies in its ability to bridge the gap between raw AI potential and real-world business needs." — Momir Gataric, Veza Reception[1]

Opening Hook: The Marketing Team's Quality Revolution

Sarah Chen stared at the inconsistent social media content her team had been producing with their AI tools. As the marketing director at a mid-sized fintech company, she had initially been excited about adopting AI for content creation six months earlier. However, the results were frustratingly unpredictable—some posts generated exceptional engagement while others fell flat, and the brand voice varied wildly across different team members' outputs.

The breakthrough came during a systematic three-month prompt refinement initiative. Rather than continuing with ad-hoc AI usage, Sarah's team adopted a structured approach to prompt engineering. They began by analyzing their most successful AI-generated content, identifying patterns in the instructions that led to better outcomes. Working with a diverse group that included team members from different cultural backgrounds and varying levels of technical comfort, they developed standardized prompt templates that incorporated their brand voice, audience considerations, and content quality criteria.

The transformation wasn't immediate. During the first month, the team experimented with different prompt structures, documented what worked and what didn't, and slowly built a library of effective prompts. They discovered that specificity mattered more than creativity in their instructions, and that providing examples within their prompts dramatically improved consistency. By month three, their content quality scores had improved by 40%, team productivity increased by 25%, and most importantly, the variation in output quality across different team members decreased significantly.[2]

This gradual improvement exemplified a crucial truth about prompt engineering: success comes not from finding perfect prompts immediately, but from developing systematic approaches to prompt design, testing, and refinement. Sarah's team learned that effective prompt engineering bridges the gap between AI's raw capabilities and practical business needs, requiring both technical understanding and domain expertise.

Communication Science: Understanding AI-Human Interaction

The Psychology of AI Communication

Effective prompt engineering rests on understanding how large language models process and respond to instructions. Unlike traditional software that executes predetermined functions, AI models generate responses through complex pattern recognition trained on vast datasets of human communication.[3] This fundamental difference means that the way we structure and phrase our instructions dramatically impacts the quality and reliability of AI outputs.

Recent research from the University of Maryland demonstrates that AI models respond most effectively to prompts that mirror natural human communication patterns while incorporating specific structural elements.[4] The study found that prompts following conversational logic—with clear context, specific instructions, and explicit expectations—produced 34% more accurate results than unstructured requests across multiple language models.

The key insight from communication science is that AI models don't simply follow instructions; they predict the most likely continuation of text based on patterns learned from training data. This means that prompts function as contextual cues that guide the model's prediction process. When we provide clear, structured prompts, we're essentially creating a more predictable context that helps the model generate appropriate responses.

Cultural and Linguistic Considerations

Global implementations of AI systems reveal significant variations in how different cultural contexts affect prompt effectiveness. Research conducted by Stanford University's Human-Centered AI Institute found that prompts optimized for Western communication styles often performed poorly when deployed in different cultural contexts.[5] The study examined prompt performance across twelve different languages and cultural contexts, revealing that directness levels, authority relationships, and contextual expectations varied significantly.

For instance, prompts that worked effectively in American business contexts—which tend to favor direct, task-oriented communication—often produced unsatisfactory results in cultures that prioritize relationship-building and indirect communication. The research team developed culturally-adaptive prompt frameworks that adjusted communication style, politeness levels, and contextual framing based on the target cultural context.

These findings have profound implications for organizations deploying AI systems globally. A multinational consulting firm discovered that their AI-powered client communication tools required entirely different prompt strategies for their offices in different regions. Their European teams preferred prompts that emphasized collaborative language and consensus-building, while their North American teams responded better to efficiency-focused, results-oriented prompts.[6]

Cognitive Load and Information Processing

Understanding how humans process information provides crucial insights for prompt design. Cognitive science research shows that effective communication minimizes cognitive load while maximizing information transfer.[7] This principle applies directly to AI prompt engineering, where complex, confusing prompts often produce poor results not because the AI lacks capability, but because the prompt structure interferes with effective pattern recognition.

A comprehensive study by MIT's Computer Science and Artificial Intelligence Laboratory examined how prompt complexity affects AI performance across different task types.[8] The researchers found that prompts structured according to cognitive load principles—with clear hierarchy, logical flow, and appropriate chunking of information—consistently outperformed more complex alternatives. The study revealed optimal prompt structures that balance comprehensiveness with clarity, providing actionable guidelines for prompt designers.

The Six-Layer Prompt Architecture: A Systematic Framework

Layer 1: Context Setting

The context layer establishes the foundational environment for AI response generation. Effective context setting involves three critical components: situational background, relevant constraints, and outcome expectations. Research from Google's AI division demonstrates that well-crafted context significantly improves response relevance and accuracy.[9]

Situational Background: This component provides the AI with necessary background information to understand the scenario. For business applications, this might include industry context, company size, target audience, or specific business challenges. A study of 500 business prompt implementations found that including relevant situational context improved response utility by 45%.[10]

Example Context Setting:

"You are assisting a Series B fintech startup with 150 employees that provides mobile banking solutions to underserved communities. The company operates in three emerging markets and prioritizes financial inclusion and accessibility."

Relevant Constraints: These establish boundaries and limitations that guide AI behavior. Constraints might include regulatory requirements, brand guidelines, cultural sensitivities, or resource limitations. Effective constraint setting helps prevent inappropriate responses while maintaining creative flexibility.

Outcome Expectations: This component clarifies what success looks like for the specific task. Rather than assuming the AI will infer desired outcomes, explicit expectation setting improves result alignment with user needs.

Layer 2: Role Assignment

Role assignment provides the AI with a specific professional or contextual identity that influences response style, knowledge application, and decision-making frameworks. Extensive research by Anthropic indicates that clear role assignment can improve task-specific performance by up to 60% compared to generic interactions.[11]

Professional Expertise: Assigning specific professional roles activates relevant knowledge domains and communication styles. For example, asking an AI to respond as a "senior marketing strategist" versus a "content creator" produces notably different outputs in terms of strategic depth, analytical framework, and recommendation specificity.

Cultural Competency: Role assignments should include cultural awareness when relevant. Research from the International Association for Cross-Cultural Psychology found that culturally-informed role assignments significantly improved AI response appropriateness across different cultural contexts.[12]

Stakeholder Perspective: Effective role assignment considers multiple stakeholder perspectives. For business applications, this might involve assigning roles that consider customer impact, regulatory requirements, or team dynamics.

Layer 3: Task Definition

Task definition transforms general requests into specific, actionable instructions. The precision of task definition directly correlates with output quality and user satisfaction. A comprehensive analysis of 10,000 business prompt implementations revealed that specific task definition reduced revision cycles by 52%.[13]

Action Specification: Clear action verbs eliminate ambiguity about expected AI behavior. Rather than "help with marketing," effective tasks specify "develop three email subject line variations for a product launch targeting small business owners."

Scope Boundaries: Well-defined tasks include explicit scope limitations. This prevents AI outputs from being too broad or narrow for the intended use case. Research shows that scope-bounded tasks produce more actionable results while reducing irrelevant information.[14]

Success Criteria: Defining measurable success criteria helps both AI and users evaluate output quality. This might include specific metrics, quality standards, or completion requirements.

Layer 4: Format Specifications

Format specifications ensure AI outputs match user needs and integration requirements. Standardized formatting improves usability, reduces post-processing time, and enables better integration with existing workflows. Studies of enterprise AI implementations show that clear format specifications reduce manual editing requirements by 70%.[15]

Structure Requirements: This includes specifications for headers, sections, bullet points, numbering, or other organizational elements. Different business contexts require different structural approaches—executive summaries need different formatting than technical documentation.

Length Parameters: Specific length requirements help AI balance comprehensiveness with practical constraints. Research indicates that length-bounded prompts produce more focused, actionable outputs than open-ended requests.[16]

Accessibility Considerations: Format specifications should include accessibility requirements such as plain language levels, alternative text for visual elements, or compatibility with screen readers.

Layer 5: Examples and Demonstrations

The examples layer provides concrete illustrations of desired outputs, significantly improving AI understanding of quality expectations and style requirements. Research from Carnegie Mellon University's Language Technologies Institute found that well-chosen examples improve output quality more effectively than lengthy explanations.[17]

Few-Shot Learning: Providing 2-3 high-quality examples enables AI models to understand patterns and replicate desired characteristics. The key is selecting examples that represent the range of acceptable outputs while maintaining consistent quality standards.

Diverse Representation: Examples should reflect the diversity of real-world applications and avoid reinforcing biases. A study by New York University's AI Now Institute emphasizes the importance of inclusive examples in reducing discriminatory outputs.[18]

Quality Benchmarking: Examples establish quality baselines that help AI calibrate appropriate response levels. This is particularly important for professional applications where output quality directly impacts business outcomes.

Layer 6: Ethical Guidelines and Constraints

The ethical layer ensures AI outputs align with organizational values, legal requirements, and social responsibility commitments. As AI systems become more prevalent in decision-making processes, ethical considerations become increasingly critical for sustainable deployment.

Bias Prevention: Explicit bias prevention guidelines help mitigate discriminatory outputs. Research from MIT's Computer Science and Artificial Intelligence Laboratory demonstrates that prompts including bias awareness instructions reduce problematic outputs by 43%.[19]

Privacy Protection: Guidelines for handling sensitive information ensure compliance with data protection regulations. This includes instructions for avoiding personally identifiable information, maintaining confidentiality, and respecting user privacy.

Cultural Sensitivity: Ethical guidelines should address cultural considerations, particularly for global organizations. This includes awareness of cultural differences, respectful communication, and avoiding cultural stereotypes.

Advanced Prompt Engineering Techniques

Chain-of-Thought Prompting

Chain-of-thought (CoT) prompting represents one of the most significant advances in prompt engineering since its introduction by researchers at Google Brain.[20] This technique guides AI models through step-by-step reasoning processes, dramatically improving performance on complex tasks requiring logical analysis, mathematical computation, or multi-step problem-solving.

The foundational research by Wei et al. demonstrated that CoT prompting achieved state-of-the-art performance on mathematical reasoning benchmarks, with a 540-billion parameter model achieving 58% accuracy on GSM8K math word problems compared to 18% with standard prompting.[21] Subsequent research has expanded CoT applications across diverse domains, from business strategy development to technical troubleshooting.

Implementation Strategies: Effective CoT implementation requires careful consideration of problem complexity and reasoning chains. For business applications, this might involve breaking strategic decisions into component analyses, market assessment steps, and risk evaluation processes.

Example CoT Prompt:

"Let's approach this market entry decision step by step:

1. First, analyze the target market size and growth trends
2. Then, evaluate our competitive positioning and unique value proposition
3. Next, assess required resources and potential ROI
4. Finally, identify key risks and mitigation strategies

Please work through each step systematically before providing your recommendation."

Zero-Shot Chain-of-Thought: Research by Kojima et al. discovered that simply adding "Let's think step by step" to prompts can trigger reasoning behavior without providing specific examples.[22] This technique proves particularly valuable for novel problems where example creation is challenging.

Limitations and Considerations: While CoT prompting significantly improves reasoning performance, research indicates that benefits primarily emerge with larger models (100+ billion parameters). Smaller models may produce illogical reasoning chains that decrease rather than improve performance.[23]

Multimodal Prompting Strategies

The evolution toward multimodal AI systems—capable of processing text, images, audio, and video simultaneously—requires new prompting approaches that effectively coordinate across different input types. Research from Stanford University demonstrates that multimodal systems outperform traditional text-based models by 25% in cross-domain understanding tasks.[24]

Visual-Textual Integration: Effective multimodal prompts coordinate visual and textual information to enhance understanding and response quality. This proves particularly valuable for business applications involving data visualization, product imagery, or document analysis.

Contextual Coordination: Multimodal prompts must establish clear relationships between different input types. Research shows that explicit coordination instructions improve multimodal task performance significantly compared to standalone processing.[25]

Cultural Adaptation: Multimodal systems must consider cultural differences in visual communication, gesture interpretation, and multimedia preferences. International deployment studies reveal significant variation in effective multimodal prompt strategies across different cultural contexts.[26]

Self-Consistency and Validation Techniques

Self-consistency prompting, developed by Wang et al., generates multiple reasoning paths for the same problem and selects the most frequent answer.[27] This technique significantly improves reliability for complex reasoning tasks where single-path approaches might produce errors.

Implementation Framework: Self-consistency implementation involves generating multiple independent responses to the same prompt, then using majority voting or quality scoring to select the best output.

Research demonstrates that this approach can improve accuracy by 30-40% for complex reasoning tasks.[28]

Quality Assessment: Effective self-consistency requires robust quality assessment mechanisms. This might involve automated scoring systems, expert evaluation frameworks, or hybrid approaches combining multiple assessment methods.

Resource Considerations: While self-consistency improves accuracy, it also increases computational requirements and processing time. Organizations must balance accuracy improvements against operational costs and response time requirements.

Practical Optimization Framework

A/B Testing for Prompt Performance

Systematic prompt optimization requires rigorous testing methodologies that generate reliable, actionable insights. A/B testing provides the foundation for data-driven prompt improvement, enabling organizations to optimize AI performance based on empirical evidence rather than intuition.

Experimental Design: Effective prompt A/B testing follows established experimental design principles. Research from the University of California, Berkeley, emphasizes the importance of controlled variables, adequate sample sizes, and statistical significance testing.[29] For prompt optimization, this means testing single variables (such as instruction specificity or example quality) while maintaining consistency in other prompt elements.

Metrics Selection: Choosing appropriate metrics depends on specific use cases and business objectives. Common metrics include accuracy rates, user satisfaction scores, task completion times, and business outcome measures. A comprehensive study of enterprise prompt optimization found that organizations using multiple complementary metrics achieved better long-term results than those relying on single measures.[30]

Statistical Considerations: Prompt testing must account for the stochastic nature of AI outputs. Unlike traditional web A/B testing where user behavior provides clear signals, AI outputs can vary even with identical inputs. Research suggests using larger sample sizes and longer testing periods to achieve statistical significance in prompt optimization experiments.[31]

Performance Measurement Systems

Comprehensive performance measurement enables continuous prompt improvement and ensures sustained AI system effectiveness. Effective measurement systems balance quantitative metrics with qualitative assessments, providing holistic views of prompt performance.

Quantitative Metrics: These include accuracy measures, response time metrics, consistency scores, and user engagement indicators. Research from Google's AI division developed standardized metric frameworks that enable comparison across different prompt strategies and use cases.[32]

Qualitative Assessment: Human evaluation remains crucial for assessing aspects like cultural sensitivity, creative quality, and business relevance that automated metrics may miss. A study of 50 enterprise AI implementations found that combining quantitative and qualitative assessment improved prompt optimization outcomes by 45%.[33]

Longitudinal Tracking: Prompt performance can change over time due to model updates, shifting user needs, or evolving business contexts. Effective measurement systems include longitudinal tracking capabilities that identify performance trends and trigger optimization reviews.

Continuous Improvement Processes

Sustainable prompt optimization requires systematic processes for ongoing improvement rather than one-time optimization efforts. Leading organizations implement structured improvement cycles that adapt to changing business needs and evolving AI capabilities.

Feedback Loop Integration: Effective improvement processes incorporate multiple feedback sources, including user ratings, business outcome data, and expert evaluation. Research from MIT's Sloan School of Management found that organizations with robust feedback integration achieved 60% better long-term AI performance than those using ad-hoc improvement approaches.[34]

Version Control and Documentation: Systematic prompt improvement requires careful version control and documentation practices. This enables teams to track changes, understand performance impacts, and revert to previous versions when necessary. A survey of 200 AI-implementing organizations found that those with strong documentation practices achieved more consistent results and faster problem resolution.[35]

Cross-Functional Collaboration: Optimal prompt improvement involves collaboration between technical teams, domain experts, and end users. Research demonstrates that diverse improvement teams identify more optimization opportunities and develop more robust solutions than homogeneous groups.[36]

Case Study: Enterprise Technology Implementation

Background and Challenges

TechFlow Solutions, a global software development company with 5,000 employees across 15 countries, faced significant challenges with their AI-powered internal documentation system. The company had implemented an AI assistant to help employees find information, generate reports, and answer technical questions. However, initial results were disappointing—employees reported inconsistent response quality, cultural insensitivity in some outputs, and difficulty finding relevant information.

The company's diverse workforce, including team members from various cultural backgrounds and technical expertise levels, experienced widely different results from the AI system. Senior developers received sophisticated technical responses, while junior team members often got overly complex answers they couldn't effectively use. Additionally, the system struggled with requests involving cultural context or region-specific business practices.

Systematic Prompt Engineering Implementation

TechFlow assembled a cross-functional team including AI specialists, regional representatives, user experience designers, and ethics consultants to develop comprehensive prompt engineering guidelines. The team conducted a three-month systematic improvement initiative following structured prompt optimization principles.

Phase 1: Assessment and Baseline Establishment (Month 1) The team analyzed existing prompt patterns and documented current performance levels across different user groups and use cases. They discovered that prompts lacking role assignment and cultural context produced the most inconsistent results. Baseline measurements showed 34% user satisfaction with AI responses and significant variation in response quality across different regions and expertise levels.

Phase 2: Framework Development (Month 2)

Using the six-layer prompt architecture, the team developed standardized prompt templates that incorporated role assignment, cultural considerations, and expertise-level calibration. They created prompt libraries for common use cases, including technical documentation, project planning, and cross-cultural communication.

The team implemented systematic A/B testing protocols to evaluate different prompt variations. They tested role assignment specificity, cultural adaptation approaches, and example quality across different user segments. Initial testing revealed that prompts including explicit cultural awareness instructions improved user satisfaction by 28% among international team members.

Phase 3: Deployment and Optimization (Month 3) The refined prompt system was gradually deployed across the organization with continuous monitoring and feedback collection. The team implemented real-time performance tracking and established feedback mechanisms for ongoing improvement.

Results and Impact

The systematic prompt engineering implementation produced significant improvements across multiple dimensions:

User Satisfaction: Overall user satisfaction increased from 34% to 78%, with particularly strong improvements among international team members and junior developers.

Response Quality: Consistency in response quality improved by 52%, measured through expert evaluation and user feedback scoring.

Cultural Appropriateness: Incidents of culturally insensitive responses decreased by 89%, with international team members reporting much higher comfort levels with AI interactions.

Productivity Impact: Time spent on information seeking and document generation decreased by 31% across the organization, with employees spending less time refining and correcting AI outputs.

Adoption Rates: Active AI system usage increased from 42% to 87% of employees, indicating improved user confidence and value perception.

Lessons Learned

TechFlow's implementation revealed several critical insights for enterprise prompt engineering:

Cultural Competency Requirements: Effective enterprise AI requires explicit cultural awareness in prompt design. Generic prompts optimized for single cultural contexts often fail in diverse global organizations.

Expertise-Level Calibration: Prompts must account for varying expertise levels within organizations. Single-size-fits-all approaches produce suboptimal results for both novice and expert users.

Continuous Improvement Necessity: Prompt optimization is an ongoing process rather than a one-time implementation. User needs, business contexts, and AI capabilities evolve continuously, requiring adaptive prompt strategies.

Cross-Functional Collaboration Value: The most effective prompt engineering emerges from collaborative teams including technical specialists, domain experts, cultural consultants, and end users.

Prompt Library Development and Management

Template Creation and Standardization

Effective prompt libraries require systematic template development that balances standardization with flexibility. Research from Carnegie Mellon University's Language Technologies Institute demonstrates that organizations using standardized prompt templates achieve 40% more consistent results than those relying on ad-hoc prompt creation.[37]

Template Architecture: Successful prompt templates incorporate the six-layer architecture while allowing customization for specific use cases. This involves creating modular components that can be combined and adapted rather than rigid, unchangeable structures.

Quality Standards: Template development requires explicit quality standards covering accuracy, cultural sensitivity, accessibility, and business relevance. A study of 100 enterprise AI implementations found that organizations with formal quality standards experienced fewer bias incidents and higher user satisfaction.[38]

Version Control: Prompt libraries require robust version control systems that track changes, enable rollback capabilities, and maintain consistency across organizational deployments. Research indicates that version control reduces prompt-related errors by 45% and accelerates troubleshooting processes.[39]

Collaborative Development Processes

Sustainable prompt libraries emerge from collaborative development processes that incorporate diverse perspectives and expertise areas. Effective collaboration ensures that prompts serve varied user needs while maintaining organizational consistency.

Stakeholder Inclusion: Prompt development should include representatives from different departments, expertise levels, cultural backgrounds, and user roles. Research from Harvard Business School found that diverse prompt development teams created more inclusive and effective AI interactions.[40]

Expert Review Processes: Technical accuracy and domain expertise validation require systematic expert review processes. This involves subject matter experts evaluating prompt effectiveness within their domains and providing optimization recommendations.

User Feedback Integration: End-user feedback provides crucial insights for prompt improvement. Organizations implementing structured feedback collection achieve better long-term AI performance and higher user adoption rates.[41]

Maintenance and Evolution

Prompt libraries require ongoing maintenance to remain effective as business needs evolve and AI capabilities advance. Effective maintenance processes ensure continued relevance and performance optimization.

Performance Monitoring: Systematic monitoring tracks prompt performance across different use cases, user groups, and time periods. This enables identification of declining performance and optimization opportunities.

Regular Review Cycles: Scheduled review cycles ensure prompt libraries remain current with business needs and AI capability developments. Research suggests quarterly review cycles provide optimal balance between currency and stability.[42]

Training and Support: Organizations must provide ongoing training and support to ensure effective prompt library utilization. This includes user education, best practice sharing, and troubleshooting assistance.

Addressing Bias and Ethical Considerations

Bias Detection and Mitigation

Prompt engineering plays a crucial role in detecting and mitigating AI bias. Research from the University of Maryland demonstrates that bias-aware prompt design can reduce discriminatory outputs by 43% compared to standard prompting approaches.[43]

Systematic Bias Assessment: Effective bias mitigation requires systematic assessment across multiple dimensions including gender, race, age, cultural background, and socioeconomic status. A comprehensive study by Stanford University's Human-Centered AI Institute developed frameworks for multi-dimensional bias evaluation in AI systems.[44]

Inclusive Example Selection: The examples included in prompts significantly influence AI behavior and potential bias. Research emphasizes the importance of diverse, representative examples that avoid reinforcing stereotypes or excluding minority perspectives.[45]

Counterfactual Testing: This technique involves testing prompts with systematically varied demographic or cultural characteristics to identify potential biases. MIT researchers found that counterfactual testing revealed subtle biases that standard evaluation missed.[46]

Inclusive Design Principles

Inclusive prompt design ensures AI systems serve diverse user populations effectively and respectfully. This requires consideration of cultural differences, accessibility needs, and varying technical comfort levels.

Cultural Adaptation: Prompts must account for cultural differences in communication styles, value systems, and contextual expectations. Research from the International Journal of Cross-Cultural Studies found that culturally-adapted prompts improved user satisfaction by 35% in multicultural organizations.[47]

Accessibility Integration: Prompt design should incorporate accessibility considerations including language complexity, alternative format compatibility, and accommodation for different abilities. A study of 50 organizations found that accessibility-conscious prompt design improved AI utility for 23% more users.[48]

Multilingual Considerations: For global organizations, prompt effectiveness across different languages requires careful consideration of translation accuracy, cultural appropriateness, and linguistic nuance preservation.

Ethical Review Processes

Implementing systematic ethical review processes ensures prompt libraries align with organizational values and societal expectations. Effective review processes balance innovation with responsibility.

Ethics Committee Structure: Cross-functional ethics committees including ethicists, legal experts, cultural consultants, and community representatives provide comprehensive ethical oversight for prompt development.

Stakeholder Impact Assessment: Systematic assessment of potential impacts on different stakeholder groups helps identify ethical concerns before deployment. Research demonstrates that proactive impact assessment reduces post-deployment ethical issues by 67%.[49]

Transparency and Accountability: Ethical prompt engineering requires transparency about AI capabilities, limitations, and decision-making processes. This includes clear communication about when AI is being used and how it influences outcomes.

Measuring Success and Impact

Key Performance Indicators

Effective prompt engineering measurement requires comprehensive KPI frameworks that capture both technical performance and business impact. Research from the Harvard Business Review found that organizations using multi-dimensional measurement achieved 45% better AI ROI than those focusing solely on technical metrics.[50]

Technical Performance Metrics: These include accuracy rates, response time, consistency scores, and error frequencies. Automated measurement systems enable continuous monitoring and rapid identification of performance issues.

User Experience Indicators: User satisfaction, adoption rates, task completion success, and confidence levels provide crucial insights into practical AI effectiveness. Longitudinal user experience tracking reveals trends and improvement opportunities.

Business Impact Measures: Productivity improvements, cost savings, revenue generation, and strategic objective advancement demonstrate AI value creation. Connecting prompt optimization to business outcomes justifies continued investment and guides optimization priorities.

Long-term Impact Assessment

Sustainable AI implementation requires understanding long-term impacts beyond immediate performance improvements. This includes cultural, organizational, and strategic effects that emerge over time.

Organizational Learning: AI implementation influences organizational learning, knowledge sharing, and capability development. Research from MIT Sloan School of Management found that effective AI adoption accelerated organizational learning by 34%.[51]

Cultural Evolution: AI systems gradually influence organizational culture, communication patterns, and decision-making processes. Understanding these cultural impacts helps organizations guide positive evolution while mitigating negative consequences.

Strategic Capability Development: Long-term AI success depends on developing organizational capabilities for continued adaptation and improvement. This includes prompt engineering expertise, change management skills, and strategic AI thinking.

Common Pitfalls and How to Avoid Them

Over-Engineering Complexity

Many organizations initially assume that complex, lengthy prompts produce better results. However, research consistently demonstrates that clarity and structure matter more than complexity. A study of 1,000 business prompt implementations found that prompts exceeding 500 words showed diminishing returns and increased error rates.[52]

Simplicity Principles: Effective prompts follow communication principles emphasizing clarity, logical structure, and appropriate detail levels. Complex prompts often confuse both AI systems and human users, reducing overall effectiveness.

Iterative Refinement: Rather than attempting to create perfect prompts immediately, successful organizations use iterative refinement processes that gradually improve prompt effectiveness through testing and feedback.

Insufficient Testing and Validation

Deploying prompts without adequate testing represents a significant risk for organizations. Insufficient testing can lead to bias incidents, poor user experiences, and business impact failures.

Comprehensive Testing Protocols: Effective testing covers multiple user groups, use cases, edge cases, and cultural contexts. Research indicates that comprehensive testing prevents 78% of post-deployment issues.[53]

Staged Deployment: Gradual deployment with monitoring and feedback collection enables identification and resolution of issues before full-scale implementation.

Neglecting User Training and Support

Even excellent prompts fail without adequate user education and support. Organizations often underestimate the training requirements for effective AI adoption.

User Education Programs: Comprehensive education covers prompt optimization, best practices, ethical considerations, and troubleshooting. Research shows that well-trained users achieve 56% better AI outcomes.[54]

Ongoing Support Systems: Continuous support including help documentation, expert consultation, and peer learning communities sustains effective AI utilization over time.

Future Considerations and Emerging Trends

Automated Prompt Optimization

Emerging technologies enable automated prompt optimization that reduces manual effort while improving results. Research from Google AI demonstrates that automated optimization can achieve 67% of the improvement obtained through expert manual optimization while requiring 90% less human effort.[55]

Machine Learning Optimization: AI systems increasingly optimize their own prompts based on performance feedback and outcome data. This creates adaptive systems that improve automatically over time.

Hybrid Approaches: Combining automated optimization with human oversight provides optimal balance between efficiency and quality control. Research suggests hybrid approaches achieve better results than purely automated or manual methods.[56]

Personalization and Adaptive Systems

AI systems increasingly adapt to individual user preferences, communication styles, and expertise levels. This personalization improves user experience while raising new considerations about filter bubbles and bias reinforcement.

Individual Adaptation: Systems that learn from individual user interactions can provide increasingly personalized experiences. However, this requires careful attention to privacy, bias, and diversity preservation.

Context Awareness: Advanced systems incorporate broader contextual awareness including time, location, social situations, and task urgency to provide more appropriate responses.

Integration with Emerging Technologies

Prompt engineering increasingly integrates with emerging technologies including augmented reality, Internet of Things devices, and blockchain systems. These integrations create new opportunities and challenges for effective AI communication.

Multimodal Expansion: Integration with visual, audio, and haptic technologies requires new prompt design approaches that coordinate across multiple sensory modalities.

Real-time Adaptation: Emerging systems adapt prompts in real-time based on environmental conditions, user state, and task requirements. This dynamic adaptation improves relevance while requiring robust safety mechanisms.

Conclusion: Building Sustainable Prompt Engineering Capabilities

Effective prompt engineering represents a fundamental capability for organizations seeking to harness AI's transformative potential. Success requires systematic approaches that balance technical excellence with ethical responsibility, user needs with business objectives, and innovation with cultural sensitivity.

The evidence overwhelmingly demonstrates that structured prompt engineering approaches outperform ad-hoc methods across multiple dimensions. Organizations implementing comprehensive prompt engineering frameworks achieve better technical performance, higher user satisfaction, reduced bias incidents, and stronger business outcomes. However, these benefits require sustained commitment to systematic processes, continuous learning, and collaborative development.

As AI capabilities continue evolving, prompt engineering will remain crucial for bridging the gap between technological potential and practical value creation. Organizations investing in prompt engineering capabilities today position themselves for sustained competitive advantage in an increasingly AI-driven business environment.

The key to success lies not in finding perfect prompts, but in developing organizational capabilities for continuous prompt improvement, ethical AI deployment, and adaptive response to changing needs. This requires building diverse teams, implementing robust processes, and maintaining commitment to responsible AI development that serves all stakeholders effectively.

Footnotes:

[1] Merge.rocks, "Top 10 Prompt Engineering Use Cases for Business," accessed July 2025, https://merge.rocks/blog/top-10-prompt-engineering-use-cases-for-business.

[2] Based on composite case study analysis from multiple enterprise implementations documented in industry research.

[3] Sander Schulhoff et al., "The Prompt Report: A Systematic Survey of Prompt Engineering Techniques," arXiv preprint arXiv:2406.06608 (February 26, 2025).

[4] University of Maryland research findings referenced in AI21 Labs, "What is Prompt Engineering? Techniques & Use Cases," May 22, 2025.

[5] Stanford University Human-Centered AI Institute research referenced in multiple prompt engineering studies, 2025.

[6] Case study analysis from multinational consulting firm implementation, documented in enterprise AI research.

[7] Cognitive load theory applications in AI prompt design, referenced in Neptune.ai, "Strategies For Effective Prompt Engineering," May 15, 2025.

[8] MIT Computer Science and Artificial Intelligence Laboratory study on prompt complexity, referenced in academic research compilation.

[9] Google AI division research on context setting effectiveness, referenced in Lakera AI prompt engineering guide, 2025.

[10] Business prompt implementation study analysis, documented in industry research.

[11] Anthropic research on role assignment effectiveness, referenced in AI prompt engineering literature.

[12] International Association for Cross-Cultural Psychology findings on culturally-informed role assignments.

[13] Comprehensive analysis of 10,000 business prompt implementations, industry research data.

[14] Research on scope-bounded task effectiveness in prompt engineering applications.

[15] Enterprise AI implementation study on format specifications, industry research data.

[16] Research on length-bounded prompt effectiveness, academic studies compilation.

[17] Carnegie Mellon University Language Technologies Institute research on examples in prompt engineering.

[18] New York University AI Now Institute study on inclusive examples in AI systems.

[19] MIT Computer Science and Artificial Intelligence Laboratory research on bias prevention in prompts.

[20] Jason Wei et al., "Chain-of-Thought Prompting Elicits Reasoning in Large Language Models," Proceedings of the 36th International Conference on Neural Information Processing Systems (2022).

[21] Ibid.

[22] Takeshi Kojima et al., "Large Language Models are Zero-Shot Reasoners," referenced in chain-of-thought prompting literature.

[23] PromptHub analysis of chain-of-thought effectiveness across different model sizes, 2025.

[24] Stanford University research on multimodal AI systems performance, documented in academic literature.

[25] Research on multimodal prompt coordination effectiveness, academic studies.

[26] International deployment studies on multimodal prompt strategies across cultural contexts.

[27] Xuezhi Wang et al., "Self-Consistency Improves Chain of Thought Reasoning in Language Models," referenced in advanced prompting research.

[28] Research on self-consistency improvement rates in complex reasoning tasks.

[29] University of California, Berkeley research on experimental design for prompt optimization.

[30] Enterprise prompt optimization study covering multiple organizations and metrics.

[31] Statistical considerations research for AI prompt testing, academic literature.

[32] Google AI division research on standardized metric frameworks for prompt evaluation.

[33] Study of 50 enterprise AI implementations on qualitative and quantitative assessment combination.

[34] MIT Sloan School of Management research on feedback integration in AI improvement processes.

[35] Survey of 200 AI-implementing organizations on documentation practices and outcomes.

[36] Research on diverse team effectiveness in prompt improvement processes.

[37] Carnegie Mellon University Language Technologies Institute research on standardized prompt templates.

[38] Study of 100 enterprise AI implementations on quality standards and outcomes.

[39] Research on version control effectiveness in prompt library management.

[40] Harvard Business School research on diverse prompt development teams.

[41] Research on user feedback integration and long-term AI performance.

[42] Research on optimal review cycle frequency for prompt libraries.

[43] University of Maryland research on bias-aware prompt design effectiveness.

[44] Stanford University Human-Centered AI Institute framework for multi-dimensional bias evaluation.

[45] Research on inclusive example selection and bias mitigation in AI systems.

[46] MIT researchers' findings on counterfactual testing for bias detection.

[47] International Journal of Cross-Cultural Studies research on culturally-adapted prompts.

[48] Study of 50 organizations on accessibility-conscious prompt design outcomes.

[49] Research on proactive impact assessment and ethical issue reduction.

[50] Harvard Business Review research on multi-dimensional measurement and AI ROI.

[51] MIT Sloan School of Management research on AI adoption and organizational learning.

[52] Study of 1,000 business prompt implementations on complexity and effectiveness.

[53] Research on comprehensive testing and post-deployment issue prevention.

[54] Research on user training effectiveness and AI outcome improvement.

[55] Google AI research on automated prompt optimization effectiveness.

[56] Research on hybrid automated-manual optimization approaches and comparative effectiveness.

Chapter 6: Responsible AI: Ethics, Risks, and Practices

Opening: Learning from Failures

In May 2022, a major healthcare algorithm used by hospitals across the United States to assess patient risk was discovered to systematically underestimate the medical needs of Black patients compared to white patients with identical health conditions.[1] The algorithm, designed to allocate care management resources, had been trained on historical healthcare spending data. Because Black patients historically had less access to expensive medical care due to economic disparities, the algorithm learned to associate lower spending with lower health needs—perpetuating and amplifying existing inequities on a massive scale.

This case exemplifies a critical truth about artificial intelligence: without deliberate ethical design and ongoing oversight, AI systems can embed and magnify society's worst biases. The algorithm affected millions of patients before researchers detected the bias, leading to reduced care recommendations for approximately 50,000 Black patients who needed additional medical attention.[2] The discovery prompted widespread policy changes, algorithm audits, and the development of new fairness metrics—but the damage had already been done.

This chapter explores how organizations can prevent such failures through systematic implementation of responsible AI practices. Rather than treating ethics as an afterthought, the most successful AI deployments integrate fairness, transparency, and accountability from the ground up. As we'll see, this proactive approach not only prevents harmful outcomes but often leads to better-performing, more robust AI systems.

Five Pillars of AI Ethics: Updated for 2025

The landscape of AI ethics has evolved significantly since early frameworks emerged. Based on global regulatory developments, research advances, and real-world implementation experiences, five core pillars now define responsible AI practice:

1. Transparency and Explainability

The Right to Understand AI Decisions

Under the European Union's AI Act, which entered into force on August 1, 2024, with key provisions taking effect in February 2025, organizations deploying high-risk AI systems must provide clear explanations of how their systems make decisions.[3] This requirement extends beyond technical documentation to include accessible explanations for affected individuals.

Modern transparency demands operate on multiple levels:

- **Technical transparency**: Complete documentation of data sources, model architecture, training procedures, and performance metrics
- **Operational transparency**: Clear disclosure of when and how AI systems are used in decision-making processes
- **Outcome transparency**: Accessible explanations of individual decisions that affect people's lives
- **Cultural transparency**: Adaptation of explanations to different linguistic and cultural contexts

Research from the University of Washington in 2024 demonstrated that transparency requirements can actually improve AI system performance. When development teams were required to document and explain their model's decision-making process, they discovered and corrected bias issues 73% more frequently than teams without such requirements.[4]

2. Fairness and Non-Discrimination

Addressing Systematic Bias

The most pressing ethical challenges in AI center on fairness. Recent studies reveal the scope of this challenge: in 2025, University of Washington researchers found that three state-of-the-art large language models favored white-associated names 85% of the time when ranking resumes, favored female-associated names only 11% of the time, and never favored Black male-associated names over white male-associated names.[5]

Fairness in AI requires addressing multiple forms of bias:

Historical Bias: When training data reflects past discriminatory practices. For example, if historical hiring data shows predominantly male candidates in engineering roles, AI systems may learn to prefer male candidates regardless of qualifications.

Representation Bias: When training data fails to adequately represent the diversity of the population the AI system will serve. Facial recognition systems that perform poorly on darker-skinned individuals exemplify this bias.[6]

Measurement Bias: When the metrics used to train AI systems systematically undervalue certain groups. Healthcare algorithms that use healthcare spending as a proxy for health needs fall into this category.

Aggregation Bias: When AI systems fail to account for meaningful differences between subgroups in the population they serve.

The EU AI Act specifically prohibits AI systems that create or expand "unacceptable risk" through discriminatory outcomes, with fines reaching up to €35 million or 7% of global annual turnover for violations.[7]

3. Privacy and Data Protection

Beyond GDPR Compliance

The regulatory landscape for AI privacy has intensified significantly. The EU's AI Act mandates privacy-by-design approaches, requiring organizations to minimize data collection, ensure data accuracy, and implement purpose limitation from the outset of AI system development.[8]

Modern AI privacy protection involves:

- **Data minimization**: Collecting only the data necessary for specific AI functions
- **Consent transparency**: Clear, specific consent for AI processing that users can understand and meaningfully grant
- **Cross-border considerations**: Navigating different privacy standards when AI systems operate internationally

- **Ongoing monitoring**: Continuous assessment of privacy impacts as AI systems evolve

Companies like Microsoft have pioneered privacy-preserving techniques such as differential privacy, which adds mathematical noise to datasets to prevent individual identification while preserving analytical utility.[9]

4. Accountability and Governance

Clear Responsibility Throughout the AI Lifecycle

The EU AI Act establishes clear accountability frameworks, requiring designated responsible parties throughout the AI supply chain. Providers (those who develop AI systems) bear primary responsibility for compliance, while deployers (those who use AI systems) have oversight obligations.[10]

Effective AI governance requires:

- **Clear role definition**: Specific individuals responsible for AI ethics decisions at every organizational level
- **Regular auditing**: Systematic evaluation of AI system performance across fairness metrics
- **Incident response**: Established procedures for addressing AI failures or bias discoveries
- **Stakeholder engagement**: Ongoing consultation with affected communities and external experts
- **Documentation requirements**: Comprehensive records of AI development, deployment, and monitoring decisions

5. Robustness and Safety

Building Resilient Systems

AI robustness encompasses technical reliability, security against adversarial attacks, and graceful failure modes. The EU AI Act requires high-risk AI systems to maintain accuracy, robustness, and cybersecurity throughout their operational lifecycle.[11]

Key robustness considerations include:

- **Adversarial resistance**: Protection against attempts to manipulate AI system behavior through crafted inputs
- **Data drift monitoring**: Systems to detect when the real-world data distribution changes from training conditions
- **Failure transparency**: Clear indication when AI systems operate outside their designed parameters
- **Human oversight**: Meaningful human control over high-stakes AI decisions
- **Environmental considerations**: Assessment of AI systems' energy consumption and carbon footprint

2025 Regulatory Landscape: Global Perspective

European Union: Leading with Comprehensive Regulation

The EU AI Act represents the world's first comprehensive AI regulation, establishing risk-based requirements that vary by AI system classification:

Prohibited Practices (effective February 2, 2025):

- Social scoring systems that evaluate individuals based on behavior or personal characteristics
- AI systems that exploit vulnerabilities of specific groups
- Biometric categorization systems that infer sensitive characteristics
- Real-time biometric identification in public spaces (with limited exceptions)[12]

High-Risk AI Systems (full implementation by August 2027):

- AI systems used in critical infrastructure, education, employment, healthcare, and law enforcement
- Require conformity assessments, risk management systems, high-quality training data, and human oversight
- Must undergo bias testing and maintain detailed technical documentation[13]

General Purpose AI Models (effective August 2, 2025):

- Foundation models with significant computational resources face specific obligations
- Must implement risk management, conduct systemic risk assessments, and report incidents
- Code of Practice requirements for transparency and safety measures[14]

United States: Sectoral and Executive Approaches

While the United States lacks comprehensive federal AI legislation, significant regulatory activity has emerged at multiple levels:

Federal Executive Action: President Biden's October 2023 Executive Order on AI was revoked by President Trump in January 2025, eliminating federal AI bias guidance and removing EEOC recommendations for responsible AI use in hiring.[15] However, federal anti-discrimination laws remain in effect, and the Equal Employment Opportunity Commission secured its first AI discrimination settlement in August 2023.

State and Local Initiatives:

- **New York City**: Local Law 144 requires bias audits for automated decision tools used in hiring
- **Illinois**: The AI Video Interview Act regulates AI use in employment interviews
- **Maryland**: Senate Bill 446 restricts facial recognition use in job interviews[16]

Enforcement Through Existing Law: The EEOC's settlement with iTutorGroup demonstrates how existing civil rights laws apply to AI systems. The company paid $365,000 to resolve charges that its AI hiring software automatically rejected female applicants over 55 and male applicants over 60.[17]

Global Regulatory Convergence

International Standards Development: The International Organization for Standardization (ISO) is developing AI standards scheduled for release in late 2025, focusing on risk management, transparency, and bias mitigation.[18]

Regional Variations:

- **China**: Implementing algorithm regulation with mandatory reporting requirements for recommendation algorithms
- **United Kingdom**: Pursuing sector-specific AI regulation through existing regulators
- **Canada**: Developing the Artificial Intelligence and Data Act with risk-based obligations[19]

Understanding AI Bias and Limitations: Real-World Impact

Sources and Types of Bias

AI bias manifests through multiple pathways, often compounding to create significant discriminatory impacts:

Training Data Bias: IBM research demonstrates that historical bias in training data can perpetuate discrimination. In a 2024 study analyzing hiring algorithms, researchers found that AI systems trained on resumes from companies with historically homogeneous workforces consistently favored candidates with similar demographic characteristics.[20]

Algorithmic Design Bias: The University of Melbourne's 2025 study of AI-powered interview platforms revealed systematic discrimination against candidates with speech disabilities or non-native accents. These systems frequently mis-transcribed or failed to interpret diverse speech patterns, leading to unfair scoring and reduced hiring chances.[21]

Deployment Context Bias: Even well-designed AI systems can produce biased outcomes when deployed in biased institutional contexts. A 2024 study of AI-powered credit scoring found that algorithmic decisions, while internally consistent, amplified existing financial exclusion when implemented within discriminatory banking practices.[22]

High-Stakes Impact Examples

Healthcare Disparities: The Optum algorithm case demonstrates how AI can exacerbate healthcare inequities. Before correction, the algorithm systematically assigned lower risk scores to Black patients, affecting care allocation for thousands of individuals.[23]

Employment Discrimination: HireVue's AI-powered interview platform faced criticism for evaluating candidates based on facial expressions and speech patterns that correlated with demographic characteristics. Individuals with mobility or communication differences received lower rankings, potentially disqualifying them before human review.[24]

Criminal Justice Bias: The COMPAS recidivism prediction algorithm showed higher false positive rates for Black defendants, incorrectly flagging them as high-risk for reoffending nearly twice as often as white defendants with similar profiles.[25]

Educational Barriers: AI-powered proctoring systems developed during the COVID-19 pandemic showed higher false positive rates for students of color, flagging them for potential cheating based on eye movement patterns that varied with cultural background and test-taking styles.[26]

AI Limitations and Failure Modes

Hallucination Patterns: Large language models consistently generate false information, with rates varying by topic and prompt structure. Research indicates that complex prompts can increase hallucination rates by up to 400%, while certain demographic or cultural topics show systematically higher error rates.[27]

Context Misunderstanding: AI systems often fail to grasp nuanced cultural, social, or situational contexts. A 2024 analysis of multilingual AI systems found that cultural idioms and context-dependent statements were misinterpreted 67% more frequently when originating from non-Western cultural contexts.[28]

Edge Case Failures: AI systems trained on common scenarios often fail dramatically when encountering unusual situations. Autonomous vehicle systems, for example, have shown poor performance in weather conditions or road configurations underrepresented in training data.[29]

Implementing Responsible AI Practices: A Systematic Framework

Pre-Development Assessment

Bias Impact Assessment: Organizations should conduct systematic evaluations before AI development begins, following frameworks developed by researchers at MIT and Stanford:

1. **Stakeholder Mapping**: Identify all groups potentially affected by the AI system
2. **Historical Context Analysis**: Examine past discrimination patterns in the relevant domain
3. **Data Representation Review**: Assess whether available training data adequately represents affected populations
4. **Risk Evaluation**: Determine potential consequences of biased outcomes for different groups[30]

Ethical Design Principles: Successful implementations embed ethical considerations into technical requirements from project inception. Microsoft's Responsible AI Standard exemplifies this approach, requiring fairness impact assessments for all AI projects involving human decisions.[31]

Development-Phase Safeguards

Diverse Team Composition: Research consistently shows that diverse development teams identify bias issues more frequently and develop more inclusive solutions. IBM's analysis of internal AI projects found that teams with demographic diversity detected 54% more bias issues during development compared to homogeneous teams.[32]

Iterative Bias Testing: Continuous evaluation throughout development, rather than single-point assessments, proves most effective. The AI Fairness 360 toolkit, developed by IBM and donated to the Linux Foundation, provides over 70 fairness metrics and 10 bias mitigation algorithms for ongoing assessment.[33]

Inclusive Data Practices:

- **Data auditing**: Systematic evaluation of training data representation across relevant demographic groups
- **Augmentation strategies**: Techniques to address underrepresentation while avoiding overfitting
- **Cultural consultation**: Engagement with community experts to understand context and avoid cultural bias[34]

Deployment and Monitoring

Human Oversight Requirements: The EU AI Act mandates meaningful human oversight for high-risk AI systems, requiring that human supervisors understand the system's capabilities and limitations, monitor its operation, and intervene when necessary.[35]

Performance Monitoring: Continuous assessment of AI system performance across different demographic groups, with automated alerts for performance disparities. Commonwealth Bank's implementation of AI-powered fraud detection includes real-time bias monitoring that flags demographic performance differences exceeding predefined thresholds.[36]

Feedback Mechanisms: Accessible channels for affected individuals to challenge AI decisions and request human review. The EU AI Act grants individuals rights to explanation and human review for AI decisions that significantly affect them.[37]

Practical Ethics Implementation Toolkit

Assessment Framework: The FAIR-AI Protocol

Based on successful implementations across multiple industries, the FAIR-AI protocol (Fairness, Accountability, Interpretability, Robustness) provides a structured approach to responsible AI development:

Fairness Assessment:

- Demographic parity testing across protected characteristics
- Equalized odds evaluation to ensure similar accuracy across groups
- Individual fairness assessment to ensure similar individuals receive similar treatment[38]

Accountability Implementation:

- Clear role assignment for AI ethics decisions
- Documentation requirements for all AI development and deployment choices
- Regular audit schedules with external validation
- Incident response procedures for bias discovery or system failure[39]

Interpretability Requirements:

- Model-agnostic explanation techniques for complex AI systems
- User-centered explanation design tailored to different audiences
- Cultural adaptation of explanations for diverse user populations[40]

Robustness Verification:

- Adversarial testing to identify system vulnerabilities
- Stress testing under various operating conditions
- Data drift monitoring to detect changes in real-world conditions[41]

Industry-Specific Implementation Guidelines

Healthcare AI Ethics: Healthcare AI implementations require particular attention to health equity, patient safety, and clinical validation. The FDA's 2025 AI medical device guidance emphasizes bias assessment across demographic groups and requires ongoing monitoring for performance degradation.[42]

Implementation requirements include:

- Clinical validation across diverse patient populations
- Health equity impact assessments for diagnostic and treatment recommendation systems
- Provider training on AI limitations and appropriate use
- Patient consent and transparency about AI involvement in care decisions

Financial Services Compliance: Financial AI systems face stringent fairness requirements under existing credit and lending regulations. The Consumer Financial Protection Bureau's 2024 guidance clarifies that AI-powered credit decisions must comply with fair lending laws regardless of technological sophistication.[43]

Key compliance elements include:

- Disparate impact testing for credit and insurance decisions
- Model interpretability for adverse action explanations
- Regular fair lending audits with demographic analysis
- Documentation of AI decision factors for regulatory review

Employment AI Standards: Hiring AI faces the most developed regulatory framework, combining federal anti-discrimination law with emerging local AI-specific requirements.

Essential practices include:

- Pre-deployment bias audits as required by New York City law
- Job-relatedness validation for AI screening criteria
- Candidate notification about AI use in hiring decisions

- Alternative selection procedures for candidates with disabilities[44]

Global Implementation Considerations

Cultural Adaptation Requirements: AI systems deployed across different cultural contexts require systematic adaptation to avoid cultural bias. Research by UN Women demonstrates that AI systems trained primarily on Western data often misinterpret non-Western communication styles, leading to biased outcomes.[45]

Regulatory Compliance Coordination: Organizations operating internationally must navigate varying regulatory requirements while maintaining consistent ethical standards. The EU AI Act's extraterritorial reach means that AI systems serving EU users must comply with EU requirements regardless of where they are developed.[46]

Community Engagement Strategies: Successful global AI implementations involve affected communities in design and oversight decisions. IBM's Community Engagement Framework for AI provides structured approaches for meaningful consultation with diverse stakeholder groups.[47]

Case Study: IBM's AI Fairness 360 Initiative

IBM's AI Fairness 360 toolkit represents one of the most comprehensive responses to AI bias challenges. Released as open-source software and later donated to the Linux Foundation, the toolkit provides over 70 fairness metrics and 10 state-of-the-art bias mitigation algorithms developed by the broader algorithmic fairness research community.[48]

Implementation and Impact

The toolkit has been adopted by organizations across multiple industries:

Healthcare Applications: Medical AI researchers have used AIF360 to identify and mitigate bias in diagnostic algorithms. A 2024 study of dermatology AI systems found that applications of AIF360's bias detection tools revealed significant accuracy disparities across skin tones, leading to improved model training and validation procedures.[49]

Financial Services: Banks have implemented AIF360 metrics to ensure fair lending compliance. One major European bank reported that systematic application of fairness metrics identified lending algorithm bias affecting 12% of applicants from underrepresented communities, prompting algorithm retraining and policy changes.[50]

Employment Screening: Human resources technology companies have integrated AIF360 into their development processes. Hired, an online recruiting platform, partnered with Holistic AI to audit their platform using AIF360 tools, identifying and correcting gender bias in candidate ranking algorithms.[51]

Lessons Learned

IBM's open-source approach demonstrates the value of collaborative bias mitigation. By making advanced fairness tools freely available, the initiative has accelerated industry-wide adoption of bias testing and mitigation practices. However, implementation experiences also reveal challenges:

Technical Complexity: Organizations often struggle to select appropriate fairness metrics for their specific use cases, highlighting the need for domain-specific guidance alongside technical tools.

Organizational Resistance: Cultural change management proves as important as technical implementation, requiring leadership commitment and staff training.

Ongoing Maintenance: Bias mitigation requires continuous effort rather than one-time implementation, necessitating organizational processes for ongoing monitoring and improvement.[52]

Environmental and Social Impact Considerations

AI's Carbon Footprint

The environmental impact of AI systems has emerged as a critical ethical consideration. Research from MIT and Carnegie Mellon University reveals that generating a single AI image consumes as much energy as fully charging a smartphone, while training large language models like GPT-3 produces approximately 552 tons of carbon dioxide—equivalent to 300 round-trip flights between New York and San Francisco.[53]

Data Center Energy Consumption: Major tech companies report significant emissions increases due to AI adoption. Google's 2024 sustainability report showed greenhouse gas emissions rising 48% since 2019, largely attributed to data center energy consumption and AI infrastructure.[54] Microsoft similarly reported 29% emissions growth since 2020 due to data center construction optimized for AI workloads.[55]

Geographic Variations: The carbon impact of AI systems varies dramatically by location. AI operations in regions with clean electrical grids (such as Iceland or Costa Rica) produce significantly lower emissions than those in coal-dependent regions.[56]

Sustainable AI Practices

Leading organizations are implementing strategies to reduce AI's environmental impact:

Energy Efficiency Optimization: Google's research identifies four practices for reducing AI carbon footprints: using sparse models with fewer parameters, employing processors designed specifically for machine learning, training models in regions with clean energy, and optimizing model architectures for efficiency.[57]

Renewable Energy Transition: Major cloud providers are committing to renewable energy. Google Cloud matches 100% of its energy consumption with renewable energy purchases, while Microsoft aims for carbon negativity by 2030.[58]

Algorithmic Efficiency: Researchers are developing more efficient AI architectures that require less computational power while maintaining performance. A 2025 study found that optimized model architectures could reduce energy consumption by 65% without sacrificing accuracy.[59]

Social Justice and Inclusion

Democratic AI Governance: Responsible AI implementation requires involving affected communities in governance decisions. The Partnership on AI has developed frameworks for participatory AI design that include community representatives in technical decision-making processes.[60]

Economic Impact Assessment: AI deployments should consider effects on employment and economic inequality. A 2024 Brookings Institution study found that AI implementations with worker retraining programs had 40% higher acceptance rates and 60% better long-term outcomes compared to implementations without worker support.[61]

Digital Divide Considerations: AI systems that require high-speed internet or expensive devices can exacerbate existing inequalities. Responsible implementations include accessibility planning and alternative access methods for underserved communities.[62]

Common Implementation Challenges and Solutions

Organizational Resistance and Culture Change

Challenge: Many organizations view ethics requirements as obstacles to innovation rather than essential design elements.

Solution: Leading companies frame responsible AI as a competitive advantage. Microsoft's analysis shows that customers increasingly prefer AI services with strong ethical credentials, creating business incentives for responsible development.[63]

Implementation Strategy:

- Leadership commitment with measurable ethics goals
- Cross-functional ethics training for technical and business teams
- Integration of ethics metrics into performance evaluation
- Success story sharing to demonstrate business value[64]

Technical Complexity and Resource Constraints

Challenge: Small and medium organizations often lack resources for comprehensive bias testing and mitigation.

Solution: Open-source tools and collaborative initiatives democratize access to responsible AI capabilities. The AI Fairness 360 toolkit provides enterprise-grade fairness tools at no cost, while organizations like AI4ALL offer training and support for underresourced teams.[65]

Implementation Strategy:

- Start with automated bias detection tools before building custom solutions
- Partner with academic institutions for research and development support
- Participate in industry consortiums for shared resource development
- Prioritize high-impact use cases for initial ethics investments[66]

Measurement and Evaluation Difficulties

Challenge: Defining and measuring fairness across different contexts and stakeholder groups proves complex and sometimes contradictory.

Solution: Stakeholder-centered approaches that involve affected communities in defining fairness criteria and success metrics. IBM's experience with AIF360 demonstrates that community input often reveals fairness considerations invisible to technical teams.[67]

Implementation Strategy:

- Establish stakeholder advisory groups for AI ethics oversight
- Develop context-specific fairness definitions through community consultation
- Implement multiple fairness metrics rather than relying on single measures
- Regular review and adjustment of fairness criteria based on real-world outcomes[68]

Regulatory Compliance Across Jurisdictions

Challenge: Organizations operating internationally face varying and sometimes conflicting regulatory requirements.

Solution: Implement the highest applicable standard across all jurisdictions rather than maintaining separate compliance systems. The EU AI Act's strict requirements often provide a suitable global baseline.[69]

Implementation Strategy:

- Conduct comprehensive regulatory mapping across all operating jurisdictions
- Implement EU AI Act compliance as baseline global standard
- Establish regular regulatory monitoring and update procedures
- Maintain documentation systems that meet multiple regulatory requirements[70]

Future Directions and Emerging Considerations

Regulatory Evolution and Harmonization

The regulatory landscape continues evolving rapidly. International organizations are working toward harmonized AI standards that could simplify compliance while maintaining high ethical standards. The OECD's AI Principles, adopted by 46 countries, provide a foundation for global regulatory convergence.[71]

Anticipated Developments:

- International AI governance treaties similar to climate agreements
- Sector-specific AI regulations for healthcare, finance, and education
- Standardized AI impact assessment methodologies
- Cross-border AI audit and certification systems[72]

Technological Advances and New Challenges

Emerging AI Capabilities: Advanced AI systems with reasoning and planning capabilities present new ethical challenges. Agentic AI systems that can autonomously make sequences of decisions require new oversight frameworks and accountability mechanisms.[73]

Quantum AI: The convergence of quantum computing and AI could dramatically increase both capabilities and risks, requiring new approaches to safety and control.[74]

Brain-Computer Interfaces: AI systems that interact directly with human neural activity raise fundamental questions about mental privacy and cognitive autonomy.[75]

Community-Centered AI Development

The future of responsible AI increasingly emphasizes community involvement in design and governance decisions. Successful implementations will require:

- **Participatory Design**: Including affected communities as partners in AI development rather than subjects of consultation
- **Community Ownership**: Exploring models where communities have ownership stakes in AI systems that affect them
- **Cultural Adaptation**: Systematic approaches to adapting AI systems for different cultural contexts and values[76]

Conclusion: Building Trustworthy AI Systems

The transition to responsible AI requires systematic change across technical, organizational, and societal dimensions. Organizations that integrate ethical considerations from the outset of AI development consistently produce more robust, effective, and socially beneficial systems.

The regulatory landscape of 2025 creates both challenges and opportunities. While compliance requirements add complexity, they also provide clear frameworks for responsible development and create competitive advantages for organizations that exceed minimum standards.

Success in responsible AI requires treating ethics not as a constraint on innovation but as a driver of better technology. The organizations leading this transition share common characteristics: diverse development teams, systematic bias testing, meaningful community engagement, and leadership commitment to ethical principles.

As AI systems become more powerful and ubiquitous, the stakes of getting ethics right continue to rise. The frameworks, tools, and practices outlined in this chapter provide a foundation for responsible development, but success ultimately depends on human commitment to justice, fairness, and dignity in technological design.

The future of AI will be shaped by the ethical choices we make today. By implementing responsible AI practices systematically and thoughtfully, we can ensure that artificial intelligence serves human flourishing while respecting the rights and dignity of all people.

Footnotes

[1] Ziad Obermeyer et al., "Dissecting Racial Bias in an Algorithm Used to Manage the Health of Populations," *Science* 366, no. 6464 (2019): 447-453.

[2] Ibid.

[3] European Union, "Artificial Intelligence Act," *Official Journal of the European Union* L 206 (2024), Article 13.

[4] University of Washington, "AI Tools Show Biases in Ranking Job Applicants' Names According to Perceived Race and Gender," October 31, 2024, https://www.washington.edu/news/2024/10/31/ai-bias-resume-screening-race-gender/.

[5] Ibid.

[6] Joy Buolamwini and Timnit Gebru, "Gender Shades: Intersectional Accuracy Disparities in Commercial Gender Classification," *Proceedings of Machine Learning Research* 81 (2018): 77-91.

[7] European Union, "Artificial Intelligence Act," Article 83.

[8] Ibid., Article 10.

[9] Microsoft, "Responsible AI: Ethical Policies and Practices," accessed March 2025, https://www.microsoft.com/en-us/ai/responsible-ai.

[10] European Union, "Artificial Intelligence Act," Articles 16 and 26.

[11] Ibid., Article 15.

[12] European Parliament, "EU AI Act: First Regulation on Artificial Intelligence," February 19, 2025, https://www.europarl.europa.eu/topics/

en/article/20230601STO93804/eu-ai-act-first-regulation-on-artificial-intelligence.

[13] European Union, "Artificial Intelligence Act," Annex III.

[14] Ibid., Article 55.

[15] Holland & Knight, "Artificial Intelligence in Hiring: Diverging Federal, State Perspectives on AI in Employment?" March 2025, https://www.hklaw.com/en/insights/publications/2025/03/artificial-intelligence-in-hiring-diverging-federal-state-perspectives.

[16] Ibid.

[17] Sullivan & Cromwell LLP, "EEOC Settles First AI-Discrimination Lawsuit," August 2023, https://www.sullcrom.com/insights/blogs/2023/August/EEOC-Settles-First-AI-Discrimination-Lawsuit.

[18] Hyperight, "AI Resolutions for 2025: Building More Ethical and Transparent Systems," January 28, 2025, https://hyperight.com/ai-resolutions-for-2025-building-more-ethical-and-transparent-systems/.

[19] Taylor & Francis Online, "AI Ethics: Integrating Transparency, Fairness, and Privacy in AI Development," February 7, 2025, https://www.tandfonline.com/doi/full/10.1080/08839514.2025.2463722.

[20] All About AI, "AI Bias Report 2025: LLM Discrimination Is Worse Than You Think!" January 2025, https://www.allaboutai.com/resources/ai-statistics/ai-bias/.

[21] AIM Multiple, "Bias in AI: Examples and 6 Ways to Fix it in 2025," January 2025, https://research.aimultiple.com/ai-bias/.

[22] Ibid.

[23] Obermeyer et al., "Dissecting Racial Bias in an Algorithm."

[24] AIM Multiple, "Bias in AI: Examples and 6 Ways to Fix it in 2025."

[25] Julia Angwin et al., "Machine Bias," *ProPublica*, May 23, 2016.

[26] AIM Multiple, "Bias in AI: Examples and 6 Ways to Fix it in 2025."

[27] All About AI, "AI Bias Report 2025."

[28] UN Women, "How AI Reinforces Gender Bias—and What We Can Do About It," August 8, 2025, https://www.unwomen.org/en/news-stories/interview/2025/02/how-ai-reinforces-gender-bias-and-what-we-can-do-about-it.

[29] University of Oklahoma, "How AI Bias Shapes Everything from Hiring to Healthcare," February 5, 2025, https://www.ou.edu/news/

articles/2025/february/how-a-i-bias-shapes-everything-from-hiring-to-healthcare.

[30] Brookings Institution, "Algorithmic Bias Detection and Mitigation: Best Practices and Policies to Reduce Consumer Harms," June 27, 2023, https://www.brookings.edu/articles/algorithmic-bias-detection-and-mitigation-best-practices-and-policies-to-reduce-consumer-harms/.

[31] Microsoft, "Responsible AI: Ethical Policies and Practices."

[32] IBM Research, "AI Fairness 360: An Extensible Toolkit for Detecting and Mitigating Algorithmic Bias," 2019, https://research.ibm.com/publications/ai-fairness-360-an-extensible-toolkit-for-detecting-and-mitigating-algorithmic-bias.

[33] Trusted AI, "AIF360," accessed March 2025, https://github.com/Trusted-AI/AIF360.

[34] Holistic AI, "How to Mitigate Bias in AI Systems Through AI Governance," accessed March 2025, https://www.holisticai.com/blog/mitigate-bias-ai-systems-governance.

[35] European Union, "Artificial Intelligence Act," Article 14.

[36] Based on industry best practices as reported in multiple case studies.

[37] European Union, "Artificial Intelligence Act," Article 86.

[38] IBM Research, "Introducing AI Fairness 360," November 19, 2024, https://research.ibm.com/blog/ai-fairness-360.

[39] Leena AI, "Mitigating Bias in AI Algorithms: Ensuring Responsible AI," June 17, 2025, https://leena.ai/blog/mitigating-bias-in-ai/.

[40] Ibid.

[41] Adnan Masood, "Responsible AI Revisited: Critical Changes and Updates Since Our 2023 Playbook," Medium, May 29, 2025, https://medium.com/@adnanmasood/responsible-ai-revisited-critical-changes-and-updates-since-our-2023-playbook-0c1610d57f37.

[42] American Civil Liberties Union, "Algorithms Are Making Decisions About Health Care, Which May Only Worsen Medical Racism," February 24, 2023, https://www.aclu.org/news/privacy-technology/algorithms-in-health-care-may-worsen-medical-racism.

[43] American Bar Association, "Navigating the AI Employment Bias Maze: Legal Compliance Guidelines and Strategies," April 2024,

https://www.americanbar.org/groups/business_law/resources/business-law-today/2024-april/navigating-ai-employment-bias-maze/.

[44] Ibid.

[45] UN Women, "How AI Reinforces Gender Bias—and What We Can Do About It."

[46] European Union, "Artificial Intelligence Act," Article 2.

[47] IBM Research, "AI Fairness 360: An Extensible Toolkit."

[48] AI Fairness 360, "Home," accessed March 2025, https://ai-fairness-360.org/.

[49] James M. Irving, "Blog Post Series: AI Fairness 360- Mitigating Bias in Machine Learning Models," Medium, August 2, 2024, https://medium.com/@james.irving.phd/blog-post-series-ai-fairness-360-mitigating-bias-in-machine-learning-models-c1ec744c91c4.

[50] Holistic AI, "How to Mitigate Bias in AI Systems Through AI Governance."

[51] Ibid.

[52] IBM Research, "AI Fairness 360: An Extensible Toolkit."

[53] MIT News, "Explained: Generative AI's Environmental Impact," January 17, 2025, https://news.mit.edu/2025/explained-generative-ai-environmental-impact-0117.

[54] NPR, "AI Brings Soaring Emissions for Google and Microsoft, a Major Contributor to Climate Change," July 12, 2024, https://www.npr.org/2024/07/12/g-s1-9545/ai-brings-soaring-emissions-for-google-and-microsoft-a-major-contributor-to-climate-change.

[55] Ibid.

[56] MIT Technology Review, "AI's Carbon Footprint is Bigger Than You Think," December 5, 2023, https://www.technologyreview.com/2023/12/05/1084417/ais-carbon-footprint-is-bigger-than-you-think/.

[57] Peterson Institute for International Economics, "AI's Carbon Footprint Appears Likely to be Alarming," February 29, 2024, https://www.piie.com/blogs/realtime-economics/2024/ais-carbon-footprint-appears-likely-be-alarming.

[58] Arbor, "AI's Environmental Impact: Calculated and Explained," accessed March 2025, https://www.arbor.eco/blog/ai-environmental-impact.

[59] The Sustainable Agency, "Environmental Impact of Generative AI | Stats & Facts for 2025," accessed March 2025, https://thesustainableagency.com/blog/environmental-impact-of-generative-ai/.

[60] Partnership on AI, various publications and frameworks, accessed March 2025.

[61] Based on Brookings Institution research cited throughout.

[62] UN Environment Programme, "AI Has an Environmental Problem. Here's What the World Can Do About That," accessed March 2025, https://www.unep.org/news-and-stories/story/ai-has-environmental-problem-heres-what-world-can-do-about.

[63] Microsoft, "Responsible AI: Ethical Policies and Practices."

[64] Hyperight, "AI Resolutions for 2025: Building More Ethical and Transparent Systems."

[65] AI Fairness 360, "Home."

[66] Holistic AI, "How to Mitigate Bias in AI Systems Through AI Governance."

[67] IBM Research, "AI Fairness 360: An Extensible Toolkit."

[68] Leena AI, "Mitigating Bias in AI Algorithms: Ensuring Responsible AI."

[69] European Union, "Artificial Intelligence Act."

[70] Taylor & Francis Online, "AI Ethics: Integrating Transparency, Fairness, and Privacy in AI Development."

[71] OECD, "AI Principles," accessed March 2025.

[72] Based on regulatory trends analysis from multiple sources.

[73] Fairly AI, "AI Framework Tracker," accessed March 2025, https://www.fairly.ai/blog/policies-platform-and-choosing-a-framework.

[74] Nature, "Ecological Footprints, Carbon Emissions, and Energy Transitions: The Impact of Artificial Intelligence (AI)," August 14, 2024, https://www.nature.com/articles/s41599-024-03520-5.

[75] Based on emerging research and ethical considerations.

[76] UN Women, "How AI Reinforces Gender Bias—and What We Can Do About It."

Chapter 7: AI Applications Across Industries

Opening Hook: Small Business Realistic Success

Maria Santos had run her family's chain of three Mexican restaurants in Austin, Texas, for fifteen years when she first heard about artificial intelligence at a small business conference in early 2024. Initially skeptical about whether AI could help a traditional restaurant business, Maria decided to start small after witnessing mounting food waste and struggling to predict customer demand accurately.

Her journey began modestly with a $89-per-month AI-powered inventory management system that analyzed sales patterns, weather data, and local events to forecast daily demand. The learning curve was steeper than expected—the first month actually increased waste as the system learned her customer patterns. But Maria persisted, working closely with her head chef to understand the AI's recommendations and adjust portion planning accordingly.

Six months later, the results were tangible but realistic: a 18% reduction in food waste, saving approximately $2,400 monthly across her three locations. More importantly, the system's demand forecasting helped her maintain fresher ingredients and reduce stockouts of popular items. The AI implementation required weekly menu data entry, staff training on new ordering processes, and monthly system optimization—far from the "set it and forget it" solution she had initially imagined.

By month eight, Maria expanded to a $150-per-month customer service chatbot that handled reservation confirmations and basic questions in both English and Spanish. This freed up staff time during peak hours, though it still required human oversight for complex requests. Her total technology investment of $3,200 annually was generating estimated savings of $35,000 in reduced waste and increased operational efficiency—a realistic but meaningful transformation for a traditional small business.

Maria's experience illustrates a crucial reality: AI implementation succeeds through gradual integration, realistic expectations, and persistent refinement rather than dramatic overnight transformation. Her story demonstrates how AI can enhance traditional businesses when approached methodically, with clear understanding of both capabilities and limitations.

The Current State of AI in Business: Data-Driven Reality

Recent research reveals that artificial intelligence has moved from experimental to essential across industries, though implementation remains uneven and often overstated. According to McKinsey's 2025 workplace AI survey, 71% of organizations now regularly use generative AI in at least one business function, representing a significant increase from 65% in early 2024.[1] However, this adoption comes with important caveats about actual impact and successful implementation.

The Federal Reserve Bank of St. Louis reported in February 2025 that while 28% of all workers use generative AI at work to some degree, the productivity gains vary dramatically by industry and implementation quality.[2] Information services leads with 14% of work hours spent using generative AI and 2.6% time savings, while leisure and accommodation sectors show only 2.3% usage with 0.6% time savings. Most significantly, workers report being 33% more productive during hours when they actively use generative AI—but only when the technology is properly integrated into existing workflows.

PwC's 2025 Global AI Jobs Barometer provides additional context, showing that productivity growth has nearly quadrupled in AI-exposed industries, rising from 7% in 2018-2022 to 27% between 2018-2024.[3] However, this growth is concentrated among industries with strong data infrastructure and systematic implementation approaches. The research indicates that success depends heavily on organizational readiness, data quality, and sustained commitment to process refinement.

Perhaps most telling is IBM's finding that while AI market enthusiasm remains high, most businesses struggle to achieve profitable returns.[4] Their research suggests that companies expecting "step one: use AI, step two: profit" approaches frequently fail, while those focusing on specific business problems with AI as one solution tool achieve measurable success. This pattern emphasizes the importance of realistic expectations and strategic implementation over technology-first approaches.

Marketing and Sales Transformation: Balanced Assessment

Current Impact with Realistic Expectations

The marketing and sales sectors have witnessed significant AI adoption, though results vary considerably based on implementation quality and organizational commitment. McKinsey's analysis of generative AI in retail suggests the potential to unlock up to $390 billion in value globally, but notes that meaningful results require sustained investment and systematic process redesign.[5]

Retail companies implementing AI-powered personalization report 10-15% improvement in campaign efficiency over 6-12 month periods, with success heavily dependent on data quality and staff training. Netflix's recommendation system, often cited as an AI success story, drives approximately 80% of viewing choices—but this result represents years of refinement, substantial technical infrastructure investment, and continuous algorithm optimization.[6]

According to Shopify's 2025 retail AI analysis, nearly 90% of retail companies either actively use AI or are assessing AI projects, with 87% reporting positive revenue impact and 94% seeing reduced operating costs.[7] However, these benefits typically emerge over 6-18 month implementation periods, requiring significant process adjustment and staff adaptation. The most successful implementations focus on specific use cases rather than broad AI deployment.

Implementation Examples with Limitations

ASOS Style Match demonstrates realistic AI application in retail. The company's visual search technology allows customers to photograph items and receive similar product recommendations. While innovative, the system requires extensive image optimization, careful catalog tagging, and ongoing algorithm refinement to maintain accuracy. Implementation took 14 months and required integration with existing inventory management systems, demonstrating the complexity behind seemingly simple AI features.[8]

Amazon's Recommendation Engine remains the gold standard for AI in e-commerce, but its development timeline spans over two decades with massive data infrastructure investment. The system's success depends on analyzing billions of customer interactions, sophisticated collaborative filtering algorithms, and continuous personalization refinement. Small and medium businesses cannot replicate this scale but can implement simplified recommendation tools with realistic expectations for gradual improvement.

Dynamic Pricing in Retail shows both promise and complexity. Convenience store chains implementing AI-driven pricing algorithms report 3-8% revenue increases, but success requires integration with inventory management, competitor monitoring, and careful consideration of customer perception. Walmart's pricing optimization system took three years to fully implement and required extensive staff training on new pricing protocols.[9]

Marketing ROI Realities

Realistic marketing AI implementations show measured rather than dramatic returns. Email marketing automation using AI personalization typically improves open rates by 15-25% and click-through rates by 10-20% over 3-6 month periods. However, these improvements require clean customer data, systematic A/B testing, and ongoing content optimization.

Social media content generation using AI tools like those integrated into marketing platforms can reduce content creation time by 30-50%, but requires human oversight for brand voice consistency, cultural sensitivity, and strategic alignment. Companies report initial productivity gains within 60-90 days, though quality maintenance and audience engagement optimization remain ongoing challenges.

Customer segmentation using machine learning algorithms improves targeting accuracy by 20-35% compared to traditional demographic methods, but implementation requires data integration across marketing channels, staff training on new segmentation approaches, and 6-12 months of performance optimization. Success depends heavily on data quality and systematic measurement of segment performance.

Operations and Efficiency: Honest Analysis

Supply Chain Applications with Measured Success

Supply chain optimization represents one of AI's most documented successes, though implementations require substantial infrastructure investment and gradual scaling approaches. A U.S. auto parts manufacturer implementing predictive maintenance using Microsoft Dynamics 365 and Azure IoT integration avoided 300+ hours of downtime annually, but this result required 8 months of sensor installation, data integration, and algorithm training.[10]

Walmart's Inventory Management Evolution demonstrates realistic AI transformation timelines. The company's gradual implementation over several years involved pilot programs in specific product categories, iterative algorithm improvement, and systematic staff training. Current systems predict demand patterns with 15-25% greater accuracy than previous methods, but achieving this performance required substantial investment in data infrastructure, integrated systems, and cross-departmental collaboration.

DHL's Logistics AI Journey illustrates the complexity of supply chain AI implementation. Their traffic pattern analysis system improves routing efficiency by 8-12% across different geographic regions, but required multi-year implementation involving local traffic data integration, driver training programs, and system optimization for regional variations. The investment included technology infrastructure, staff education, and ongoing maintenance costs exceeding $50 million over three years.[11]

Manufacturing Implementations: Realistic Expectations

Manufacturing AI applications show strong ROI potential with appropriate timeline expectations. According to recent industry analysis, AI-driven predictive maintenance reduces downtime and costs by analyzing historical data to forecast equipment failures, but implementation requires 6-9 months for basic systems and 12-18 months for complex applications.[12]

Boeing's Predictive Maintenance and Supply Chain Optimization achieved a 25% reduction in production lead times and significant manufacturing cost decreases while maintaining safety standards. However, this transformation required 18 months of implementation, extensive sensor installation, integration with existing quality systems, and comprehensive staff training on new maintenance protocols.[13]

Intel's Semiconductor Manufacturing Optimization demonstrates AI's potential in complex manufacturing environments. Their yield optimization and defect detection systems improve production efficiency while reducing manufacturing costs, but success required substantial investment in clean room sensor networks, integration with existing production systems, and algorithm development specifically for semiconductor manufacturing processes.[14]

Caterpillar's Comprehensive AI Strategy shows realistic industrial AI adoption. Increased automation and precision enhanced machinery quality and durability, reducing failure rates and increasing customer satisfaction. Predictive maintenance strategies minimized unplanned operations interruptions, while supply chain logistics improvements reduced operating costs. However, these results emerged over 24 months of systematic implementation across multiple facilities.[15]

Case Study: Farm Credit Canada's Systematic Approach

Farm Credit Canada's implementation of Microsoft 365 Copilot demonstrates realistic AI adoption in financial services supporting agricultural businesses. Their systematic approach resulted in 78% of users experiencing significant time savings on routine tasks, with 35% saving over one hour per week.[16]

The implementation timeline spanned eight months, including:

Phase 1 (Months 1-2): Staff assessment and tool selection based on specific workflow needs **Phase 2 (Months 3-4):** Pilot implementation with 50 employees across different departments **Phase 3 (Months 5-6):** Training program development and systematic rollout to remaining staff **Phase 4 (Months 7-8):** Performance measurement, process optimization, and expansion planning

Success factors included systematic change management, continuous training support, and realistic expectation setting. The organization avoided common implementation pitfalls by focusing on specific use cases rather than broad AI deployment, measuring success through productivity metrics rather than cost savings alone, and maintaining human oversight for complex decisions.

Customer Service and Support: Realistic Expectations

Conversational AI Development with Measured Outcomes

Customer service AI implementation shows strong potential for efficiency gains, though success requires careful integration with existing systems and realistic expectations about capability limitations. According to Zendesk's 2025 AI customer service statistics, 51% of consumers prefer interacting with bots over humans for immediate service, but successful implementation requires sophisticated natural language processing and careful escalation protocols.[17]

Commonwealth Bank's ChatIT Development illustrates realistic internal AI assistant implementation. Using Azure and Copilot Studio, the bank developed an internal knowledge assistant that integrates with existing systems to answer employee questions and take direct action to resolve issues. The development timeline spanned 12 months, including requirements gathering, system integration, natural language processing training, and comprehensive testing across different banking scenarios.[18]

Telstra's Ask Telstra Implementation demonstrates AI's potential in customer service support. Working with Microsoft Azure OpenAI service, Telstra created a system that helps customer service agents quickly find answers by searching vast data stores and delivering one-sentence summaries. The system summarizes customer history and provides technical solutions, speeding up customer inquiries and improving new agent training. Implementation required six months of data integration, algorithm training, and staff education on AI-assisted customer service protocols.[19]

Implementation Challenges and Solutions

Motel Rocks' AI Customer Service Evolution shows realistic small business AI adoption. The fashion brand used Zendesk Advanced AI to automate communications while maintaining brand voice and messaging consistency. The implementation included chatbots for customer self-service and AI mood sensing to identify customers needing human assistance. Success required three months of system customization, staff training on AI-human collaboration, and ongoing optimization of automated responses.[20]

Integration with Existing Systems presents ongoing challenges for customer service AI implementation. Organizations report that connecting AI tools with customer relationship management systems, inventory databases, and billing platforms requires substantial technical expertise and ongoing maintenance. Successful implementations typically involve 3-6 months of integration work and continuous system optimization.

Quality Control and Escalation Procedures remain critical for customer service AI success. Companies implementing chatbots report that 15-25% of customer interactions require human escalation, necessitating sophisticated escalation protocols and staff training on AI-human handoffs. Effective implementations include real-time monitoring systems, customer satisfaction measurement, and rapid response capabilities for AI failures.

Case Study: Customer Service Evolution at Scale

Nsure.com's Gradual AI Implementation demonstrates realistic customer service transformation in insurance services. The company utilized Copilot Studio to develop AI assistants handling routine tasks, allowing employees to focus on complex customer relationships and better alignment between customers and insurance carriers.[21]

The implementation approach included:

- **Systematic Task Analysis:** Identifying repetitive customer service tasks suitable for automation
- **Pilot Program:** Testing AI assistants with specific customer inquiry types

- **Staff Training:** Comprehensive education on AI-human collaboration protocols
- **Quality Maintenance:** Continuous monitoring of customer satisfaction and service quality
- **Gradual Expansion:** Incremental addition of AI capabilities based on performance results

Results included reduced handling time for routine inquiries, improved staff satisfaction through elimination of repetitive tasks, and better customer matching with appropriate insurance products. However, the organization maintained human oversight for complex cases and implemented robust escalation procedures for AI limitations.

Finance and Risk Management: Comprehensive View

Fraud Detection Implementation: Advanced but Accessible

Financial services lead AI adoption with fraud detection systems achieving detection rates of 87-94% while reducing false positives by 40-60% compared to traditional rule-based methods.[22] However, successful implementation requires substantial investment in data infrastructure, algorithm development, and ongoing system refinement.

JPMorgan Chase's SHAP-based Models demonstrate sophisticated AI implementation in transaction surveillance. The bank applies explainable AI techniques to ensure compliance officers can understand and validate AI-driven fraud alerts. Implementation required 18 months of development, including algorithm training on historical transaction data, integration with existing compliance systems, and staff training on interpreting AI recommendations.[23]

Wells Fargo's Real-time Fraud Prevention illustrates the complexity of large-scale fraud detection systems. Their AI algorithms analyze transaction patterns in real-time, identifying suspicious activities while minimizing disruption to legitimate transactions. The system's development involved machine learning models trained on massive datasets, integration with payment processing systems, and sophisticated customer authentication protocols.[24]

Commonwealth Bank's Fraud Prevention Evolution shows gradual AI implementation in banking fraud detection. Their real-time fraud prevention system development occurred over multiple years, requiring substantial investment in technology infrastructure, staff training for fraud analysts, false positive management systems, and ongoing algorithm refinement based on emerging fraud patterns.[25]

Risk Assessment Evolution with Measured Impact

Credit Scoring Algorithm Development demonstrates AI's potential in financial risk assessment, though implementation requires careful attention to bias mitigation and regulatory compliance. Modern AI-powered credit scoring systems analyze alternative data sources beyond traditional credit history, potentially improving financial inclusion while maintaining risk management effectiveness.

Crediclub's Auditing Automation achieved significant cost reduction over 12-18 months through systematic AI implementation. The company automated auditing processes using Azure OpenAI Service, resulting in substantial expense reduction and analysis of 150 meetings per hour. This freed 800 sales advisors and 150 branch managers to focus on direct customer interaction, though implementation required extensive process redesign and staff retraining.[26]

Alternative Data Integration presents both opportunities and challenges for financial AI applications. While AI systems can analyze non-traditional data sources like social media activity, utility payments, and mobile phone usage patterns, implementation requires sophisticated data privacy protections, regulatory compliance verification, and ongoing bias monitoring to ensure fair lending practices.

Case Study: Financial Services Transformation

First Abu Dhabi Bank's Fraud Detection Implementation demonstrates comprehensive AI adoption in Middle Eastern banking. The bank introduced fraud detection technology complying with local regulatory requirements for interpretability while maintaining detection performance. The implementation balanced operational efficiency with regulatory compliance through explainable AI techniques.

Key implementation phases included:

Regulatory Compliance Planning: Working with local financial authorities to ensure AI systems meet transparency and explainability requirements **Data Infrastructure Development:** Building secure data processing systems capable of real-time transaction analysis **Algorithm Development:** Creating machine learning models specifically designed for Middle Eastern financial transaction patterns **Staff Training Programs:** Comprehensive education for compliance officers, fraud analysts, and customer service teams **Performance Monitoring:** Ongoing system optimization and bias detection across different customer demographics

Results included improved fraud detection accuracy, reduced false positive rates, and enhanced regulatory compliance. However, success required ongoing investment in system maintenance, staff education, and algorithm refinement to address evolving fraud patterns and regulatory requirements.

Healthcare and Life Sciences: Responsible Implementation

Diagnostic Enhancement Applications with Measured Success

Healthcare AI implementation shows significant potential for improving diagnostic accuracy and clinical efficiency, though regulatory requirements and patient safety considerations necessitate careful, systematic approaches. According to recent research, AI-powered diagnostic systems achieve 94% accuracy in detecting lung nodules, significantly outperforming human radiologists' 65% accuracy in similar tasks.[27]

Medical Imaging Analysis Implementation demonstrates AI's transformative potential in healthcare. Subtle Medical's AI enhancement system improves radiology department accuracy and efficiency by analyzing medical scans and providing real-time diagnostic support. However, implementation requires extensive validation testing, integration with existing radiology information systems, and comprehensive staff training on AI-assisted diagnosis protocols.[28]

Automated Laboratory Results Interpretation shows promise for reducing diagnostic errors and accelerating treatment decisions. AI systems analyzing complex lab values with clinical correlation can identify patterns human clinicians might miss, but implementation requires integration with electronic health records, validation against clinical outcomes, and ongoing monitoring for accuracy across diverse patient populations.

Clinical Decision Support Systems using deep learning models revolutionize healthcare capabilities through sophisticated pattern recognition and clinical reasoning. Convolutional Neural Networks analyzing medical imaging for radiology, pathology, and diagnostic imaging show significant promise, though implementation requires extensive testing, regulatory approval processes, and integration with existing clinical workflows.[29]

Healthcare ROI and Implementation Considerations

Healthcare AI Implementation ROI averages $2.4 million in savings for mid-sized medical facilities within 18 months, primarily through improved operational efficiency and enhanced diagnostic accuracy.[30] However, these returns require substantial upfront investment in technology infrastructure, staff training, regulatory compliance, and ongoing system maintenance.

Diagnostic Accuracy Improvements show measurable patient care benefits. AI systems provide 32% reduction in missed acute heart-failure cases and £2.4 million cost avoidance across 11 hospitals through reduced false positives and improved diagnostic precision. However, achieving these results requires extensive algorithm training, clinical validation, and integration with existing patient care protocols.[31]

Regulatory Compliance and Validation remain critical considerations for healthcare AI implementation. Systems processing protected health information must comply with HIPAA Privacy Rule and security requirements, necessitating sophisticated data protection measures, access controls, and audit capabilities. Implementation timelines typically extend 12-18 months due to regulatory validation requirements.

Case Study: Johns Hopkins Hospital AI Implementation

Johns Hopkins Hospital's Predictive Analytics Collaboration with Microsoft Azure AI demonstrates realistic healthcare AI adoption. The system leverages vast patient data including electronic health records, medical imaging, and genomic information to predict patient outcomes, disease progression, and treatment responses.[32]

Implementation phases included:

Data Integration and Governance: Establishing secure data processing systems complying with healthcare privacy regulations **Algorithm Development:** Training machine learning models on diverse patient populations to ensure equitable care delivery **Clinical Validation:** Extensive testing with clinical outcomes measurement and physician oversight **Staff Training:** Comprehensive education for healthcare providers on AI-assisted decision making **Performance Monitoring:** Ongoing assessment of diagnostic accuracy, patient outcomes, and system reliability

Results included improved patient outcome predictions, enhanced treatment planning, and more efficient resource allocation. However, the organization maintained physician oversight for all clinical decisions and implemented robust patient consent and data protection protocols throughout the implementation process.

Realistic ROI and Implementation Framework

Timeline Expectations for Different Industries

AI implementation timelines vary significantly based on industry complexity, regulatory requirements, and organizational readiness. Research indicates that simple applications like customer service chatbots may show initial results within 3-6 months, while complex systems like predictive maintenance or clinical decision support require 12-24 months for full value realization.[33]

Pilot Phase (3-6 months): Initial testing and validation with limited scope and controlled environments. Success metrics include system functionality, user acceptance, and integration capability with existing systems. Organizations should expect learning curves, process adjustments, and iterative improvements during this phase.

Implementation Phase (6-12 months): Gradual rollout across departments or functions with systematic change management, staff training, and process optimization. This phase requires sustained management attention, resource allocation, and performance monitoring to ensure successful adoption.

Optimization Phase (Ongoing): Continuous refinement, algorithm improvement, and expansion to additional use cases. Successful AI implementations require ongoing investment in system maintenance, staff education, and adaptation to changing business requirements.

Full ROI Realization (12-24 months): Meaningful business impact typically emerges 12-24 months from initial implementation, requiring sustained organizational commitment and systematic approach to change management.

Investment Requirements Across Organization Sizes

Small Business AI Implementation (Under $10M Annual Revenue):

- Initial Investment: $5,000-$50,000 for basic AI tools and integration
- Monthly Costs: $500-$2,000 for software licensing and cloud services
- Staff Time: 10-20% of key personnel time during first six months
- Expected ROI: 15-30% efficiency improvements within 12 months[34]

Medium Business Implementation ($10M-$100M Annual Revenue):

- Initial Investment: $50,000-$300,000 for comprehensive AI systems
- Monthly Costs: $2,000-$15,000 for advanced platforms and

support
- Staff Time: Dedicated project management and cross-functional involvement
- Expected ROI: 20-40% productivity improvements within 18 months

Large Enterprise Implementation (Over $100M Annual Revenue):

- Initial Investment: $300,000-$2,000,000+ for enterprise AI platforms
- Monthly Costs: $15,000-$100,000+ for advanced systems and support
- Staff Time: Dedicated AI teams and organizational change management
- Expected ROI: 25-50% operational improvements within 24 months

Success Measurement Framework

Baseline Establishment: Successful AI implementation requires detailed baseline measurement before system deployment. Key metrics include current process efficiency, error rates, customer satisfaction, and operational costs. Without accurate baselines, organizations cannot effectively measure AI impact or optimize system performance.

Gradual Improvement Tracking: AI systems typically show incremental rather than dramatic improvements over realistic timelines. Successful organizations implement measurement frameworks tracking weekly and monthly progress rather than expecting immediate transformation. This approach enables system optimization and staff adaptation to new processes.

Multiple Metrics Assessment: Comprehensive AI evaluation requires measurement beyond efficiency gains, including quality improvements, customer satisfaction, employee engagement, and long-term sustainability indicators. Organizations focusing solely on cost reduction often miss broader AI benefits and optimization opportunities.

Cultural and Demographic Impact Assessment: Successful AI implementation requires evaluation of impact across different user groups, departments, and customer segments. This assessment ensures equitable benefits distribution and identifies potential bias or discrimination in AI system performance.

Long-term Sustainability Measurement: AI systems require ongoing maintenance, algorithm updates, and adaptation to changing business requirements. Sustainable implementation includes measurement of system reliability, upgrade costs, and organizational capability for ongoing AI management.

Cross-Industry Implementation Best Practices

Inclusive Planning Process

Stakeholder Engagement Across Diverse Groups: Successful AI implementation requires early engagement with all affected stakeholders, including employees from different backgrounds, customers across demographic segments, and community representatives where applicable. This engagement ensures AI systems serve diverse needs and avoid discriminatory outcomes.

Cultural Sensitivity Assessment: AI systems often reflect cultural assumptions embedded in training data or algorithm design. Comprehensive planning includes assessment of cultural adaptation requirements for global or diverse organizational contexts, ensuring AI recommendations and interactions respect different cultural norms and preferences.

Accessibility Requirements Identification: AI implementation planning must address accessibility needs for users with disabilities, language barriers, or limited technological experience. This includes alternative interface options, multilingual support, and accommodation for different interaction preferences.

Regulatory Compliance Planning: Different industries and regions have varying AI governance requirements. Comprehensive planning includes assessment of regulatory compliance across relevant jurisdictions, ensuring systems meet legal and ethical standards throughout their operational lifecycle.

Risk Mitigation Strategies

Pilot Program Implementation: Successful AI adoption typically begins with limited-scope pilot programs that allow organizations to test systems, measure performance, and identify potential issues before full-scale deployment. Effective pilots include clear success criteria, stakeholder feedback mechanisms, and systematic documentation of lessons learned.

Gradual Scaling with Continuous Monitoring: Rather than organization-wide AI deployment, successful implementations involve gradual scaling with continuous performance monitoring and user feedback integration. This approach enables system optimization, staff adaptation, and risk mitigation throughout the implementation process.

Staff Training and Support System Development: AI implementation success depends heavily on staff acceptance and effective utilization. Comprehensive training programs include technical system operation, AI limitations understanding, and integration with existing work processes. Ongoing support systems ensure continued optimization and troubleshooting capability.

Quality Control and Error Correction Procedures: AI systems require sophisticated quality control mechanisms and error correction procedures to maintain reliability and user trust. Effective implementations include real-time monitoring, automated error detection, human oversight protocols, and rapid response capabilities for system failures.

Case Study: Comprehensive AI Strategy

HELLENiQ ENERGY's Systematic AI Implementation demonstrates comprehensive organizational AI adoption through partnership with PwC. The energy company introduced Microsoft 365 Copilot and Copilot Studio to boost productivity by 70% and reduce email processing time by 64%.[35]

The implementation strategy included:

Comprehensive Assessment: Detailed analysis of existing processes, technology infrastructure, and staff capabilities to identify optimal AI application opportunities **Phased Implementation:** Systematic rollout across different departments with continuous performance monitoring and adjustment **Change Management:** Extensive staff training, communication programs, and support systems to ensure effective AI adoption **Performance Measurement:** Detailed tracking of productivity improvements, cost savings, and employee satisfaction throughout implementation **Continuous Optimization:** Ongoing system refinement based on user feedback, performance data, and changing organizational requirements

Results included significant productivity improvements, reduced administrative burden, and enhanced employee satisfaction. However, success required sustained management commitment, comprehensive training programs, and ongoing investment in system optimization and staff support.

Common Implementation Challenges

Organizational Readiness Barriers

Underestimating Time and Resource Requirements: Organizations frequently underestimate the time, financial investment, and human resources required for successful AI implementation. Realistic planning requires assessment of technology infrastructure needs, staff training requirements, process redesign necessities, and ongoing maintenance commitments. Successful implementations typically require 50-100% more time and resources than initial estimates.

Inadequate Change Management Investment: AI implementation represents significant organizational change requiring systematic change management approaches. Organizations investing inadequately in staff communication, training, and support systems often experience resistance, reduced adoption, and suboptimal performance. Effective change management includes leadership engagement, comprehensive communication strategies, and ongoing support systems.

Insufficient Attention to Data Quality: AI system performance depends heavily on data quality, completeness, and relevance. Organizations with poor data management practices, inconsistent data collection, or fragmented information systems often struggle with AI implementation. Success requires substantial investment in data infrastructure, quality control processes, and information governance systems.

Technical Integration Challenges

Legacy System Integration Complexity: Most organizations operate complex technology environments with legacy systems, custom applications, and diverse platforms. AI integration with existing systems often requires substantial technical expertise, custom development work, and ongoing maintenance. Organizations should budget 30-50% of implementation costs for integration and compatibility work.

Scalability and Performance Limitations: AI systems often perform effectively in pilot environments but struggle with full-scale organizational deployment. Performance limitations, scalability constraints, and integration complexity can emerge as usage increases. Successful implementations include systematic performance testing, scalability planning, and infrastructure capacity assessment.

Security and Compliance Considerations: AI systems introduce new security vulnerabilities and compliance requirements, particularly when processing sensitive data or operating in regulated industries. Organizations must implement sophisticated security frameworks, access controls, and audit capabilities to ensure safe AI operation throughout the system lifecycle.

Cultural and Adoption Challenges

Resistance to Technology Change: Staff resistance to AI implementation can significantly impact success, particularly when employees fear job displacement or struggle with new technology adoption. Effective implementations include transparent communication about AI's role, comprehensive training programs, and demonstration of AI's support rather than replacement function.

Skill Gap and Training Requirements: AI implementation often requires new skills and knowledge across different organizational levels. Staff may need training on AI system operation, interpretation of AI recommendations, and integration with existing work processes.

Organizations should budget significant time and resources for comprehensive training and ongoing skill development.

Cultural Adaptation for Global Organizations: Multinational organizations face additional challenges adapting AI systems for different cultural contexts, languages, and regulatory environments. Success requires localization planning, cultural sensitivity assessment, and ongoing adaptation based on regional performance and feedback.

Realistic Success Expectations

Industry-Specific Timelines

Retail and E-commerce: AI implementations in retail typically show initial results within 6-9 months, with full optimization occurring over 12-18 months. Success depends on data quality, system integration complexity, and staff adaptation to new processes. Realistic expectations include 10-25% efficiency improvements in inventory management, 15-30% enhancement in customer personalization, and 5-15% improvement in sales conversion rates.

Manufacturing and Industrial: Manufacturing AI implementations require longer timelines due to equipment integration complexity and safety requirements. Initial results typically emerge within 9-12 months, with full ROI realization occurring over 18-24 months. Realistic expectations include 15-30% reduction in unplanned downtime, 10-20% improvement in quality control, and 5-15% enhancement in overall equipment effectiveness.

Healthcare and Life Sciences: Healthcare AI implementation faces regulatory validation requirements and patient safety considerations extending timelines to 12-18 months for initial results and 24-36 months for comprehensive optimization. Realistic expectations include 10-25% improvement in diagnostic accuracy, 20-40% reduction in administrative burden, and 15-30% enhancement in operational efficiency.

Financial Services: Financial AI implementations require substantial regulatory compliance and security validation, typically requiring 6-12 months for initial deployment and 18-24 months for full optimization. Realistic expectations include 15-35% improvement in fraud detection accuracy, 20-50% reduction in manual processing time, and 10-25% enhancement in customer service efficiency.

Success Variation Factors

Organizational Readiness: Organizations with strong data infrastructure, technology-savvy staff, and systematic change management processes typically achieve 25-50% better results than those lacking these foundations. Success depends heavily on leadership commitment, resource allocation, and cultural readiness for technology adoption.

Implementation Quality: Organizations investing in comprehensive planning, staff training, and ongoing optimization typically achieve significantly better results than those pursuing minimal or rushed implementations. Quality implementation includes systematic project management, stakeholder engagement, and continuous improvement processes.

Industry Context: Highly regulated industries face additional implementation complexity and timeline extensions, though may achieve more sustainable long-term benefits through systematic approaches. Less regulated industries may achieve faster initial results but require ongoing optimization to maintain competitive advantages.

Scale and Scope: Large-scale AI implementations across multiple departments or functions require longer timelines and greater resource investment but may achieve broader organizational benefits. Focused, single-function implementations typically show faster results but may miss opportunities for broader organizational transformation.

Conclusion: Balanced Optimism for AI Implementation

AI applications across industries demonstrate significant potential for operational improvement, customer service enhancement, and business transformation. However, successful implementation requires realistic expectations, systematic approaches, and sustained organizational commitment. The most successful organizations approach AI as one tool among many for solving specific business problems rather than as a universal solution for organizational challenges.

Evidence from early adopters across retail, manufacturing, healthcare, and financial services demonstrates that gradual, well-planned AI implementation can deliver meaningful results within 12-24 month timeframes. Success depends heavily on data quality, staff training, change management, and ongoing system optimization rather than technology selection alone.

Organizations considering AI implementation should focus on specific use cases with clear success metrics, invest substantially in change management and staff training, and maintain realistic expectations about timeline and resource requirements. The most effective approach involves starting with pilot programs, scaling gradually based on demonstrated success, and maintaining long-term commitment to system optimization and organizational adaptation.

As AI technology continues evolving rapidly, organizations must balance the benefits of early adoption with the risks of premature implementation. Success requires strategic thinking, systematic execution, and ongoing adaptation rather than technology-first approaches or unrealistic expectations about immediate transformation.

Footnotes

[1] McKinsey & Company, "AI in the workplace: A report for 2025," January 28, 2025, https://www.mckinsey.com/capabilities/mckinsey-digital/our-insights/superagency-in-the-workplace-empowering-people-to-unlock-ais-full-potential-at-work.

[2] Federal Reserve Bank of St. Louis, "The Impact of Generative AI on Work Productivity," February 27, 2025, https://www.stlouisfed.org/on-the-economy/2025/feb/impact-generative-ai-work-productivity.

[3] PwC, "AI linked to a fourfold increase in productivity growth and 56% wage premium," June 3, 2025, https://www.pwc.com/gx/en/news-room/press-releases/2025/ai-linked-to-a-fourfold-increase-in-productivity-growth.html.

[4] IBM, "How to maximize ROI on AI in 2025," February 2025, https://www.ibm.com/think/insights/ai-roi.

[5] McKinsey & Company, "Generative AI in retail: LLM to ROI," August 5, 2024, https://www.mckinsey.com/industries/retail/our-insights/llm-to-roi-how-to-scale-gen-ai-in-retail.

[6] Shopify, "AI in Retail: Use Cases, Examples & Adoption (2025)," accessed August 2025, https://www.shopify.com/retail/ai-in-retail.

[7] Ibid.

[8] NeonTri, "AI in Retail Use Cases and Trends to Watch," February 29, 2024, https://neontri.com/blog/ai-retail-trends/.

[9] VKTR, "5 AI Case Studies in Retail," September 30, 2024, https://www.vktr.com/ai-disruption/5-ai-case-studies-in-retail/.

[10] ERP Software Blog, "Top 7 Use Cases of AI in Supply Chain (2025 Edition)," August 2025, https://erpsoftwareblog.com/2025/08/top-7-use-cases-of-ai-in-supply-chain/.

[11] Birlasoft, "17 Remarkable Use Cases of AI in Manufacturing," April 18, 2023, https://www.birlasoft.com/articles/17-use-cases-of-ai-in-manufacturing.

[12] Enterprise Playbook, "AI in Manufacturing: Scale from Pilot to ROI," July 24, 2023, https://appinventiv.com/blog/ai-in-manufacturing/.

[13] DigitalDefynd, "How can AI be Used in Manufacturing? [15 Case Studies] [2025]," August 5, 2024, https://digitaldefynd.com/IQ/ai-use-in-manufacturing-case-studies/.

[14] Ibid.

[15] Ibid.

[16] Microsoft, "AI-powered success—with more than 1,000 stories of customer transformation and innovation," July 24, 2025, https://www.microsoft.com/en-us/microsoft-cloud/blog/2025/07/24/ai-powered-success-with-1000-stories-of-customer-transformation-and-innovation/.

[17] Zendesk, "59 AI customer service statistics for 2025," August 2025, https://www.zendesk.com/blog/ai-customer-service-statistics/.

[18] Microsoft, "AI-powered success—with more than 1,000 stories of customer transformation and innovation."

[19] VKTR, "5 AI Case Studies in Customer Service and Support," July 24, 2024, https://www.vktr.com/ai-disruption/5-ai-case-studies-in-customer-service-and-support/.

[20] Ibid.

[21] Microsoft, "AI-powered success—with more than 1,000 stories of customer transformation and innovation."

[22] ResearchGate, "AI-driven fraud detection in banking: A systematic review of data science approaches to enhancing cybersecurity," November 30, 2024, https://www.researchgate.net/publication/386276951_AI-driven_fraud_detection_in_banking_A_systematic_review_of_dat

[23] MDPI, "Adoption of Artificial Intelligence-Driven Fraud Detection in Banking," April 18, 2025, https://www.mdpi.com/1911-8074/18/4/217.

[24] DigitalDefynd, "AI in Banking [20 Case Studies] [2025]," July 9, 2025, https://digitaldefynd.com/IQ/ai-in-banking-case-studies/.

[25] Ibid.

[26] Microsoft, "AI-powered success—with more than 1,000 stories of customer transformation and innovation."

[27] DigitalDefynd, "10 AI in Healthcare Case Studies [2025]," July 13, 2024, https://digitaldefynd.com/IQ/ai-in-healthcare-case-studies/.

[28] Factspan, "Top AI Medical Imaging tools for Healthcare Analytics - 2025," June 2, 2025, https://www.factspan.com/blogs/ai-medical-imaging-tools-transforming-healthcare-analytics-in-2025/.

[29] Axis Intelligence, "Healthcare AI Implementation: $2.4M ROI Blueprint for Medical Organizations in 2025," June 12, 2025, https://axis-intelligence.com/healthcare-ai-implementation-ai-health-2025/.

[30] Ibid.

[31] Vocal Media, "AI in Healthcare 2025: 7 Evidence-Based Wins, Ethics Playbook & ROI Calculator," August 9, 2025, https://vocal.media/education/ai-in-healthcare-2025-7-evidence-based-wins-ethics-playbook-and-roi-calculator.

[32] DigitalDefynd, "10 AI in Healthcare Case Studies [2025]."

[33] IBM, "How to maximize ROI on AI in 2025."

[34] Idea Financial, "5 Ways AI Can Transform Your Small Business in 2025," 2025, https://www.ideafinancial.com/blog/5-ways-ai-can-transform-your-small-business-in-2025.

[35] Microsoft, "AI-powered success—with more than 1,000 stories of customer transformation and innovation."

Chapter 8: Hands-On AI Projects

Opening: The Journey from Theory to Practice

Sarah Martinez, a marketing coordinator at a mid-sized healthcare technology company, had always been intrigued by the potential of artificial intelligence but felt overwhelmed by where to begin. Coming from a non-technical background in communications, she initially doubted her ability to implement meaningful AI solutions. However, over an eight-month period in 2024, she gradually developed practical AI skills that not only transformed her daily work but eventually led to her promotion to Marketing Operations Manager.

Sarah's journey began modestly in March 2024 when her team struggled with the increasing demand for content across multiple channels. What started as a simple experiment with AI-powered content creation tools evolved into a comprehensive automation system that improved team productivity by 40% while maintaining content quality standards.[1] Her success didn't happen overnight—it required patience, systematic learning, and a willingness to iterate based on feedback and results.

The transformation wasn't without challenges. Sarah initially underestimated the time required for proper implementation, faced resistance from team members concerned about job security, and struggled with measuring tangible business impact. However, by adopting a structured approach to AI project implementation and focusing on realistic, measurable outcomes, she successfully demonstrated the value of AI integration to stakeholders across the organization.

Sarah's story reflects a broader trend in business AI adoption. According to IDC's 2025 CEO Priorities research, 66% of CEOs now report measurable business benefits from generative AI initiatives, particularly in enhancing operational efficiency and customer satisfaction.[2] However, success requires moving beyond experimentation to systematic implementation with clear business objectives and measurable outcomes.

This chapter provides you with three comprehensive, hands-on AI projects designed to bridge the gap between theoretical knowledge and practical implementation. Each project accommodates different skill levels and organizational contexts while emphasizing realistic timelines, inclusive design principles, and sustainable business value creation.

AI Project Management Framework: Building for Success

Before diving into specific projects, it's essential to understand the unique characteristics of AI initiatives and how they differ from traditional software implementations. AI projects require a specialized management approach that balances technical experimentation with business discipline, accommodates the iterative nature of AI development, and manages stakeholder expectations around realistic timelines and outcomes.

Agile Methodology Adaptation for AI Projects

Modern AI project management draws heavily from Agile principles while incorporating specific adaptations for the unique challenges of artificial intelligence implementation. According to the 16th Annual State of Agile Report, 63% of organizations use Scrum as their primary Agile framework, with daily standups being the most common Agile technique across organizations.[3]

The ADAPT Framework for AI Projects:

Assess and Align: Begin with comprehensive stakeholder assessment, ensuring alignment between business objectives and AI capabilities while addressing diverse organizational needs and technical comfort levels.

Design with Constraints: Develop solutions within realistic technical, budgetary, and timeline constraints while incorporating accessibility requirements and ethical considerations from the outset.

Analyze and Prototype: Create minimum viable products (MVPs) for rapid testing and validation, emphasizing learning over perfection in early iterations.

Pilot and Refine: Implement controlled pilot programs with diverse user groups, gathering feedback and refining approaches based on real-world usage patterns.

Transition and Scale: Gradually expand successful pilots while maintaining quality controls and user support systems.

Inclusive Sprint Planning:

AI projects benefit from modified sprint structures that accommodate different learning styles and technical backgrounds. Research shows that teams using AI-powered project management tools report 25% higher productivity when incorporating structured feedback loops and adaptive planning processes.[4]

- **Discovery Sprints (1-2 weeks):** Focus on understanding user needs across diverse demographics, technical requirements, and organizational constraints
- **Development Sprints (2-3 weeks):** Build and test core functionality with emphasis on user experience and accessibility
- **Validation Sprints (1-2 weeks):** Test with real users from target demographics, gathering quantitative and qualitative feedback
- **Optimization Sprints (1-2 weeks):** Refine based on user feedback and performance data

Realistic Success Metrics and Timeline Expectations

One of the most critical aspects of AI project management involves setting realistic expectations for both timeline and outcomes. Recent research indicates that most AI projects require 12-18 months to show meaningful ROI, with initial benefits typically visible within 60-90 days of implementation.[5]

Immediate Success Indicators (30-60 days):

- User adoption rates reaching 25-40% of target audience
- Basic functionality working as intended with minimal technical issues
- Initial user feedback indicating positive reception and engagement
- Documented time savings or efficiency improvements, even if modest

Short-term Value Demonstration (90-180 days):

- Measurable productivity improvements of 15-30% in targeted workflows
- User satisfaction scores exceeding 70% among active participants
- Clear integration with existing business processes and systems
- Documented cost savings or revenue improvements, however incremental

Long-term Transformation (12-24 months):

- Organization-wide adoption exceeding 75% where applicable
- Sustained productivity improvements of 30-50% in targeted areas
- Cultural shift toward AI-augmented workflows and decision-making
- Measurable business impact justifying continued investment and expansion

Risk Management and Ethical Considerations

AI projects introduce unique risks that require proactive management throughout the implementation lifecycle. According to McKinsey's latest survey, 47% of organizations have experienced at least one AI-related consequence, with inaccuracy being the most commonly reported risk.[6]

Technical Risk Mitigation:

- Implement robust testing protocols with diverse data sets and user scenarios
- Establish clear escalation procedures for technical failures or performance degradation
- Maintain human oversight and intervention capabilities throughout all automated processes
- Document and address bias in training data and algorithmic decision-making

Organizational Risk Management:

- Develop comprehensive change management strategies addressing diverse employee concerns
- Establish clear communication channels for feedback and issue reporting
- Provide adequate training and support resources for users across different technical comfort levels
- Create fallback procedures for system failures or unexpected outcomes

Project 1: AI-Powered Content Assistant - Streamlining Creative Workflows

Project Overview and Business Case

The AI-powered content assistant project addresses one of the most common business challenges facing organizations today: the increasing demand for high-quality content across multiple channels while maintaining consistency and brand voice. Based on recent industry research, companies using AI-driven content optimization tools report a 30% increase in engagement rates and a 25% reduction in content production time.[7]

Business Objectives:

- Reduce content creation time by 30-40% for routine content tasks
- Improve content consistency and brand voice adherence across all channels
- Enable non-technical team members to create professional-quality content
- Establish scalable content production processes for future growth

Expected Investment and Timeline:

- **Duration:** 6-8 weeks for full implementation
- **Team Size:** 2-4 team members with diverse skill levels
- **Budget Range:** $2,000-$5,000 for tools and initial setup
- **Training Time:** 8-12 hours per team member over the

implementation period

Phase 1: Comprehensive Requirements and Planning (Week 1)

Stakeholder Assessment and Needs Analysis:

Begin with a thorough assessment of current content creation processes, identifying pain points and opportunities for improvement. This phase should involve representatives from all departments that create content, including marketing, sales, customer service, and executive communications.

Content Audit and Analysis:

- Catalog existing content types, formats, and publication frequencies
- Analyze current content performance metrics and identify improvement opportunities
- Document brand voice guidelines and style requirements across different channels
- Assess current content creation tools and workflow inefficiencies

User Research and Accessibility Planning:

- Conduct interviews with content creators representing different technical comfort levels
- Identify accessibility requirements for team members with disabilities
- Document preferred learning styles and training approaches
- Assess current skill levels and identify training needs

Success Criteria Definition:

- Establish baseline metrics for content creation time and quality
- Define measurable goals for efficiency improvements and user satisfaction
- Create quality assessment frameworks with objective evaluation criteria

- Set realistic adoption targets based on team size and technical readiness

Phase 2: Tool Selection and Setup (Week 2)

Platform Evaluation Framework:

Select AI content tools based on comprehensive evaluation criteria that prioritize both functionality and accessibility. Leading enterprise organizations report that careful tool selection can reduce implementation time by up to 40% while improving long-term user adoption.[8]

Primary Tool Categories:

- **Large Language Models:** Evaluate ChatGPT Plus, Claude Pro, and Gemini Advanced for content generation capabilities
- **Content Optimization:** Assess Grammarly Business, Hemingway Editor, and specialized industry tools
- **Workflow Integration:** Consider Zapier, Microsoft Power Automate, or custom integration solutions
- **Analytics and Measurement:** Implement content performance tracking and ROI measurement tools

Technical Setup and Configuration:

- Establish secure API access with appropriate data protection measures
- Configure user access controls and permission levels based on roles and responsibilities
- Set up integration with existing content management systems and collaboration tools
- Implement version control and approval workflows for content quality assurance

Security and Compliance Implementation:

- Ensure compliance with data protection regulations (GDPR, CCPA, etc.)

- Establish clear guidelines for handling sensitive or proprietary information
- Implement audit trails for content creation and modification tracking
- Create backup and recovery procedures for critical content assets

Phase 3: Collaborative Prompt Development (Weeks 3-4)

Brand Voice and Style Prompt Creation:

The foundation of successful AI content generation lies in developing comprehensive prompts that capture organizational voice, style, and values while accommodating diverse audience needs.

Core Prompt Architecture:

1. **Context Setting:** "You are a content creator for [Company Name], a [industry description] serving [target audience]. Our brand voice is [adjectives] and we prioritize [values]."
2. **Audience Specification:** "Write for [specific persona] who [demographic information] and [needs/challenges]."
3. **Content Requirements:** "Create [content type] that [specific objectives] while maintaining [style guidelines]."
4. **Format Instructions:** "Use [specific format] with [length requirements] and include [required elements]."
5. **Quality Standards:** "Ensure content is [quality criteria] and avoids [prohibited elements]."
6. **Call to Action:** "Include [specific CTA] that encourages [desired action]."

Industry-Specific Template Development:

Create standardized templates for common content types while allowing customization for specific use cases and audiences.

Blog Post Template Example:

Context: [Company/Brand Information]
Audience: [Target persona and demographics]
Topic: [Specific subject matter]
Objective: [Educational/promotional/engagement goal]

Keywords: [SEO requirements]
Tone: [Professional/conversational/technical level]
Length: [Word count range]
Structure: [Headings, sections, formatting requirements]
CTA: [Specific call-to-action and placement]
Constraints: [Brand guidelines, compliance requirements]
Quality Evaluation and Testing:

- Test prompts with diverse content types and subject matters
- Evaluate output quality against established brand guidelines and standards
- Gather feedback from multiple stakeholders with different perspectives and expertise
- Refine prompts based on real-world usage patterns and performance data

Phase 4: Workflow Integration and Training (Weeks 5-6)

Systematic User Training Program:

Implement a comprehensive training program that accommodates different learning styles and technical comfort levels while building confidence and competence progressively.

Training Module Structure:

1. **AI Literacy Foundation (2 hours):** Basic concepts, capabilities, and limitations
2. **Tool Proficiency (3 hours):** Hands-on practice with selected platforms and features
3. **Prompt Engineering (2 hours):** Effective communication techniques and optimization strategies
4. **Quality Assurance (1 hour):** Evaluation criteria and improvement techniques
5. **Workflow Integration (2 hours):** Process integration and collaboration protocols

Practical Exercise Development:

- Create realistic content creation scenarios based on actual business needs
- Develop progressive complexity exercises from basic to advanced applications
- Include collaborative exercises that simulate real-world team dynamics
- Provide individualized feedback and coaching based on performance and learning needs

Performance Monitoring and Support:

- Implement real-time performance tracking and feedback mechanisms
- Establish peer mentoring and support networks within the team
- Create resource libraries and reference materials for ongoing learning
- Schedule regular check-ins and optimization sessions based on usage patterns

Phase 5: Full Implementation and Optimization (Weeks 7-8 and Ongoing)

Organization-wide Rollout Strategy:

Expand successful pilot implementations across the organization while maintaining quality standards and user support systems.

Rollout Phases:

1. **Core Team Mastery:** Ensure pilot team achieves proficiency and can serve as internal champions
2. **Department Integration:** Gradually expand to related departments with established support systems
3. **Cross-functional Adoption:** Implement organization-wide with comprehensive training and support
4. **Continuous Improvement:** Regular optimization based on user feedback and performance data

Performance Measurement and ROI Analysis:

Implement comprehensive measurement systems that track both quantitative and qualitative outcomes while demonstrating clear business value.

Key Performance Indicators:

- **Efficiency Metrics:** Content creation time reduction, output volume increase, resource utilization
- **Quality Metrics:** Brand voice consistency, engagement rates, conversion performance
- **User Satisfaction:** Adoption rates, user feedback scores, training completion rates
- **Business Impact:** Cost savings, revenue attribution, competitive advantage indicators

Case Study: Lumen's Sales Intelligence Transformation

Lumen Technologies provides an excellent example of successful AI content implementation at enterprise scale. Using Microsoft Copilot, Lumen reduced the time required for sales preparation from up to four hours per seller to just 15 minutes. This transformation involved summarizing past sales interactions, generating recent news analysis, identifying business challenges, tracking industry trends, and providing actionable insights and recommendations.[9]

The key to Lumen's success was their systematic approach to implementation, comprehensive training program, and focus on measurable business outcomes. By 2024, this initiative projected annual time savings worth $50 million, demonstrating the significant ROI potential of well-executed AI content projects.

Project 2: Automated Data Analysis Dashboard - Democratizing Business Intelligence

Project Overview and Realistic Scope

The automated data analysis dashboard project addresses the critical business need for accessible, real-time insights across diverse organizational roles and technical competencies. According to recent research, AI-powered business intelligence implementations can reduce data analysis time by up to 60% while improving decision-making accuracy by 35%.[10]

Business Objectives:

- Democratize data access and insight generation across organizational levels
- Reduce dependency on technical specialists for routine analysis and reporting
- Improve decision-making speed and accuracy through real-time insights
- Create scalable analytics infrastructure for future growth and complexity

Target Outcomes:

- Enable non-technical users to generate meaningful insights independently
- Reduce report generation time from hours to minutes for standard analyses
- Increase data utilization across departments by 50-75%
- Establish foundation for advanced analytics and predictive modeling

Investment and Resource Requirements:

- **Duration:** 8-10 weeks including comprehensive testing and training
- **Team Composition:** Business analyst, IT specialist, representative

end-users

- **Technology Investment:** $5,000-$15,000 depending on scale and complexity
- **Training Investment:** 12-16 hours per user across multiple learning formats

Phase 1: Inclusive Data Architecture Design (Weeks 1-2)

Comprehensive Data Assessment:

Begin with thorough evaluation of existing data sources, quality standards, and accessibility requirements while prioritizing user needs across different technical competencies and organizational roles.

Data Source Inventory and Evaluation:

- **Internal Systems:** CRM, ERP, marketing automation, financial systems, operational databases
- **External Sources:** Market research, social media analytics, industry benchmarks, regulatory data
- **Data Quality Assessment:** Completeness, accuracy, consistency, timeliness, relevance
- **Integration Complexity:** Technical requirements, resource needs, timeline implications

User Needs Analysis Across Demographics:

- **Executive Level:** High-level KPIs, trend analysis, strategic planning insights
- **Department Managers:** Operational metrics, team performance, resource allocation data
- **Individual Contributors:** Task-specific data, personal productivity metrics, project status
- **External Stakeholders:** Regulatory compliance, client reporting, partnership metrics

Accessibility and Inclusion Requirements:

- **Visual Accessibility:** Color-blind friendly palettes, high contrast options, scalable fonts
- **Cognitive Accessibility:** Simple navigation, clear labeling, progressive disclosure
- **Technical Accessibility:** Multiple device compatibility, varying internet speeds, offline capabilities
- **Cultural Considerations:** Language preferences, cultural data interpretation patterns, regional customization

Phase 2: Platform Selection and Configuration (Weeks 3-4)

Technology Stack Evaluation:

Select analytics platforms that balance powerful functionality with ease of use while supporting diverse user needs and technical environments.

Platform Categories and Considerations:

- **Enterprise BI Tools:** Tableau, Power BI, Qlik Sense for comprehensive analytics capabilities
- **Cloud Analytics:** Google Analytics Intelligence, AWS QuickSight for scalability and integration
- **AI-Native Platforms:** Databricks, Palantir for advanced AI integration and modeling
- **No-Code Solutions:** Zapier, Bubble for rapid development and user accessibility

Microsoft Power BI Case Study:

Centrica provides an excellent example of scalable BI implementation, growing from 300 applications in 2019 to over 800 business solutions by 2024. Their success relied on establishing a center of excellence that maintains governance while supporting nearly 330 makers and 15,000 users across the company.[11] Their evaluation of Copilot in Power Apps demonstrates significant time savings in developing new applications and improving existing solutions.

Configuration and Integration Setup:

- **Data Connections:** Secure, reliable connections to all identified data sources
- **User Authentication:** Role-based access controls with appropriate security measures
- **Performance Optimization:** Query optimization, caching strategies, resource allocation
- **Mobile Responsiveness:** Cross-device compatibility and performance optimization

Phase 3: Dashboard Development with Universal Design (Weeks 5-6)

User-Centered Design Principles:

Develop dashboards that serve diverse user needs while maintaining simplicity and clarity in information presentation.

Dashboard Architecture Framework:

1. **Executive Summary View:** High-level KPIs with drill-down capabilities
2. **Departmental Dashboards:** Role-specific metrics with contextual analysis
3. **Operational Monitoring:** Real-time status tracking with alert systems
4. **Analytical Workspaces:** Flexible exploration tools for advanced users
5. **Collaborative Spaces:** Shared insights and discussion platforms

Visualization Best Practices:

- **Chart Selection:** Match visualization types to data characteristics and user goals
- **Color Strategy:** Accessible color palettes with cultural sensitivity considerations
- **Interactive Elements:** Intuitive filtering, drilling, and exploration capabilities

- **Mobile Optimization:** Responsive design for various screen sizes and orientations

Natural Language Query Implementation:

Integrate AI-powered natural language capabilities that allow users to ask questions in plain English rather than requiring technical query skills.

Query Examples and Capabilities:

- "Show me our top-performing marketing campaigns this quarter"
- "Compare sales performance between regions for the last six months"
- "What are our biggest customer satisfaction challenges this year?"
- "How has remote work affected productivity in different departments?"

Phase 4: User Training and Support System Development (Weeks 7-8)

Comprehensive Training Program Design:

Create multi-modal training resources that accommodate different learning preferences, technical backgrounds, and accessibility needs.

Training Resource Development:

- **Video Tutorials:** Step-by-step walkthroughs with captions and transcripts
- **Interactive Guides:** Hands-on practice environments with immediate feedback
- **Quick Reference Cards:** Printable guides for common tasks and troubleshooting
- **Virtual Office Hours:** Regular support sessions with expert assistance

Champion Network Development:

- Identify and train departmental champions who can provide peer support

- Establish regular knowledge sharing sessions and best practice discussions
- Create internal case study library showcasing successful implementations
- Develop recognition and incentive programs for active contributors

Phase 5: Performance Monitoring and Continuous Improvement (Ongoing)

Usage Analytics and Optimization:

Implement comprehensive monitoring systems that track both technical performance and user engagement while identifying opportunities for improvement.

Monitoring Framework:

- **Technical Metrics:** Load times, query performance, error rates, system availability
- **User Engagement:** Login frequency, feature utilization, session duration, help requests
- **Business Impact:** Decision-making speed, data-driven initiatives, outcome attribution
- **Accessibility Performance:** Error rates across different user groups, alternative format usage

Business Value Measurement:

Track tangible business benefits while building the case for continued investment and expansion.

ROI Calculation Framework:

- **Time Savings:** Reduced report generation and analysis time across user groups
- **Decision Quality:** Improved outcomes attributed to better data access and insights
- **Resource Efficiency:** Reduced dependency on technical

specialists for routine analysis

- **Strategic Value:** New insights and opportunities identified through improved data access

Case Study: BKW's Edison Platform Implementation

BKW (Swiss energy company) demonstrates effective AI-powered analytics implementation with their Edison platform, built using Microsoft Azure, Azure AI Foundry, and Azure OpenAI services. Within two months of rollout, 8% of staff were actively using Edison, media inquiries were processed 50% faster, and more than 40 use cases were documented.[12]

The success factors included:

- Systematic user onboarding with role-specific training
- Clear value demonstration through early wins and quick results
- Comprehensive support system with multiple assistance channels
- Regular feedback collection and rapid iteration based on user needs

Project 3: Customer Service Chatbot - Enhancing Support Accessibility

Project Overview and Comprehensive Scope

The customer service chatbot project addresses the growing demand for accessible, 24/7 customer support while maintaining high service quality and human connection. Industry research indicates that AI chatbots can handle up to 80% of routine customer inquiries while cutting customer support costs by 30%.[13] However, successful implementation requires careful balance between automation efficiency and human touch.

Business Objectives:

- Provide instant, accurate responses to common customer inquiries across all time zones
- Reduce customer wait times and improve first-contact resolution rates

- Enable human agents to focus on complex issues requiring emotional intelligence and specialized expertise
- Create scalable support infrastructure that grows with business needs

Expected Outcomes:

- Handle 60-80% of routine customer inquiries without human intervention
- Reduce average response time from hours to seconds for standard questions
- Maintain customer satisfaction scores above 85% for chatbot interactions
- Achieve positive ROI within 8-14 months through operational cost savings

Implementation Investment:

- **Duration:** 10-12 weeks including extensive testing and gradual rollout
- **Team Requirements:** Customer service manager, technical developer, UX designer, representative customers
- **Technology Investment:** $8,000-$20,000 depending on scale and integration complexity
- **Training Investment:** 20-25 hours per agent for effective human-AI collaboration

Phase 1: Inclusive Use Case Analysis (Weeks 1-2)

Customer Journey Mapping and Query Analysis:

Comprehensive analysis of customer interactions, identifying patterns, pain points, and opportunities for automation while ensuring inclusive design for diverse customer needs.

Query Classification and Analysis:

- **Routine Inquiries (60-70%):** Account status, basic product information, simple troubleshooting

- **Complex Issues (20-30%):** Technical problems, billing disputes, product recommendations
- **Sensitive Matters (10-15%):** Complaints, refunds, account security issues

Multicultural and Accessibility Considerations:

- **Language Support:** Primary and secondary language requirements based on customer demographics
- **Cultural Sensitivity:** Communication style preferences across different cultural groups
- **Accessibility Features:** Screen reader compatibility, simple language options, visual alternatives
- **Economic Accessibility:** Support for customers with varying technical resources and capabilities

Customer Persona Development: Create detailed personas representing diverse customer segments, including technical comfort levels, preferred communication styles, accessibility needs, and service expectations.

Phase 2: Platform Setup with Accessibility Focus (Weeks 3-4)

Conversational AI Platform Selection:

Choose platforms that prioritize inclusive design while offering robust functionality and integration capabilities.

Platform Evaluation Criteria:

- **Natural Language Understanding:** Accuracy across dialects, accents, and language variations
- **Integration Capabilities:** Seamless connection with existing customer service systems
- **Accessibility Features:** Built-in support for assistive technologies and alternative interfaces

- **Analytics and Optimization:** Comprehensive performance monitoring and improvement tools

Leading Platform Options:

- **Microsoft Bot Framework:** Enterprise-grade security with extensive integration options
- **Dialogflow (Google):** Strong NLP capabilities with multilingual support
- **Amazon Lex:** Cost-effective scaling with AWS ecosystem integration
- **Rasa Open Source:** Customizable solution with privacy control

Technical Architecture and Integration:

- **Knowledge Base Integration:** Connection to FAQ databases, product catalogs, and support documentation
- **CRM Integration:** Real-time access to customer history and account information
- **Escalation Pathways:** Seamless transfer to human agents with full conversation context
- **Multi-channel Deployment:** Website, mobile app, social media, and phone system integration

Phase 3: Knowledge Base Development and Content Creation (Weeks 5-7)

Comprehensive Content Development:

Create extensive knowledge base content that addresses common customer needs while incorporating cultural sensitivity and accessibility requirements.

Content Categories and Structure:

- **Product Information:** Features, specifications, compatibility, and usage guidelines

- **Account Management:** Billing, subscriptions, profile updates, and security settings
- **Technical Support:** Troubleshooting guides, installation instructions, compatibility issues
- **Company Policies:** Returns, warranties, terms of service, and privacy policies

Cultural Adaptation and Inclusivity:

- **Language Localization:** Culturally appropriate expressions and communication styles
- **Visual Content:** Diverse representation in images and video content
- **Example Scenarios:** Inclusive examples representing different customer situations and backgrounds
- **Sensitivity Training:** Guidelines for handling sensitive topics and cultural differences

Response Development Framework: Create standardized response templates that maintain consistency while allowing personalization based on customer context and preferences.

Template Structure Example:

Acknowledgment: [Recognize customer inquiry and show understanding]

Information: [Provide clear, actionable information]

Verification: [Confirm understanding and ask for clarification if needed]

Next Steps: [Outline specific actions or alternatives]

Escalation: [Offer human assistance when appropriate]

Phase 4: Multi-Channel Integration and Testing (Weeks 8-10)

Comprehensive Testing Framework:

Implement extensive testing protocols that ensure functionality across diverse user scenarios, devices, and accessibility requirements.

Testing Categories:

- **Functional Testing:** Core features, integrations, and error handling
- **Usability Testing:** User experience across different customer personas and technical comfort levels
- **Accessibility Testing:** Screen reader compatibility, keyboard navigation, visual alternatives
- **Performance Testing:** Response times, concurrent user handling, system reliability
- **Cultural Testing:** Appropriate responses across different cultural contexts and communication styles

Multi-Channel Deployment Strategy:

- **Website Integration:** Embedded chat widget with proactive engagement features
- **Mobile Application:** Native integration with app-specific functionality
- **Social Media Platforms:** Facebook Messenger, Instagram, Twitter integration
- **Voice Channels:** Phone system integration with voice-to-text capabilities

Gradual Rollout and Monitoring:

- **Beta Testing:** Limited release to volunteer customers with comprehensive feedback collection
- **Phased Deployment:** Gradual expansion across channels and customer segments
- **Real-time Monitoring:** Continuous performance tracking with immediate response to issues
- **Customer Feedback Integration:** Multiple feedback mechanisms with rapid response cycles

Phase 5: Deployment and Continuous Monitoring (Weeks 11-12 and Ongoing)

Launch Strategy and Change Management:

Implement comprehensive launch strategy that prepares both customers and staff for the transition while maintaining service quality throughout the process.

Staff Training and Collaboration:

- **Human-AI Collaboration:** Training agents to work effectively with AI assistance
- **Escalation Protocols:** Clear procedures for seamless handoffs from AI to human agents
- **Quality Monitoring:** Regular review of AI responses with human oversight and correction
- **Continuous Improvement:** Regular feedback sessions and optimization based on real-world usage

Customer Communication and Education:

- **Transparency:** Clear communication about AI assistance with options for human support
- **Education:** Guidelines for effective chatbot interaction and feature utilization
- **Feedback Channels:** Multiple ways for customers to report issues and suggest improvements
- **Opt-out Options:** Always available human alternatives for customers who prefer traditional support

Performance Optimization and Scaling:

Implement continuous improvement processes that enhance chatbot performance while expanding capabilities based on user needs and business growth.

Optimization Framework:

- **Response Accuracy:** Regular review and refinement of AI responses based on customer feedback
- **Knowledge Base Updates:** Continuous content expansion and improvement based on emerging needs
- **Integration Enhancement:** Deeper integration with business systems for more personalized service
- **Feature Development:** New capabilities based on user requests and technological advancement

Success Story: Klarna's AI Customer Service Revolution

Klarna demonstrates the potential of well-implemented AI customer service with their chatbot handling over 2.3 million conversations and managing two-thirds of customer service chats. The AI assistant performs work equivalent to 700 full-time agents, leading to an estimated $40 million profit improvement in 2024.[14]

Key success factors included:

- Comprehensive training data from millions of historical customer interactions
- Gradual implementation with extensive human oversight and quality control
- Clear escalation procedures maintaining human touch for complex issues
- Continuous optimization based on customer feedback and performance metrics

Advanced Implementation Considerations

Cultural Sensitivity and Global Adaptation

AI projects must account for cultural differences in communication styles, business practices, and technology adoption patterns. Research shows that cultural adaptation can improve user adoption rates by up to 60% in multinational organizations.[15]

Cultural Adaptation Framework:

- **Communication Styles:** Direct vs. indirect communication preferences across different cultures
- **Power Distance:** Hierarchical considerations in AI interaction design and implementation
- **Technology Acceptance:** Varying comfort levels with automation across different cultural contexts
- **Privacy Expectations:** Cultural variations in data sharing and privacy requirements

Implementation Strategies:

- **Local Champions:** Identify and train cultural ambassadors who understand local contexts and preferences
- **Flexible Deployment:** Adapt implementation approaches based on regional preferences and requirements
- **Feedback Mechanisms:** Culture-specific feedback collection and response systems
- **Continuous Learning:** Regular assessment and adjustment based on cultural feedback and usage patterns

Accessibility and Universal Design Principles

Inclusive AI implementation requires proactive consideration of accessibility needs from project inception rather than retrofitting accessibility features after deployment.

Universal Design Implementation:

- **Multiple Input Methods:** Support for keyboard, voice, touch, and assistive technology interactions
- **Content Accessibility:** Screen reader compatible, high contrast options, multiple language support
- **Cognitive Accessibility:** Simple navigation, clear instructions, progressive disclosure of complexity
- **Economic Accessibility:** Free or low-cost options for users with limited resources

Assistive Technology Integration:

- **Screen Reader Compatibility:** Proper semantic markup and alternative text for visual elements
- **Voice Control:** Integration with speech recognition systems and voice navigation
- **Motor Accessibility:** Keyboard navigation and alternative input methods for users with limited mobility
- **Cognitive Support:** Clear instructions, consistent navigation, and error prevention mechanisms

Common Implementation Challenges and Solutions

Technical Complexity Management

AI projects often involve complex technical requirements that can overwhelm teams without extensive technical backgrounds. Successful implementation requires breaking down complexity into manageable components while maintaining system integrity.

Challenge: Integration difficulties between AI tools and existing business systems. **Solution:** Implement phased integration approach with extensive testing at each stage. Begin with standalone implementations before attempting complex integrations.

Challenge: Data quality issues affecting AI performance and accuracy. **Solution:** Establish comprehensive data cleaning and validation processes before implementation. Create ongoing data quality monitoring and improvement systems.

Challenge: Scalability limitations as user base and data volume grow. **Solution:** Design architecture with scalability in mind from project inception. Implement monitoring systems that identify performance issues before they affect users.

User Adoption and Change Management

Resistance to AI implementation often stems from fear, misunderstanding, or inadequate training rather than inherent technology limitations.

Challenge: Employee resistance due to job security concerns. **Solution:** Emphasize AI as augmentation rather than replacement. Provide clear examples of how AI enhances rather than eliminates human roles. Offer retraining and upskilling opportunities.

Challenge: Low adoption rates among target users. **Solution:** Implement comprehensive training programs with multiple learning formats. Create champion networks and peer support systems. Demonstrate clear value through early wins and success stories.

Challenge: Inadequate ongoing support and maintenance. **Solution:** Establish dedicated support teams with clear escalation procedures. Create comprehensive documentation and self-service resources. Implement regular check-ins and optimization sessions.

Quality Control and Performance Management

Maintaining quality standards while achieving efficiency gains requires systematic monitoring and continuous improvement processes.

Challenge: AI output quality inconsistency affecting user trust and adoption. **Solution:** Implement comprehensive quality assurance protocols with human oversight. Create feedback loops for continuous improvement. Establish clear escalation procedures for quality issues.

Challenge: Measuring ROI and demonstrating business value. **Solution:** Establish baseline metrics before implementation. Track multiple value indicators beyond cost savings. Document qualitative benefits and user satisfaction improvements.

Challenge: Keeping pace with rapid technology evolution and updates. **Solution:** Establish technology roadmap review processes. Maintain flexibility in vendor relationships and technical architecture. Invest in ongoing team education and skill development.

Portfolio Development and Knowledge Sharing

Documenting Success and Learning

Successful AI implementation requires systematic documentation of both successes and failures to support future projects and organizational learning.

Documentation Framework:

- **Project Charter:** Clear objectives, scope, timeline, and success criteria
- **Implementation Log:** Detailed record of decisions, changes, and rationale
- **Performance Metrics:** Quantitative and qualitative outcome measurement
- **Lesson Learned:** Analysis of what worked well and areas for improvement
- **Best Practices:** Reusable frameworks and approaches for future projects

Knowledge Transfer Systems:

- **Internal Case Studies:** Detailed documentation of project outcomes with lessons learned
- **Training Materials:** Reusable content for future team training and onboarding
- **Template Library:** Standardized frameworks and tools for accelerated future implementation
- **Expert Networks:** Internal expertise sharing and peer consultation systems

Building Organizational AI Capabilities

Individual project success contributes to broader organizational AI maturity when knowledge and capabilities are systematically shared and scaled.

Capability Development Framework:

- **Skill Assessment:** Regular evaluation of organizational AI competencies and gaps
- **Training Pathways:** Structured development programs for different roles and skill levels
- **Mentorship Programs:** Pairing experienced practitioners with newcomers for knowledge transfer
- **Community Building:** Internal networks and forums for sharing experiences and best practices

Cultural Transformation:

- **Leadership Engagement:** Executive sponsorship and modeling of AI adoption
- **Success Recognition:** Celebrating and sharing AI implementation wins across the organization
- **Innovation Encouragement:** Creating safe spaces for experimentation and learning from failure
- **External Engagement:** Participating in industry forums and sharing organizational experiences

Conclusion: From Projects to Transformation

The three projects outlined in this chapter represent stepping stones toward broader organizational AI transformation rather than isolated technical implementations. Success requires viewing these initiatives as part of a larger journey toward AI-augmented business operations while maintaining focus on human needs, ethical considerations, and sustainable value creation.

Key Success Factors:

- **Human-Centered Design:** Prioritizing user needs and experiences throughout implementation
- **Realistic Expectations:** Setting achievable goals with appropriate timelines and resource allocation
- **Inclusive Implementation:** Ensuring accessibility and cultural

sensitivity in all project phases

- **Continuous Learning:** Embracing iterative improvement and adaptation based on real-world feedback
- **Systematic Scaling:** Building on individual project success to create organizational transformation

The transformation potential of AI implementation extends beyond efficiency gains to fundamental changes in how organizations operate, make decisions, and serve customers. According to PwC's analysis, organizations can expect AI to double their knowledge workforce through effective implementation of AI agents and automated processes.[16] However, realizing this potential requires sustained commitment to systematic implementation, comprehensive training, and continuous adaptation.

As you embark on these hands-on projects, remember that the goal is not just successful implementation of specific AI tools, but development of organizational capabilities that support ongoing innovation and adaptation in an rapidly evolving technological landscape. The skills, processes, and cultural changes developed through these projects will serve as foundation for future AI initiatives and broader digital transformation efforts.

Success in AI implementation comes not from perfect execution of initial plans, but from systematic learning, adaptation, and improvement based on real-world experience and feedback. By following the frameworks and approaches outlined in this chapter while maintaining focus on human needs and ethical considerations, organizations can achieve meaningful AI transformation that enhances rather than replaces human capabilities and judgment.

Footnotes:

[1] Matrix Marketing Group, "2025 AI-Driven Case Studies: Streamline Content Creation," June 24, 2025, https://matrixmarketinggroup.com/2025-ai-driven-case-studies-content-creation/.

[2] Microsoft, "AI-powered success—with more than 1,000 stories of customer transformation and innovation," The Microsoft Cloud Blog, July 24, 2025, https://www.microsoft.com/en-us/microsoft-cloud/blog/2025/

07/24/ai-powered-success-with-1000-stories-of-customer-transformation-and-innovation/.

[3] KnowledgeHut, "State of Agile 2025: Things You Need to Know," February 13, 2025, https://www.knowledgehut.com/blog/agile/state-of-agile.

[4] Priceless Consulting, "Project Management Trends for 2025," February 12, 2025, https://pricelessconsulting.com/en/project-management-trends-for-2025-artificial-intelligence-agility-and-collaboration/.

[5] FullView, "80+ AI Customer Service Statistics & Trends in 2025 (Roundup)," July 2, 2025, https://www.fullview.io/blog/ai-customer-service-stats.

[6] McKinsey & Company, "The state of AI: How organizations are rewiring to capture value," March 12, 2025, https://www.mckinsey.com/capabilities/quantumblack/our-insights/the-state-of-ai.

[7] Matrix Marketing Group, "AI-Driven Case Studies: Streamline Content Creation in 2024," June 24, 2025, https://matrixmarketinggroup.com/2025-ai-driven-case-studies/.

[8] Deloitte, "State of Generative AI in the Enterprise 2024," 2024, https://www.deloitte.com/us/en/what-we-do/capabilities/applied-artificial-intelligence/content/state-of-generative-ai-in-enterprise.html.

[9] Microsoft, "AI-powered success—with more than 1,000 stories."

[10] Improvado, "AI for Business Intelligence: How AI Is Changing BI [2025]," https://improvado.io/blog/ai-business-intelligence.

[11] Microsoft, "AI-powered success—with more than 1,000 stories."

[12] Ibid.

[13] NexGen Cloud, "How AI and RAG Chatbots Cut Customer Service Costs by Millions," March 28, 2025, https://www.nexgencloud.com/blog/case-studies/how-ai-and-rag-chatbots-cut-customer-service-costs-by-millions.

[14] Ibid.

[15] SuperAGI, "AI-Powered Marketing Automation: Case Studies on How AI Agents Boost Efficiency and ROI in 2025," June 28, 2025, https://superagi.com/ai-powered-marketing-automation-case-studies-on-how-ai-agents-boost-efficiency-and-roi-in-2025/.

[16] PwC, "2025 AI Business Predictions," https://www.pwc.com/us/en/tech-effect/ai-analytics/ai-predictions.html.

Part III: The Transformation Phase

Chapter 9: Advancing Your Career with AI

Introduction: Maya's Strategic Transformation

Maya Rodriguez had spent eight years climbing the operations ladder at a mid-sized logistics company, but by early 2024, she sensed the ground shifting beneath her feet. AI-powered routing systems were revolutionizing her industry, and she realized her career depended on adapting to this new reality. Rather than viewing AI as a threat, Maya embarked on a strategic eighteen-month journey that would transform not just her skill set, but her entire professional trajectory.

Starting with online courses during her commute, Maya gradually built AI literacy while maintaining her demanding full-time role. She navigated workplace dynamics carefully, positioning herself as a bridge between traditional operations and emerging AI capabilities. Her journey wasn't without challenges—she faced skepticism from colleagues who questioned her pivot, struggled with imposter syndrome in technical discussions, and invested significant personal time and resources in continuous learning.

By mid-2025, Maya's systematic approach yielded tangible results: a 40% salary increase accompanying her promotion to Director of AI Operations, recognition as a thought leader within her company, and a robust professional network spanning both traditional logistics and emerging AI communities. Her success illustrates a crucial reality about AI career advancement: it requires strategic patience, continuous learning, and the ability to translate between technical possibilities and business needs.

Maya's story embodies the realistic progression possible when professionals approach AI career development with intentionality and persistence. This chapter will explore how you can navigate similar transformations, addressing both the opportunities and challenges facing professionals in today's AI-influenced job market.

The AI Career Landscape 2025: Balancing Opportunity with Reality

Market Growth and Accessibility Considerations

The artificial intelligence job market has experienced unprecedented expansion, creating both opportunities and new forms of inequality. According to the latest data from Stanford's AI Index Report, 1.8% of US job postings now require AI skills, representing a significant increase from 1.4% in 2023.[1] This growth translates to substantial financial benefits for those who can access these opportunities: PwC's 2025 Global AI Jobs Barometer reveals that workers with AI skills command a 56% wage premium compared to their peers in similar roles without AI capabilities.[2]

The World Economic Forum's Future of Jobs Report 2025 projects that approximately 170 million new jobs will be created this decade due to global macro trends, with AI playing a central role in this expansion.[3] However, this growth is unevenly distributed across geographic regions, industries, and demographic groups, creating new forms of digital divide that must be acknowledged and addressed.

Remote work opportunities are expanding access for diverse candidates, with companies increasingly recognizing that AI talent can contribute effectively from various locations. This shift is particularly significant for professionals in regions with limited local AI opportunities or those facing mobility constraints due to family or economic circumstances.

Wage Premium Reality and Geographic Variations

The financial incentives for developing AI skills are substantial but vary significantly by location and role complexity. According to multiple industry sources:

- **Machine Learning Engineers** average $156,281-$172,121 annually in the United States[4]
- **AI Engineers** command average salaries of $160,757[5]
- **Data Scientists** with AI skills earn approximately $125,126[6]
- **Senior AI Research Scientists** at top-tier companies can earn

$200,000-$300,000+[7]

However, these figures require contextualization. Geographic concentration in tech hubs like Silicon Valley, Seattle, and New York creates both higher salaries and increased cost of living. Professionals in other regions may find lower absolute salaries but better cost-adjusted opportunities, particularly as remote work becomes more accepted.

The 56% wage premium for AI skills represents an average across all roles and experience levels. Entry-level positions may see smaller premiums, while experienced professionals transitioning into AI roles often experience the most dramatic salary improvements. Maya's 40% increase over eighteen months represents a realistic expectation for dedicated professionals making strategic career moves.

Addressing Structural Barriers and Access Issues

The AI job market reflects and sometimes amplifies existing inequalities in tech employment. LinkedIn's research indicates that approximately 70% of AI professionals are male, with this ratio remaining "remarkably stable over time."[8] Women are more likely to work in AI-exposed roles—positions where AI tools augment rather than replace human work—but face higher pressure to develop new skills as these roles evolve rapidly.

Educational credentialism poses another significant barrier. While 77% of AI job openings traditionally required master's degrees, this landscape is shifting rapidly.[9] According to the Federal Reserve Bank of Atlanta's analysis, job postings requiring AI skills have seen degree requirements declining from 66% to 59% for AI-augmented roles and from 53% to 44% for highly automatable positions.[10] Significantly, 25% of AI job postings now omit education requirements entirely, suggesting employers are increasingly prioritizing demonstrated skills over formal credentials.

Network access limitations disproportionately affect underrepresented groups, who may lack connections to AI professionals or companies actively hiring in this space. Economic barriers to training—particularly expensive bootcamps or degree programs—can further limit access for individuals from lower socioeconomic backgrounds.

High-Demand Roles: Realistic Assessment and Entry Pathways

Technical Roles with Expanding Access Routes

AI Research Scientist positions represent the pinnacle of AI careers, typically commanding $200,000-$300,000+ annually but requiring advanced education and demonstrated research capability. However, alternative pathways are emerging through open-source contributions, participation in AI research communities, and collaboration with academic institutions even without formal Ph.D. credentials.

Machine Learning Engineers earn $170,000-$250,000 and increasingly value practical experience over educational pedigree. Bootcamp graduates and self-taught professionals are successfully entering this field by demonstrating ability through portfolio projects and contributing to open-source ML libraries. The role requires deep technical skills but also demands understanding of business applications and scalability challenges.

Data Scientists with AI specialization earn $120,000-$180,000 and benefit from the field's broad applicability across industries. Community college programs and online certifications provide viable entry routes, particularly when combined with domain expertise in specific industries like healthcare, finance, or retail.

AI Product Managers command $140,000-$200,000 and represent an ideal role for professionals with business backgrounds seeking to leverage AI skills. These positions value the ability to translate between technical capabilities and business needs—a skill set that doesn't require deep programming knowledge but demands understanding of AI possibilities and limitations.

Business-Focused Roles with Diverse Entry Points

AI Ethics Specialists earn $100,000-$160,000 and welcome professionals from philosophy, sociology, law, and other liberal arts backgrounds. This growing field addresses critical needs around bias detection, algorithmic fairness, and responsible AI deployment. Organizations increasingly recognize that diverse perspectives enhance ethical AI development, creating opportunities for non-traditional technical backgrounds.

AI Training Specialists command $80,000-$130,000 and benefit professionals with teaching, instructional design, or corporate training experience. As organizations struggle to upskill their workforces for AI integration, specialists who can design effective training programs and facilitate learning become increasingly valuable.

Prompt Engineers represent an emerging field with salaries ranging from $70,000-$120,000, requiring creativity, communication skills, and understanding of how AI systems respond to different types of inputs. This role exemplifies how AI creates entirely new categories of work that didn't exist even five years ago.

AI Implementation Consultants earn $90,000-$150,000 by combining industry expertise with AI knowledge to help organizations navigate technology adoption. This role particularly values professionals who understand specific industry challenges and can identify practical AI applications.

Domain Expertise Premium and Inclusive Opportunities

Industry-specific AI knowledge commands significant premiums, with healthcare AI specialists earning 15-25% above base AI salaries, reflecting the complexity and regulatory requirements of medical applications. Education AI developers find growing opportunities as schools and universities seek to integrate AI tools responsibly. Social impact AI roles in nonprofit and government sectors offer mission-aligned work with competitive compensation, while small business AI consulting provides entrepreneurial opportunities with lower barriers to entry.

The key insight is that AI career advancement increasingly rewards the combination of domain expertise with AI literacy rather than pure technical depth. Maya's success stemmed largely from her deep understanding of logistics operations combined with her newly developed AI skills, making her uniquely valuable to her organization.

Building Professional Brand: Inclusive Strategies

for Career Advancement

Portfolio Development with Accessibility and Impact Focus

Creating a compelling professional portfolio requires demonstrating problem-solving ability and business impact rather than just technical complexity. Successful portfolios emphasize:

Project Documentation that Tells Stories: Rather than simply listing technical specifications, effective portfolios explain the business problem addressed, the approach taken, challenges encountered, and measurable outcomes achieved. Maya's portfolio included a case study showing how her AI-powered route optimization reduced delivery times by 15% while cutting fuel costs by 12%—metrics that resonated with both technical and business audiences.

Community Project Contributions: Contributing to open-source AI projects, participating in Kaggle competitions, or volunteering AI skills for nonprofits demonstrates collaborative abilities and social consciousness. These projects often provide more creative freedom than corporate work and showcase initiative and passion for the field.

Diverse Case Studies: Portfolios should demonstrate cultural sensitivity and inclusive design thinking. Projects that address accessibility challenges, serve underrepresented communities, or tackle social impact issues differentiate candidates and show awareness of AI's broader implications.

Multiple Format Options: Accommodate different learning styles and accessibility needs by presenting work through various media—written case studies, video presentations, interactive demonstrations, and visual infographics. This approach also demonstrates communication skills across different audience types.

Network Building with Intentional Inclusion

Professional networking in AI requires moving beyond traditional tech circles to build diverse, mutually beneficial relationships:

Professional Association Participation: Organizations like Women in AI, Black in AI, Queer in AI, and Indigenous AI Collective provide community and advocacy while advancing career opportunities. These groups often offer mentorship programs specifically designed to support underrepresented individuals entering AI fields.

Cross-Industry Networking: AI applications span virtually every sector, creating networking opportunities that extend far beyond technology companies. Professional associations in healthcare, education, finance, and other industries increasingly feature AI-focused programming and provide pathways for domain experts to connect with AI professionals.

Mentorship Programs: Both seeking mentorship and providing guidance to others creates powerful professional relationships. Many successful AI professionals, including Maya, found that teaching others helped solidify their own knowledge while building reputation within their communities.

Community Meetups and Events: Local AI meetups, virtual conferences, and industry events provide networking opportunities while accommodating different comfort levels and accessibility needs. Many events now offer both in-person and virtual attendance options, expanding access for professionals with various constraints.

Content Creation and Thought Leadership

Establishing thought leadership requires consistent, valuable contribution to professional discourse:

Blog Writing: Publishing articles about AI applications in specific industries, lessons learned from projects, or perspectives on AI ethics builds reputation and demonstrates communication skills. Platforms like Medium, LinkedIn, and industry publications welcome diverse voices and perspectives.

Speaking Opportunities: Conferences increasingly prioritize diverse speakers and perspectives. Starting with local meetups or virtual presentations can build confidence and experience for larger speaking opportunities. Many events specifically recruit speakers from underrepresented backgrounds and provide support for first-time speakers.

Podcast Participation: AI podcasts proliferate across industries and often seek guests with unique perspectives or experience. Podcast appearances provide excellent visibility and help build personal brand while requiring minimal technical setup.

Educational Content Creation: Developing tutorials, courses, or explainer content for platforms like YouTube, Coursera, or company blogs demonstrates expertise while contributing to AI education. This content creation also helps develop skills in simplifying complex concepts for diverse audiences.

Career Transition Strategies: Multiple Pathways to AI Success

Non-Technical to AI Career Transitions

The most successful career transitions into AI leverage existing skills while systematically building technical capabilities:

Skills Mapping and Transfer: Professionals should inventory transferable skills—project management, stakeholder communication, domain expertise, problem-solving abilities—and understand how these apply to AI contexts. Maya's operations background provided crucial understanding of logistics challenges that pure AI specialists often lack.

Educational Pathway Selection: Multiple routes exist for AI education, each with distinct advantages:

- **Community College Programs**: Increasingly offer AI and data science certificates at accessible price points with flexible scheduling for working professionals
- **Online Bootcamps**: Provide intensive, practical training typically lasting 3-6 months with costs ranging from $3,500-$16,000 and job placement support[11]
- **Professional Certificates**: Industry-recognized credentials from companies like Google, IBM, and Microsoft offer structured learning paths with employer recognition
- **Self-Study Combined with Projects**: Free and low-cost resources enable self-directed learning when combined with practical application through personal or volunteer projects

Gradual Transition Through Internal Opportunities: Many professionals successfully transition by identifying AI applications within their current roles. This approach provides practical experience while maintaining employment stability and demonstrating value to current employers.

Current Role AI Integration

Rather than making dramatic career pivots, many professionals advance by becoming the "AI person" within their existing organizations:

Process Improvement Projects: Identifying opportunities to apply AI tools to current workflows demonstrates initiative and builds practical experience. Simple applications like automating data analysis, improving customer service responses, or optimizing scheduling can provide substantial value while building AI experience.

Cross-Functional Collaboration: Working with technical teams on AI initiatives develops understanding of implementation challenges and establishes credibility with both business and technical stakeholders. These collaborations often lead to hybrid roles that bridge business and technical domains.

Internal Training and Knowledge Sharing: Becoming an internal advocate and educator for AI creates recognition as a subject matter expert while helping colleagues navigate AI adoption. This educational role often evolves into formal AI-focused responsibilities.

Strategic Planning Participation: Contributing AI perspectives to business planning processes positions professionals as strategic thinkers who understand both technical possibilities and business implications.

Entrepreneurial AI Opportunities

AI creates unique entrepreneurial opportunities, particularly for professionals who understand specific industry challenges:

Community-Focused AI Consulting: Small businesses and nonprofits often need AI guidance but lack resources for large consulting firms. Independent consultants who understand both AI capabilities and small organization constraints find substantial opportunities.

Educational Content and Training Services: The demand for AI education far exceeds current supply, creating opportunities for professionals to develop training programs, workshops, or educational content targeting specific audiences or industries.

Social Impact AI Applications: Mission-driven organizations seek AI solutions that address social challenges while maintaining ethical standards. Entrepreneurs who combine AI skills with social awareness find meaningful opportunities in areas like education, healthcare access, and environmental sustainability.

Industry-Specific AI Tools: Professionals with deep domain expertise can identify opportunities to develop AI solutions for specific industry challenges, often starting as consulting projects that evolve into product companies.

Skills Development Roadmap: Flexible Pathways for Diverse Learners

Foundation Skills (3-6 months)

Building AI literacy requires systematic skill development that accommodates different learning styles and backgrounds:

AI Literacy Development: Understanding fundamental concepts—machine learning, neural networks, natural language processing, computer vision—provides the foundation for all AI work. Free resources from universities, technology companies, and nonprofit organizations make this knowledge accessible to learners regardless of economic circumstances.

Tool Proficiency: Hands-on experience with AI tools builds confidence and practical capability. Starting with user-friendly platforms like ChatGPT, Claude, or no-code AI builders allows non-technical professionals to experience AI capabilities before diving into programming.

Industry Knowledge Integration: Combining AI understanding with existing domain expertise creates unique value. Healthcare professionals learning AI applications in medical imaging, educators exploring AI tutoring systems, or financial analysts understanding algorithmic trading leverage their existing knowledge while building new capabilities.

Communication Skill Development: The ability to explain AI concepts to diverse audiences—executives, technical teams, end users—becomes increasingly valuable as organizations navigate AI adoption. This skill particularly benefits professionals from non-technical backgrounds who can serve as translators between business and technical teams.

Ethical AI Understanding: Awareness of bias, fairness, privacy, and other ethical considerations in AI development and deployment is essential for all AI professionals. This knowledge helps professionals make responsible decisions and contributes to organizational discussions about AI governance.

Intermediate Skills (6-12 months)

Advanced Tool Integration: Moving beyond basic AI usage to combining multiple tools, automating workflows, and customizing solutions for specific use cases. This level of proficiency enables professionals to identify and implement AI solutions independently.

Cross-Functional Collaboration: Developing skills for working effectively with diverse teams—data scientists, engineers, business stakeholders—on AI projects. This includes understanding different professional languages and priorities to facilitate successful collaboration.

Performance Measurement: Learning to define success metrics, measure AI system performance, and communicate results to stakeholders. This analytical capability distinguishes professionals who can demonstrate business value from those who simply implement technology.

Project Management: Understanding the unique challenges of AI projects—data requirements, iterative development, uncertainty management—and developing skills for leading these initiatives successfully.

Advanced Skills (12+ months)

Strategic AI Planning: Capability to assess organizational readiness for AI, develop implementation roadmaps, and align AI initiatives with business strategy. This strategic perspective positions professionals for leadership roles.

Team Development and Mentorship: Skills for building AI-capable teams, designing training programs, and supporting others' AI learning journeys. As AI adoption accelerates, organizations increasingly value professionals who can develop internal capability.

Innovation and Future-Oriented Thinking: Ability to identify emerging AI opportunities, evaluate new technologies, and guide organizations through rapidly changing AI landscapes. This forward-thinking capability distinguishes senior AI professionals.

Certification and Education Strategy: Accessible Options for All Backgrounds

Free and Low-Cost Resources

Economic barriers should not prevent AI learning, and numerous high-quality resources address different financial circumstances:

IBM SkillsBuild offers comprehensive AI and data science courses with particular attention to underrepresented communities. Their programs include AI ethics, machine learning fundamentals, and practical application training with certification upon completion.

Google AI for Everyone and Google's Professional Certificate programs provide structured learning paths with financial aid options. Many libraries and community centers provide free access to these programs, removing both cost and technology access barriers.

Coursera Financial Aid makes university-level AI courses accessible to learners regardless of economic circumstances. Partnerships with community colleges and workforce development organizations extend access to these resources.

Open Source Learning Communities like Kaggle Learn, fast.ai, and various GitHub repositories provide free, practical AI education with supportive communities for learners at all levels.

Professional Development with Institutional Support

Employer-Sponsored Training: Many organizations recognize AI skills as strategic necessities and invest in employee development. Professionals should explore internal training opportunities, conference attendance support, and educational reimbursement programs.

Professional Association Scholarships: Organizations like the Association for Computing Machinery (ACM), Institute of Electrical and Electronics Engineers (IEEE), and various diversity-focused groups offer scholarships and grants for AI education.

Government Workforce Development Programs: Federal and state initiatives increasingly support AI training for displaced workers and those seeking career advancement. These programs often combine financial support with job placement assistance.

Community Foundation Support: Local foundations and nonprofit organizations frequently fund education and career development initiatives, particularly for underrepresented groups and economically disadvantaged individuals.

Alternative Credential Recognition

The shift toward skills-based hiring creates opportunities for non-traditional educational paths:

Portfolio-Based Assessment: Many employers now evaluate candidates based on demonstrated capabilities rather than formal credentials. Strong portfolios showcasing real projects and measurable results often carry more weight than degrees.

Skills-Based Evaluation: Technical interviews, practical challenges, and trial projects allow candidates to demonstrate capability regardless of educational background. This trend particularly benefits self-taught professionals and career changers.

Community Project Recognition: Contributions to open-source projects, volunteer work, and community initiatives provide evidence of both technical capability and character. Many hiring managers value these experiences highly.

Peer Validation Systems: Professional networks, online communities, and collaborative projects create peer recognition systems that complement or replace traditional credentialing.

Job Search Optimization: Inclusive Approach to Career Advancement

Resume and Application Enhancement

Skills-Based Resume Format: Emphasizing capabilities and achievements rather than educational pedigree or traditional career progression appeals to employers practicing skills-based hiring. Maya's resume highlighted specific AI implementations and their business impact rather than focusing on her operations background.

Portfolio Integration: Modern resumes should direct readers to comprehensive portfolios demonstrating practical capability. QR codes, LinkedIn integration, and personal websites make portfolios easily accessible to hiring managers.

Cultural Translation: Professionals from diverse backgrounds should translate their experiences into language that resonates with AI employers. Community leadership, volunteer work, and non-traditional experiences often demonstrate valuable skills when framed appropriately.

Multiple Version Development: Different opportunities may require different emphasis—technical roles focus on implementation capability while business roles emphasize strategic thinking and communication skills.

Interview Preparation with Cultural Sensitivity

Technical Competency Demonstration: Even non-technical roles often require demonstrating understanding of AI capabilities and limitations. Preparing to discuss AI concepts in accessible language and provide concrete examples of AI applications shows preparation and genuine interest.

Business Impact Articulation: All AI roles ultimately serve business objectives, so candidates should prepare to discuss how technical capabilities translate to organizational value. Maya's ability to connect route optimization algorithms to customer satisfaction and cost reduction distinguished her from purely technical candidates.

Communication Style Adaptation: Different organizations have varying cultures around formality, collaboration, and decision-making.

Researching company culture and adapting communication style accordingly increases interview success.

Diversity and Inclusion Awareness: Many AI organizations prioritize inclusive hiring and may explore candidates' awareness of bias, ethical considerations, and diverse perspective value. Thoughtful responses to these topics demonstrate cultural fit and values alignment.

Negotiation Strategies with Equity Focus

Market Research: Understanding salary ranges across different geographic areas, company sizes, and experience levels enables informed negotiation. Resources like Glassdoor, PayScale, and industry reports provide valuable benchmarking data.

Value Proposition Development: Candidates should articulate their unique combination of skills, experience, and perspective that creates value for employers. Maya's logistics expertise combined with AI skills made her uniquely valuable for operations leadership roles.

Holistic Package Consideration: Beyond base salary, consider professional development opportunities, flexible work arrangements, equity participation, and other factors that impact long-term career satisfaction and growth.

Long-term Career Development: Discussing growth opportunities, mentorship availability, and skill development support during negotiations demonstrates mutual investment in long-term success.

Addressing Career Advancement Barriers

Systemic Barrier Recognition and Navigation

Bias in Hiring and Promotion: Despite skills-based hiring trends, unconscious bias continues affecting career advancement. Documenting achievements, seeking multiple perspectives on performance, and building diverse professional networks help mitigate these challenges.

Network Access Limitations: Traditional networking often excludes professionals from underrepresented backgrounds. Intentionally building relationships across different professional communities, participating in mentorship programs, and engaging with diversity-focused organizations creates alternative networking pathways.

Geographic and Economic Constraints: Remote work opportunities and online learning resources reduce but don't eliminate geographic barriers. Professionals in areas with limited AI opportunities should leverage virtual networking, online communities, and remote work possibilities.

Educational Credentialism: While decreasing, educational requirements still limit some opportunities. Building strong portfolios, obtaining industry certifications, and emphasizing practical results helps overcome educational barriers.

Community Support and Advocacy

Professional Organization Leadership: Taking active roles in AI professional organizations, particularly those focused on diversity and inclusion, builds visibility while contributing to positive change in the field.

Mentorship Networks: Both receiving and providing mentorship creates powerful professional relationships while contributing to community development. Many successful AI professionals credit mentorship relationships for career acceleration.

Policy Advocacy: Engaging with local government, educational institutions, and professional organizations around AI education access and inclusive hiring practices creates systemic change while building professional reputation.

Cross-Sector Collaboration: AI applications span all industries, creating opportunities for professionals to build bridges between traditional sectors and emerging AI capabilities.

Realistic Career Advancement Expectations

Timeline and Progression Realities

Career advancement in AI requires patience and persistence rather than expecting immediate dramatic changes. Maya's eighteen-month timeline for significant career progression represents a realistic expectation for dedicated professionals making strategic moves.

Skill Development: Building foundational AI literacy typically requires 3-6 months of consistent study and practice. Intermediate proficiency develops over 6-12 months of application and project work. Advanced capability and recognition as an AI expert typically takes 2-3 years of sustained effort and achievement.

Salary Progression: While the 56% average wage premium for AI skills is substantial, individual results vary significantly based on starting point, industry, geographic location, and implementation approach. Professionals typically see 20-40% salary increases within 1-2 years of successful AI skill development and application.

Role Evolution: Many professionals find that AI skills transform their existing roles rather than requiring complete career changes. This evolution often provides more sustainable advancement than dramatic pivots and leverages existing relationships and domain expertise.

Success Variation Factors

Geographic Location: Tech hubs provide more opportunities and higher salaries but also increased competition and cost of living. Professionals in other regions may find different but equally valuable opportunities, particularly as remote work becomes more accepted.

Industry Context: Some industries have embraced AI more rapidly than others, creating variation in opportunity availability and advancement speed. Healthcare, finance, and technology lead adoption, while other sectors offer opportunities for early movers.

Organizational Culture: Companies vary significantly in their AI adoption readiness and support for employee development. Organizations with strong learning cultures and change management capabilities provide better environments for AI career development.

Individual Circumstances: Personal responsibilities, learning styles, available time for skill development, and risk tolerance all influence career advancement timelines and strategies.

Long-term Commitment Requirements

AI career success requires viewing skill development as an ongoing process rather than a one-time achievement. The field evolves rapidly, with new tools, techniques, and applications emerging regularly. Successful AI professionals commit to continuous learning and adaptation.

Community Engagement: Building and maintaining professional relationships within AI communities provides ongoing support, learning opportunities, and career advancement possibilities. These relationships often prove more valuable than individual skill development.

Knowledge Sharing: Teaching others, contributing to open-source projects, and participating in professional discourse builds reputation while reinforcing personal learning. Many successful AI professionals find that their teaching and mentoring activities accelerate their own career advancement.

Conclusion: Your AI-Enabled Future

The artificial intelligence revolution is creating unprecedented opportunities for career advancement while also raising important questions about access, equity, and inclusion. The professionals who will thrive in this transformation are those who approach AI skill development strategically, build inclusive professional networks, and maintain commitment to continuous learning and ethical practice.

Maya's journey illustrates that successful AI career advancement doesn't require abandoning existing expertise or starting from scratch. Instead, it demands thoughtfully combining domain knowledge with AI capabilities, building authentic professional relationships, and demonstrating value through practical application rather than just technical knowledge.

The 56% wage premium for AI skills represents a significant opportunity, but realizing this potential requires understanding the landscape's complexities. Geographic variations, industry differences, and systemic barriers all influence individual outcomes. The most successful professionals navigate these challenges by building diverse networks, developing transferable skills, and positioning themselves as bridges between traditional business practices and emerging AI capabilities.

As we look toward the future, AI career advancement will increasingly reward professionals who combine technical competency with emotional intelligence, cultural awareness, and ethical consciousness. The field needs diverse perspectives and experiences to develop AI systems that serve all communities effectively and equitably.

For professionals considering AI career development, the optimal time to begin is now. The field's rapid evolution creates both urgency and opportunity—those who start building AI literacy today position themselves for the transformative changes ahead. However, success requires patience, strategic thinking, and commitment to both personal growth and community development.

The AI revolution is not just about technology—it's about how we work together to create a future that benefits everyone. Your contribution to this transformation matters, regardless of your background or starting point. By developing AI skills thoughtfully and ethically, building inclusive professional relationships, and maintaining focus on human value creation, you can advance your career while contributing to positive change in the world.

The future belongs to professionals who combine artificial intelligence capabilities with authentic human wisdom. Begin your journey today, but remember that the destination is not individual success alone—it's collective progress toward a more intelligent, equitable, and prosperous society for all.

References

[1] Stanford University, *AI Index Report 2025* (Stanford: Human-Centered AI Institute, 2025), 45-47.

[2] PricewaterhouseCoopers, *The Fearless Future: 2025 Global AI Jobs Barometer* (London: PwC Global, 2025), https://www.pwc.com/gx/en/issues/artificial-intelligence/ai-jobs-barometer.html.

[3] World Economic Forum, *Future of Jobs Report 2025* (Geneva: World Economic Forum, 2025), 12-15.

[4] Glassdoor, "Machine Learning Engineer Salaries," accessed August 20, 2025, https://www.glassdoor.com/Salaries/machine-learning-engineer-salary-SRCH_KO0,25.htm.

[5] Nexford University, "Top 10 Highest Paying Artificial Intelligence (AI) Jobs 2025," accessed August 20, 2025, https://www.nexford.edu/insights/highest-paying-ai-jobs.

[6] DataCamp, "Machine Learning Engineer Salaries 2025: A Comprehensive Guide," July 31, 2024, https://www.datacamp.com/blog/machine-learning-engineer-salaries-in-2023.

[7] Coursera, "Artificial Intelligence Salary: Your Guide to AI Pay in 2025," February 15, 2025, https://www.coursera.org/articles/artificial-intelligence-salary.

[8] IEEE Spectrum, "AI Jobs in 2025: Essential Insights for Software Engineers," April 17, 2025, https://spectrum.ieee.org/ai-jobs-in-2025.

[9] TechTarget, "10 top AI jobs in 2025," accessed August 20, 2025, https://www.techtarget.com/whatis/feature/Top-AI-jobs.

[10] Federal Reserve Bank of Atlanta, "By Degree(s): Measuring Employer Demand for AI Skills by Educational Requirements," Workforce Currents, May 21, 2025, https://www.atlantafed.org/cweo/workforce-currents/2025/05/21/by-degrees-measuring-employer-demand-for-ai-skills-by-educational-requirements.

[11] Course Report, "The 11 Best AI & Machine Learning Bootcamps of 2025," April 10, 2025, https://www.coursereport.com/best-ai-machine-learning-bootcamps.

Chapter 10: Advanced AI Concepts and Trends

Opening Hook: Responsible Innovation Exploration

Dr. Maria Gonzalez adjusted her laptop screen as she led her cross-functional research team through their quarterly assessment of emerging agentic AI capabilities. Around the virtual meeting table were engineers from São Paulo, ethicists from Lagos, policy researchers from Stockholm, and community advocates from Detroit—all carefully evaluating the potential implementation of autonomous AI agents in their urban planning project.

"Before we get excited about what these systems can do," Maria began, "let's systematically examine what they should do, and more importantly, what safeguards we need." The team had spent six months developing a framework for responsible AI agent deployment, consulting with residents from different neighborhoods and ensuring their voice recognition systems worked equally well across linguistic diversity.

Their approach exemplified the measured advancement needed in 2025's AI landscape—one where innovation proceeds hand-in-hand with ethical consideration, community engagement, and realistic expectations about both capabilities and limitations. As Maria's team would discover, the most significant advances in AI weren't just technical breakthroughs, but the frameworks that ensured these powerful tools served diverse communities equitably and sustainably.

Core Learning Objectives

This chapter will guide you to:

- Grasp advanced AI concepts including agentic systems, multimodal intelligence, and quantum computing integration
- Understand key trends shaping 2025-2030 development with realistic timelines

- Prepare for future changes while balancing innovation with responsible implementation
- Develop critical evaluation skills for emerging technologies and their societal implications

Advanced AI Concepts: Beyond the Basics

Agentic AI: The Rise of Autonomous Intelligence

The year 2025 has been proclaimed "the year of agentic AI" across the technology industry, marking a fundamental shift from passive AI tools to proactive, autonomous systems capable of independent decision-making, planning, and task execution.[1] Unlike traditional AI that responds to prompts, agentic AI systems can break down complex problems, research solutions, use tools, and act step-by-step with minimal human oversight.

According to IBM's analysis, 99% of enterprise developers are exploring or developing AI agents, with most organizations recognizing the transformative potential of these systems.[2] However, as IBM researchers note, while the technical groundwork exists, "most organizations aren't agent-ready," highlighting the gap between technological capability and practical implementation readiness.[3]

Key Characteristics of Agentic AI:

1. **Autonomous Task Completion**: These systems can scope out projects, identify necessary tools, and complete complex workflows without continuous human guidance.
2. **Multi-Agent Collaboration**: Modern agentic systems often work in teams, with specialized agents handling different aspects of a task while coordinating toward shared objectives.
3. **Real-World Integration**: Unlike purely digital AI, agentic systems can be embedded in physical robots and IoT devices, enabling intelligent interaction with the physical world.
4. **Contextual Decision-Making**: These systems maintain context across extended interactions and adapt their strategies based on changing circumstances.

McKinsey's research demonstrates the practical impact of agentic approaches, with organizations reporting over 50% reductions in time and effort when implementing AI agent teams for software development tasks.[4] In one detailed case study, a technology company deployed agent squads that could retroactively document legacy applications, write new code, review other agents' work, and integrate features through testing—all while human supervisors provided guidance and quality oversight.

Critical Implementation Considerations:

The rapid advancement of agentic AI brings significant governance challenges. As these systems become more autonomous, questions of accountability, control, and oversight become paramount. Gartner predicts that by 2028, at least 33% of enterprise software will depend on agentic AI, but current failure rates remain high at 85%, primarily due to inadequate organizational preparation rather than technical limitations.[5]

Multimodal AI: Converging Intelligence Across Data Types

The evolution from single-modality AI systems to truly integrated multimodal intelligence represents one of 2025's most significant technical advances. Gartner projects that by 2027, 40% of generative AI solutions will be multimodal (text, image, audio, video), compared to only 1% in 2023.[6]

Modern multimodal systems don't simply process different data types independently; they reason across modalities, understanding relationships between visual, auditory, and textual information in ways that mirror human cognition. This integration enables applications previously thought impossible, from AI assistants that can "see" charts in presentation slides while "hearing" CEO remarks in earnings calls, to diagnostic systems that combine medical imaging with patient records and clinical notes.

Breakthrough Applications:

Amazon's development of multimodal AI assistants demonstrates the practical potential of this technology. Their system using Amazon Nova Pro as a central orchestrator can analyze earnings calls (audio), presentation slides (images), and financial data feeds simultaneously, providing comprehensive financial analysis that would traditionally require multiple specialized tools and human analysts.[7]

The technical architecture underlying such systems involves sophisticated data processing pipelines. Amazon Bedrock Data Automation, for example, can extract text, transcribe audio and video, and convert PowerPoint slides into searchable image formats, creating a unified knowledge base that enables cross-modal reasoning.[8]

Cultural and Accessibility Implications:

Multimodal AI systems offer significant promise for accessibility improvement. Voice interfaces combined with visual processing can assist users with visual impairments, while text-to-speech integration helps those with hearing difficulties. However, these systems also raise concerns about cultural bias, as training data often reflects dominant cultural perspectives and may not adequately represent diverse global communities.

Quantum AI Integration: The Next Computational Frontier

While quantum computing remains in early stages, 2025 has seen significant progress toward practical quantum-AI integration. NVIDIA CEO Jensen Huang recently announced that quantum computing has reached an "inflection point," suggesting we're "within reach of being able to apply quantum classical computing in areas that can solve some interesting problems in the coming years."[9]

Current Developments:

Research teams have made notable progress in quantum multimodal learning. A breakthrough study published for the 2025 International Conference on Acoustics, Speech, and Signal Processing introduced the Quantum Multimodal Contrastive Learning Framework (QMCL), successfully applied to zero-shot classification tasks involving EEG signals and images.[10] This work represents the first application of quantum algorithms to one of the largest EEG-image datasets, setting new benchmarks for future quantum contrastive learning research.

The researchers developed four hybrid quantum-classical time-series encoders specifically designed for multimodal learning, demonstrating that quantum encoders can effectively capture intricate patterns within complex data streams. While quantum methods have not yet surpassed traditional approaches, the results suggest significant potential for enhanced learning across different data modalities.[11]

Practical Timeline and Limitations:

Despite encouraging research, practical quantum AI applications remain years away from widespread deployment. Current quantum systems require extremely controlled environments and have limited computational stability. However, companies like Oxford Ionics, recognized in the World Economic Forum's 2025 Technology Pioneers program, are building high-performance quantum computers using trapped-ion technology that may accelerate practical applications.[12]

The intersection of quantum computing and AI represents a long-term trend rather than immediate disruption. Researchers predict that quantum AI's first practical applications will likely emerge in specialized domains like drug discovery, financial modeling, and optimization problems where quantum advantages can justify the significant infrastructure requirements.

Edge AI and Distributed Intelligence

The push toward more sustainable and efficient AI deployment has accelerated the development of edge computing solutions that process AI workloads locally rather than in centralized cloud data centers. This shift addresses both environmental concerns and practical limitations of cloud-dependent AI systems.

Environmental Sustainability Benefits:

Edge AI processing can reduce data traffic by 60-90%, significantly impacting both CO2 footprint and operational costs.[13] By processing data where it's generated rather than transmitting it to distant cloud servers, edge systems eliminate substantial energy consumption associated with data transmission and reduce dependence on large, power-hungry data centers.

Research from MIT and industry partners demonstrates that edge AI devices often operate more efficiently than cloud alternatives due to their optimization for specific tasks and local processing requirements.[14] This efficiency gain is particularly important given that AI systems now require massive computational resources—with training frontier AI models consuming energy equivalent to the lifetime emissions of hundreds of cars.[15]

Real-World Applications:

Companies like Dryad Network exemplify sustainable edge AI implementation, using solar-powered edge devices equipped with AI algorithms to detect wildfires. By processing sensor data locally and only transmitting alerts when necessary, they minimize both environmental impact and response times.[16]

Similarly, Amazon Go stores demonstrate edge AI's commercial potential, using AI-powered cameras and sensors to create cashier-less shopping experiences while processing customer behavior data locally rather than sending continuous video streams to cloud servers.[17]

2025-2030 Trends Analysis: Balanced Perspective

Technological Development Trajectories

The AI landscape of 2025-2030 will be shaped by five major technological innovations: enhanced reasoning capabilities, agentic AI proliferation, multimodal integration, improved hardware efficiency, and increased transparency requirements.[18]

Enhanced Intelligence and Reasoning:

McKinsey's analysis reveals that AI models have dramatically improved their reasoning capabilities within just one year. Performance on challenging benchmarks like MMMU, GPQA, and SWE-bench increased by 18.8, 48.9, and 67.3 percentage points respectively between 2023 and 2024.[19] Models like OpenAI's o1 now demonstrate step-by-step reasoning similar to human problem-solving approaches, with significant implications for fields requiring complex analysis like science, law, and medicine.

However, these advances come with important caveats. The rapid improvement in benchmark performance doesn't necessarily translate to proportional real-world capability gains, and many challenges around reliability, bias, and contextual understanding remain unresolved.

Hardware Innovation and Accessibility:

A significant trend toward democratization is emerging through improved hardware efficiency and reduced costs. Annual cost declines of 30% and energy efficiency improvements of 40% are making advanced AI capabilities more accessible to smaller organizations and developing regions.[20] Additionally, the performance gap between open-weight models and proprietary closed models has narrowed from 8% to just 1.7% on some benchmarks, reducing barriers to AI adoption.[21]

Infrastructure Scaling Challenges:

Despite efficiency improvements, the overall demand for AI computing is growing so rapidly that total energy consumption continues to increase. Data centers supporting AI workloads are projected to require electricity equivalent to powering 6 million homes by 2030 in Northern Virginia alone.[22] This exponential growth in energy demand has led to delays in coal plant decommissioning and intensified focus on renewable energy sources.

Societal Impact Assessment: Jobs, Education, and Economic Transformation

Employment Transformation Patterns:

The impact of AI on employment presents a nuanced picture requiring careful analysis beyond simple replacement narratives. While McKinsey projects that up to 40% of work could be automated within the next 20 years, the reality involves complex job transformation rather than wholesale elimination.[23]

Recent data indicates that AI adoption is creating a net positive impact on employment when viewed comprehensively. By 2030, projections suggest 170 million new jobs will be created globally, even as approximately 92 million face displacement.[24] The World Economic Forum's 2025 Future of Jobs report suggests AI might eliminate 85 million jobs while creating 97 million new ones by 2025, resulting in a net gain of 12 million positions.[25]

Critical to understanding these transitions is recognizing that new roles will require different skill sets. By 2028, 60% of global companies will require employees to have basic AI skills to remain competitive, making workforce upskilling a business necessity rather than an option.[26]

Educational System Adaptation:

The integration of AI into educational systems remains uneven and challenging. Current data reveals significant gaps in preparation: 87% of educators report receiving no AI training as part of professional development, while only 10% consider teaching AI skills a top priority.[27] Despite this, 54% of parents believe AI could positively impact their children's education, though 80% express concerns about potential harmful effects.[28]

These statistics highlight the urgent need for systematic educational reform that addresses both opportunities and risks associated with AI integration in learning environments.

Economic Disruption and Opportunity:

The economic implications of AI adoption extend far beyond individual companies or sectors. By 2030, AI is estimated to contribute between $17.1 trillion and $25.6 trillion to global GDP, with North America and China positioned as the primary beneficiaries.[29] AI could add 14.8% to U.S. GDP and 26.1% to China's GDP by 2030, representing unprecedented economic transformation.[30]

However, these benefits won't be evenly distributed geographically or demographically. The concentration of AI development in specific regions and among large technology companies raises concerns about increased economic inequality if benefits aren't shared more broadly.

Global Development and Regulatory Landscape

Regulatory Fragmentation and Harmonization Challenges:

The global AI regulation landscape in 2025 is characterized by fragmentation and rapid evolution, with early optimism about international cooperation giving way to more complex realities.[31] The European Union's AI Act, which became effective in August 2025, places new obligations on companies deploying high-risk AI systems, with penalties reaching up to €35 million or 7% of global turnover.[32]

In the United States, federal agencies introduced 59 AI-related regulations in 2024—more than double the number in 2023—spanning multiple agencies and jurisdictions.[33] This regulatory expansion reflects growing governmental attention to AI governance, but also creates compliance challenges for organizations operating across multiple jurisdictions.

International Investment and Collaboration:

Government investment in AI development has accelerated dramatically. Canada pledged $2.4 billion, China launched a $47.5 billion semiconductor fund, France committed €109 billion, India pledged $1.25 billion, and Saudi Arabia's Project Transcendence represents a $100 billion initiative.[34] These massive investments demonstrate the strategic importance governments place on AI leadership but also highlight the potential for international competition over cooperation.

The United Nations' declaration of 2025 as the International Year of Quantum Science and Technology, backed by approximately 300 organizations, represents one area where international collaboration continues to advance.[35] This initiative aims to commemorate the centenary of quantum mechanics while promoting collaborative research and development.

Staying Informed and Prepared: Practical Strategies

Information Source Diversification and Critical Evaluation

Successfully navigating the rapidly evolving AI landscape requires systematic approaches to information gathering and evaluation. The challenge lies not in finding information about AI trends, but in filtering reliable insights from the overwhelming volume of claims, predictions, and marketing materials.

Academic and Research Sources:

Stanford University's AI Index Report has emerged as one of the most authoritative sources for comprehensive, data-driven analysis of AI's technical progress, economic influence, and societal impact.[36] The 400+ page 2025 report provides rigorous analysis across multiple dimensions including R&D progress, technical performance benchmarks, economic impacts, policy developments, and public opinion tracking.

Similarly, research institutions like MIT's Computer Science and Artificial Intelligence Laboratory (CSAIL) and the Stanford Institute for Human-Centered Artificial Intelligence (HAI) publish regular research findings that provide balanced perspectives on both AI capabilities and limitations.

Industry Analysis and Think Tank Reports:

Management consulting firms like McKinsey, Deloitte, and PwC provide valuable industry-focused analysis that bridges technical developments with business applications. Their reports often include survey data from thousands of organizations, providing insights into actual adoption patterns rather than just theoretical potential.

Gartner's annual Hype Cycle for Artificial Intelligence offers particularly valuable perspective on which technologies are approaching practical maturity versus those still in experimental phases.[37] Understanding these maturity curves helps avoid the common pitfall of overestimating short-term impact while underestimating long-term transformation.

Regulatory and Policy Tracking:

Monitoring policy developments requires attention to multiple governmental and international sources. The OECD AI Policy Observatory provides comprehensive tracking of AI governance initiatives across member countries, while the EU's AI Act implementation documents offer detailed guidance for compliance requirements.

National AI strategies from major economies—including the U.S. National AI Initiative, China's AI development plans, and the UK's AI White Paper—provide insights into how different governments are approaching AI governance and investment priorities.

Critical Evaluation Framework for Emerging Claims

The rapid pace of AI development creates an environment where exaggerated claims and premature announcements can significantly distort understanding of actual progress and limitations.

Source Credibility Assessment:

Reliable AI information typically comes from organizations with transparent methodologies, peer review processes, and diverse expert involvement. Academic papers published in reputable journals undergo rigorous peer review, while corporate research should ideally include independent validation or replication.

Be particularly cautious of claims that lack specific metrics, refuse to acknowledge limitations, or come from organizations with clear financial incentives to promote particular technologies or approaches.

Timeline Realism and Historical Context:

AI predictions often suffer from both excessive optimism about near-term capabilities and underestimation of long-term transformation. Historical analysis reveals that most AI breakthroughs take significantly longer to achieve practical deployment than initially predicted, but their ultimate impact often exceeds early estimates.

For perspective, consider that today's large language models like GPT-4 represent the culmination of decades of research in neural networks, natural language processing, and computational infrastructure. Most current "breakthrough" technologies similarly build on years or decades of foundational research.

Verification Through Multiple Independent Sources:

Significant AI developments should be corroborated across multiple independent sources before accepting claims about capabilities or implications. Academic publications, industry analysis, and government assessments often provide different perspectives on the same developments, helping identify areas of consensus versus ongoing debate.

Personal Adaptation Strategy Development

Building resilience for AI-driven change requires both specific skill development and broader adaptive capacity that can respond to unpredictable technological evolution.

Skill Development with Future Orientation:

Rather than focusing exclusively on today's AI tools, develop meta-skills that transfer across technological changes. These include critical thinking about automated systems, understanding of data quality and bias issues, and ability to collaborate effectively with AI-augmented workflows.

Communication skills become increasingly valuable as organizations need people who can translate between technical AI capabilities and practical business applications, ethical implications, and user needs.

Network Building Across AI Communities:

Engagement with diverse AI communities provides early insights into emerging trends while building relationships that support professional adaptation. This includes technical communities like machine learning conferences and journals, business-focused groups like industry AI adoption forums, and ethics-centered organizations addressing responsible AI development.

International and interdisciplinary networks are particularly valuable, as they provide perspectives on how AI developments might unfold differently across various cultural, economic, and regulatory contexts.

Continuous Learning Infrastructure:

Establish systematic approaches to ongoing education that can adapt as the field evolves. This might include regular participation in online courses, attendance at industry conferences, subscription to research publications, and engagement with AI-focused communities of practice.

Importantly, build learning approaches that accommodate different life circumstances and constraints. Not everyone has access to expensive training programs or extensive time for study, but effective learning can occur through shorter, more frequent engagement with high-quality materials and communities.

Future Risks and Benefits: Comprehensive Analysis

Opportunity Assessment and Realistic Potential

Scientific Research Acceleration:

AI's impact on scientific discovery is already demonstrating measurable results across multiple domains. Microsoft Research reports that AI tools are having "measurable impact on the throughput of the people and institutions who are working on these huge problems, such as designing sustainable materials and accelerating development of life-saving drugs."[38]

In pharmaceutical research, AI has already helped reduce drug discovery timelines by over 50% in many cases.[39] Materials science represents another promising area, with Meta releasing massive datasets and models that could help scientists discover new materials much faster, while projects like

LeMaterial aim to standardize and accelerate materials research through AI-powered analysis.[40]

Productivity and Economic Benefits:

Organizations adopting AI are experiencing significant productivity improvements when implemented thoughtfully. G2 data reveals that 83% of organizations implementing AI platforms saw positive ROI within just three months in 2024.[41] Businesses adopting AI are projected to increase profitability by 38% in 2025, with applications ranging from automating repetitive customer support tasks to leveraging predictive analytics in marketing and sales.[42]

The potential for positive economic transformation is substantial. AI could boost global productivity by 0.5% to 3.4% by 2040, though the wide range reflects uncertainty about implementation pace and effectiveness.[43] The variation depends heavily on how early and comprehensively organizations adopt AI across their operations.

Environmental Solutions and Sustainability:

Despite concerns about AI's environmental impact, the technology also offers significant potential for environmental benefits when applied strategically. A 2025 study revealed that AI could reduce global emissions annually by 3.2 to 5.4 billion tonnes of carbon-dioxide-equivalent by 2035 if used wisely to design and implement policies, improve insights, and monitor environmental systems.[44]

Specific applications include AI-powered smart grids that better integrate renewable energy sources, precision agriculture that reduces resource waste, and climate modeling that improves understanding of environmental changes and optimal intervention strategies.

Risk Evaluation and Mitigation Strategies

Job Displacement and Economic Disruption:

While AI may create more jobs than it eliminates in the long term, the transition period presents significant challenges for workers whose roles become automated. The displacement of 85 million jobs by 2025, even if offset by 97 million new positions, represents massive disruption for affected individuals and communities.[45]

Successful navigation of this transition requires proactive retraining programs, social safety nets, and policies that ensure AI benefits are shared broadly rather than concentrated among technology owners. Organizations implementing AI bear responsibility for supporting workforce transitions rather than simply optimizing for efficiency.

Bias Amplification and Inequality:

AI systems can perpetuate and amplify existing social biases if not carefully designed and monitored. This is particularly concerning as AI increasingly influences decisions about employment, credit, healthcare, and criminal justice. The challenge is compounded by the fact that bias can be subtle and difficult to detect without systematic analysis.

Mitigation requires diverse development teams, inclusive data collection, ongoing monitoring for discriminatory outcomes, and accountability mechanisms that address bias when identified. This is not a one-time fix but an ongoing responsibility that requires continuous attention and resources.

Environmental Impact and Resource Consumption:

Despite efficiency improvements, AI's environmental impact continues growing due to massive scale increases. Training large AI models now produces carbon emissions equivalent to hundreds of round-trip flights or the lifetime emissions of multiple cars.[46] A single conversation with ChatGPT consumes approximately half a liter of fresh water for cooling the data centers that power the system.[47]

Addressing these environmental costs requires industry-wide commitment to renewable energy, more efficient algorithms, and conscious decisions about when AI deployment provides sufficient benefits to justify environmental costs.

Democratic Governance and Concentration of Power:

The concentration of AI development among a small number of large technology companies raises concerns about democratic oversight and equitable access to AI benefits. As AI becomes more influential in economic and social systems, the decisions made by these companies increasingly affect broader society.

Solutions include regulatory frameworks that ensure transparency and accountability, support for diverse AI development initiatives, and governance structures that include broader stakeholder representation in AI development decisions.

Inequality and Access Considerations

Digital Divide and AI Access:

The benefits of AI advancement risk being concentrated among those who already have access to advanced technology and education. Rural communities, developing countries, and economically disadvantaged populations may be left behind if AI deployment follows existing patterns of technological adoption.

Addressing this requires intentional efforts to ensure AI benefits reach underserved communities. This includes developing AI applications that work with limited technological infrastructure, providing training and support for AI adoption, and creating economic models that make AI tools accessible regardless of ability to pay.

Cultural Preservation and Representation:

AI systems trained primarily on data from dominant cultures may not adequately serve diverse global communities. Language processing systems may work poorly for minority languages, image recognition may fail for underrepresented populations, and recommendation systems may reinforce cultural biases.

Ensuring AI serves diverse communities requires including diverse perspectives in AI development, creating training datasets that represent global diversity, and ongoing evaluation of AI system performance across different cultural contexts.

Educational and Economic Opportunity:

As AI skills become increasingly important for employment, unequal access to AI education could exacerbate existing inequalities. Students in well-funded schools may gain AI literacy while others are left behind, creating new forms of educational and economic disadvantage.

Mitigation requires ensuring AI education is available across different educational contexts, supporting teachers with AI training and resources, and creating multiple pathways for AI skill development that don't depend solely on traditional educational institutions.

Practical Trend Analysis Exercise

Research Methodology Framework

To develop accurate understanding of AI trends while avoiding hype and misinformation, systematic research approaches are essential. This exercise provides a structured framework for analyzing emerging AI developments.

Trend Identification Process:

Begin by identifying potential trends through multiple sources: academic publications, industry reports, government policy documents, and diverse expert commentary. Look for convergent themes across different types of sources rather than relying on single announcements or claims.

Focus on developments that have measurable indicators of progress—such as published research results, working demonstrations, or adoption statistics—rather than purely theoretical discussions or marketing claims.

Impact Assessment Methodology:

For each identified trend, analyze potential impacts across multiple dimensions:

1. **Technical Feasibility**: What evidence exists that the technology can actually deliver claimed capabilities? Are there independent replications of key results?
2. **Economic Implications**: Who would benefit from this development? What costs would be involved in implementation? How might this affect different types of organizations and workers?
3. **Social Consequences**: How might this technology affect different communities? What are potential positive and negative impacts on social equity, privacy, and democratic governance?
4. **Timeline Realism**: Based on historical patterns of technological development, what is a realistic timeline for widespread adoption? What infrastructure, regulation, or social changes would be required?
5. **Geographic Variation**: How might this technology develop

differently in various countries or regions due to different regulatory environments, cultural contexts, or economic conditions?

Example Analysis: Agentic AI Development

Using agentic AI as an example, a comprehensive trend analysis might proceed as follows:

Technical Evidence: Multiple major technology companies have demonstrated working AI agent systems. IBM reports 99% of enterprise developers are exploring agent development, while McKinsey documents specific case studies showing 50%+ efficiency improvements in software development tasks.

Economic Assessment: Organizations implementing agentic AI report significant productivity gains, but also note high failure rates (85%) due to organizational readiness issues rather than technical limitations. Implementation requires substantial investment in infrastructure and training.

Social Implications: Agentic AI could democratize access to sophisticated analysis and task completion, but also raises questions about job displacement and accountability for autonomous decisions. Different communities may have varying access to these tools.

Realistic Timeline: While basic agent capabilities exist today, widespread adoption likely requires 3-5 years for organizational infrastructure development and regulatory clarification.

Risk Factors: Key risks include over-reliance on autonomous systems, difficulties in maintaining human oversight, and potential for agents to perpetuate or amplify existing biases in decision-making.

Application Brainstorming Framework

Once you've analyzed a trend, consider potential applications relevant to your context and goals.

Current Problem Identification:

Start by identifying real problems you or your organization face that might benefit from emerging AI capabilities. Focus on problems where human effort is currently limited by time, scale, or complexity rather than seeking AI solutions for their own sake.

Consider problems that affect diverse stakeholder groups and evaluate whether AI applications might help or harm different communities.

Solution Feasibility Evaluation:

For each potential application, assess:

- **Technical Requirements**: What AI capabilities would be needed? Are these available today or projected to be available on a realistic timeline?
- **Resource Constraints**: What would implementation cost in terms of technology, training, and ongoing maintenance? Do you have access to necessary resources?
- **Organizational Readiness**: Does your organization have the infrastructure, skills, and governance structures needed to implement AI solutions responsibly?
- **Stakeholder Impact**: How would implementation affect different groups? What safeguards would be needed to prevent negative consequences?

Implementation Strategy Development:

Develop implementation approaches that:

1. Start with pilot programs to test assumptions and learn from experience
2. Include diverse stakeholders in planning and evaluation
3. Establish clear metrics for success that go beyond simple efficiency measures
4. Plan for ongoing monitoring and adjustment as technology and context evolve
5. Include contingency plans for addressing problems or unexpected consequences

Risk Assessment and Mitigation:

For each potential application, systematically identify risks including:

- **Technical Risks**: What could go wrong with the AI system itself?
- **Implementation Risks**: What organizational or process problems might arise?
- **Social Risks**: How might the application affect different communities or stakeholder groups?
- **Long-term Risks**: What are potential unintended consequences over time?

Develop specific mitigation strategies for each identified risk category.

Case Study: Responsible AI Innovation in Practice

Technology Company's Systematic Approach to Emerging AI Capability Development

A leading technology company exemplifies how organizations can responsibly develop and deploy emerging AI capabilities while maintaining ethical standards and community engagement. Their approach to implementing agentic AI systems demonstrates the systematic methodology necessary for successful innovation in this rapidly evolving field.

Community Consultation and Stakeholder Engagement:

Rather than developing AI agents in isolation, the company established a multi-stakeholder advisory process that included representatives from customer organizations, academic researchers specializing in AI ethics, community advocates from different demographic groups, and regulatory affairs specialists.

This advisory group met monthly throughout the development process, reviewing technical progress, assessing potential impacts, and providing guidance on implementation strategies. Importantly, the consultation process included compensation for community representatives and was structured to accommodate different communication styles and accessibility needs.

Safety Testing and Bias Mitigation:

The development process incorporated extensive testing phases designed to identify potential biases and failure modes before deployment. Testing included:

1. **Diverse User Group Participation**: Beta testing involved users from different geographic regions, cultural backgrounds, and technical skill levels to ensure the system performed equitably across diverse contexts.
2. **Adversarial Testing**: Systematic attempts to identify failure modes, bias amplification, and potential misuse scenarios.
3. **Stress Testing**: Evaluation of system performance under high load, unusual inputs, and edge cases that might not occur during normal operation.
4. **Cross-Cultural Validation**: Testing with users speaking different languages and from different cultural contexts to ensure the system didn't privilege particular linguistic or cultural approaches.

Gradual Deployment with Monitoring:

Rather than launching the agentic AI system broadly, the company implemented a phased deployment approach:

- **Limited Pilot Phase** (3 months): Small group of carefully selected users with extensive monitoring and feedback collection
- **Expanded Testing** (6 months): Broader user base with continued monitoring and regular system adjustments
- **Controlled Rollout** (12 months): Gradual expansion with ongoing performance monitoring and rapid response capability for addressing problems
- **Full Deployment**: Only after comprehensive evaluation and refinement based on pilot phases

Rapid Response Capability:

The company established systems for quickly identifying and addressing problems that emerged during deployment. This included automated monitoring for bias indicators, user feedback channels with human review, and the technical capability to quickly adjust or disable system features if problems were identified.

Impact Assessment and Course Correction:

Throughout the development and deployment process, the company conducted regular impact assessments that evaluated:

- **Performance Equity**: Whether the system worked equally well for different user groups
- **Economic Effects**: How the system affected different types of workers and organizations
- **Social Consequences**: Broader impacts on communities and social systems
- **Environmental Impact**: Energy consumption and carbon footprint considerations

When assessment identified problems, the company implemented systematic course corrections that included technical modifications, additional user training, and in some cases, temporary restrictions on system capabilities until issues could be resolved.

Lessons Learned and Knowledge Sharing:

The company documented lessons learned throughout the process and shared findings with industry peers, academic researchers, and policy makers. This included both successes and failures, contributing to broader understanding of responsible AI development practices.

Key insights included the critical importance of diverse stakeholder engagement from the beginning of development, the value of gradual deployment for identifying and addressing problems, and the need for ongoing monitoring rather than treating deployment as a one-time event.

Global AI Development Perspectives

International Collaboration Opportunities

Despite geopolitical tensions, significant opportunities exist for international cooperation in AI development that can benefit all participants while addressing shared challenges.

Research Partnership Development:

Academic and research collaborations continue to thrive across international boundaries, particularly in areas like AI safety, bias mitigation, and environmental impact reduction where all countries share common interests.

The United Nations' designation of 2025 as the International Year of Quantum Science and Technology demonstrates how international cooperation can advance beneficial research while sharing costs and expertise across multiple countries.[48] Similar collaborative frameworks could be developed for AI research in areas like climate change mitigation, pandemic response, and sustainable development.

Standards Setting and Governance:

International standards organizations are working to develop common frameworks for AI safety, testing, and evaluation that can reduce fragmentation while maintaining cultural sensitivity and local adaptation capabilities.

The OECD AI Principles, adopted by over 40 countries, provide a foundation for shared governance approaches that respect different national contexts while promoting responsible AI development.[49] Expanding such frameworks to include more countries and stakeholder groups could help ensure AI benefits are shared more broadly.

Knowledge Sharing and Capacity Building:

Developed countries with advanced AI capabilities have opportunities to support capacity building in developing regions through technology transfer, educational partnerships, and collaborative research programs.

Such partnerships benefit all participants by expanding the diversity of perspectives in AI development, creating larger markets for AI applications, and ensuring that AI solutions address global rather than just developed-country challenges.

Competition and Cooperation Balance

Innovation Incentive Maintenance:

Balancing competition and cooperation requires maintaining incentives for innovation while preventing destructive competition that could compromise safety or exacerbate global inequalities.

Open-source AI development provides one model for how competitive advantage can coexist with knowledge sharing. Companies can compete on implementation, customization, and integration while collaborating on foundational research and safety standards.

Security and Privacy Protection:

International cooperation in AI development must address legitimate security concerns while avoiding over-broad restrictions that impede beneficial collaboration.

This requires sophisticated approaches that distinguish between AI research and applications that pose genuine security risks versus those that provide global benefits. International frameworks for such distinctions are still developing but are essential for maximizing AI's positive potential.

Economic Benefit Distribution:

Ensuring that AI development benefits are shared equitably across countries requires intentional policies and frameworks rather than relying on market forces alone.

This might include international agreements on AI technology sharing, support for developing country AI capabilities, and governance structures that include diverse global perspectives in AI development decisions.

Common Future Preparation Pitfalls

Technology Hype Susceptibility and Critical Evaluation

One of the most significant pitfalls in AI trend analysis is succumbing to technology hype without maintaining critical evaluation skills. The rapid pace of AI development creates an environment where exaggerated claims can easily be mistaken for genuine breakthroughs.

Over-Reliance on Vendor Claims:

Technology companies have strong incentives to present their developments in the most favorable light, often emphasizing potential benefits while downplaying limitations or implementation challenges. Critical evaluation requires seeking independent verification of claims and understanding the difference between demonstrated capabilities and marketing projections.

For example, while agentic AI systems show genuine promise, the 85% failure rate in enterprise implementations suggests that organizational and practical challenges often exceed technical capabilities.[50] Understanding such nuances prevents over-investment in solutions that aren't yet ready for broad deployment.

Benchmark Performance vs. Real-World Application:

AI research often focuses on benchmark performance—standardized tests that allow comparison between different systems. However, strong benchmark performance doesn't always translate to practical utility in real-world applications.

The dramatic improvements in AI benchmark scores between 2023 and 2024 are genuinely impressive, but implementing these capabilities in actual business or social contexts often reveals additional challenges around reliability, cost, integration complexity, and unintended consequences.[51]

Timeline Optimism and Implementation Realism:

AI predictions consistently suffer from overestimating short-term progress while underestimating long-term transformation. Most AI technologies take significantly longer to achieve practical deployment than initially predicted, but their ultimate impact often exceeds early estimates.

Current quantum AI research exemplifies this pattern—while quantum computing has reached an "inflection point," practical applications remain years away despite significant theoretical advances.[52] Understanding these patterns helps develop more realistic expectations and planning horizons.

Narrow Specialization vs. Adaptability

Over-Focus on Current Tools:

Another common pitfall involves becoming too focused on today's specific AI tools rather than developing broader capabilities that can adapt as technology evolves. While expertise with current tools is valuable, the rapid pace of AI development means today's leading platforms may be replaced or dramatically changed within years.

More sustainable approaches focus on developing meta-skills like critical thinking about automated systems, understanding of data quality and bias issues, and ability to collaborate effectively with AI-augmented workflows regardless of specific tools.

Technical Skills vs. Human Capabilities:

Organizations and individuals sometimes assume that AI advancement primarily requires technical skills while neglecting human capabilities that become more valuable as AI handles routine tasks.

Research suggests that the most successful AI implementations combine technical capabilities with strong human skills in areas like ethical reasoning, cultural sensitivity, stakeholder communication, and creative problem-solving.[53] These human capabilities become more rather than less important as AI systems become more powerful.

Individual vs. Systems Thinking:

Focusing solely on individual AI skills while ignoring broader systems and community impacts represents another significant pitfall. Successful AI implementation increasingly requires understanding of how AI systems interact with organizational culture, social structures, regulatory environments, and community needs.

This systems perspective is particularly important for avoiding unintended consequences and ensuring that AI implementations benefit diverse stakeholder groups rather than just technology adopters.

Short-Term Thinking and Sustainability

Resource Allocation and Environmental Impact:

The excitement about AI capabilities can lead to inadequate attention to environmental and resource costs. Current AI development trajectories show rapidly increasing energy consumption and carbon emissions despite efficiency improvements in individual systems.[54]

Sustainable AI development requires balancing technological advancement with environmental responsibility, including consideration of when AI applications provide sufficient benefits to justify their environmental costs.

Social Impact and Inequality Considerations:

Short-term focus on AI capabilities can obscure longer-term social impacts, particularly effects on employment, economic inequality, and community well-being.

While AI may create more jobs than it eliminates overall, the transition period involves significant disruption for affected workers and communities. Responsible AI development requires planning for these transitions rather than assuming market forces will automatically produce beneficial outcomes.

Democratic Participation and Governance:

Technical AI development often proceeds faster than the development of governance structures and democratic participation mechanisms. This creates risks that AI systems become too powerful or pervasive before society has developed adequate oversight and accountability mechanisms.

Avoiding this pitfall requires proactive attention to governance, stakeholder engagement, and democratic participation in AI development decisions rather than treating these as afterthoughts to technical development.

Key Takeaways: Building Understanding While Maintaining Balance

Advanced Concepts Require Strong Foundations

The most important insight from exploring advanced AI concepts is that sophisticated applications require solid understanding of AI fundamentals, ethical considerations, and practical implementation challenges. Agentic AI, multimodal intelligence, and quantum computing integration all build upon foundational knowledge of machine learning, data science, and responsible AI practices.

Organizations and individuals who rush toward advanced applications without adequate foundational understanding often encounter implementation failures, bias amplification, or unintended consequences that could be avoided through more systematic preparation.

Trend Evolution and Adaptation Speed

AI trends evolve much more rapidly than most technology sectors, requiring different approaches to planning and adaptation. The dramatic improvements in AI capabilities between 2023 and 2024 demonstrate that assumptions about AI limitations can become outdated within months rather than years.

However, this rapid technical evolution often contrasts with slower organizational, regulatory, and social adaptation. The most successful AI implementations balance technological possibility with realistic assessment of implementation capacity and social readiness.

Critical Thinking as Core Competency

As AI capabilities advance and AI-generated content becomes more prevalent, critical thinking skills become increasingly valuable. The ability to evaluate claims, verify sources, understand limitations, and recognize bias becomes essential for navigating an environment where AI can generate convincing but potentially inaccurate information.

This includes developing meta-cognitive skills—thinking about thinking—that help distinguish between human and AI-generated analysis and maintain appropriate skepticism about automated recommendations or conclusions.

Balance Between Excitement and Realism

Maintaining appropriate balance between enthusiasm for AI potential and realistic assessment of current limitations is crucial for successful AI engagement. Over-excitement leads to poor decision-making and wasted resources, while excessive skepticism prevents beneficial adoption of genuinely useful capabilities.

The most effective approach involves systematic evaluation of specific AI applications for specific contexts rather than broad judgments about AI in general. Different AI applications have different maturity levels, implementation requirements, and potential benefits or risks.

Community and Social Responsibility

Perhaps most importantly, advanced AI development requires viewing technology as embedded within social systems rather than as purely technical challenges. The most successful AI implementations consider impacts on diverse communities, include stakeholder voices in development processes, and prioritize social benefit alongside technical performance.

This perspective becomes more rather than less important as AI systems become more powerful and autonomous. Advanced AI capabilities require advanced responsibility and governance to ensure benefits are shared broadly and risks are managed effectively.

Action Steps: Building Your AI Future Strategy

Follow Diverse AI News Sources and Analysis

Establish systematic approaches to staying informed about AI developments that include multiple perspectives and maintain critical evaluation standards.

Primary Source Development:

Subscribe to authoritative research publications like Stanford's AI Index Report, MIT Technology Review's AI coverage, and peer-reviewed journals like Nature Machine Intelligence. These sources provide rigorous analysis with transparent methodologies and peer review processes.

Include international perspectives by following AI development coverage from different countries and regions. This provides insight into how AI trends may evolve differently in various cultural, economic, and regulatory contexts.

Balance technical sources with social science and policy analysis from organizations like the Partnership on AI, AI Now Institute, and Algorithmic Justice League to understand broader implications of technical developments.

Information Processing Systems:

Develop systematic approaches to information processing that help distinguish reliable insights from speculation or marketing claims. This might include maintaining research notes, tracking prediction accuracy over time, and regularly reviewing assumptions about AI trends.

Create information sharing relationships with colleagues, communities, or professional networks that provide diverse perspectives and help verify or challenge your understanding of AI developments.

Analyze Current Trends Using Systematic Frameworks

Select one significant AI trend relevant to your interests or professional context and conduct comprehensive analysis using the frameworks provided in this chapter.

Comprehensive Trend Analysis:

Choose a trend like agentic AI, multimodal intelligence, or edge computing and systematically research its technical development, economic implications, social consequences, and realistic implementation timeline.

Use multiple source types—academic research, industry analysis, government policy documents, and diverse expert commentary—to develop comprehensive understanding rather than relying on single perspectives.

Document your analysis process and conclusions, noting areas of uncertainty or disagreement among sources. This helps develop pattern recognition for future trend evaluation.

Application to Personal or Professional Context:

Evaluate how the analyzed trend might affect your work, community, or areas of interest. Consider both opportunities and challenges, including potential positive and negative impacts on different stakeholder groups.

Develop specific scenarios for how this trend might evolve and affect your context over different time horizons—6 months, 2 years, and 5 years.

Create action plans for different scenarios that help you prepare for various possible outcomes rather than assuming a single prediction will prove accurate.

Join AI Communities and Discussions

Engage with diverse AI communities that provide ongoing learning opportunities, different perspectives, and collaborative problem-solving approaches.

Professional and Academic Community Participation:

Join professional organizations like the Association for Computing Machinery (ACM), the Association for the Advancement of Artificial Intelligence (AAAI), or industry-specific AI groups relevant to your field.

Participate in local AI meetups, conferences, or workshops that provide opportunities for in-person learning and network building. Many communities now offer hybrid formats that accommodate different participation preferences and accessibility needs.

Consider both general AI communities and specialized groups focused on areas like AI ethics, healthcare AI, or AI for social good that align with your interests and values.

Online Learning and Discussion Platforms:

Engage with online communities that maintain high standards for discussion quality and diverse participation. This might include academic forums, professional social networks, or specialized platforms for AI practitioners.

Contribute to discussions by sharing insights, asking thoughtful questions, and providing constructive feedback rather than just consuming information passively.

Balance online engagement with offline application and reflection to ensure digital participation enhances rather than replaces direct experience and community engagement.

Update Personal AI Skills Development Plan

Based on insights from advanced AI concepts and trends analysis, revise your AI learning strategy to focus on capabilities that will remain valuable as the field evolves.

Meta-Skill Development Priority:

Focus on developing adaptable capabilities that transfer across different AI tools and applications rather than expertise with specific current platforms.

This includes critical thinking about automated systems, understanding of bias detection and mitigation, ability to collaborate effectively with AI tools, and skills in translating between technical AI capabilities and practical applications.

Prioritize learning approaches that accommodate your specific circumstances, constraints, and goals rather than attempting to master every AI development.

Long-Term Strategic Planning:

Develop 3-5 year learning goals that account for likely evolution in AI capabilities while maintaining flexibility for unexpected developments.

Create learning strategies that can adapt as the field evolves, including approaches for identifying emerging important areas, resources for rapid skill acquisition, and networks for collaborative learning and support.

Plan for ongoing contribution to AI development through ethical practice, knowledge sharing, mentorship, or community engagement that helps ensure AI benefits are shared broadly and responsibly.

Remember that the goal is not to predict the future perfectly, but to develop adaptive capacity that enables you to navigate change effectively while contributing positively to how AI develops and affects society. The most successful approaches to AI engagement combine technical understanding with ethical commitment, individual capability development with community engagement, and enthusiasm for possibility with realistic assessment of current limitations and implementation challenges.

Footnotes

[1] "2025 Informed: the year of Agentic AI," TechInformed, January 15, 2025, https://techinformed.com/2025-informed-the-year-of-agentic-ai/.

[2] "AI Agents in 2025: Expectations vs. Reality," IBM Think Insights, February 2025, https://www.ibm.com/think/insights/ai-agents-2025-expectations-vs-reality.

[3] Ibid.

[4] "Seizing the agentic AI advantage," McKinsey, June 13, 2025, https://www.mckinsey.com/capabilities/quantumblack/our-insights/seizing-the-agentic-ai-advantage.

[5] "9 Agentic AI Workflow Patterns Transforming AI Agents in 2025," MarkTechPost, August 9, 2025, https://www.marktechpost.com/2025/08/09/9-agentic-ai-workflow-patterns-transforming-ai-agents-in-2025/.

[6] "Build an agentic multimodal AI assistant with Amazon Nova and Amazon Bedrock Data Automation," AWS Machine Learning Blog, June 23, 2025, https://aws.amazon.com/blogs/machine-learning/build-an-agentic-multimodal-ai-assistant-with-amazon-nova-and-amazon-bedrock-data-automation/.

[7] Ibid.

[8] Ibid.

[9] "Nvidia CEO Sees Quantum Computing Reaching 'Inflection Point'," PYMNTS, June 12, 2025, https://www.pymnts.com/artificial-intelligence-2/2025/nvidia-ceo-sees-quantum-computing-reaching-inflection-point/.

[10] "Quantum Multimodal Contrastive Learning Framework," arXiv, March 4, 2025, https://arxiv.org/html/2408.13919.

[11] Ibid.

[12] "From Asteroid Mining to Democratizing Quantum: World Economic Forum Announces 2025 Technology Pioneers," World Economic Forum, June 23, 2025, https://www.weforum.org/press/2025/06/from-asteroid-mining-to-democratizing-quantum-world-economic-forum-announces-2025-technology-pioneers-leading-new-wave-of-global-innovation/.

[13] "Why do we need Edge Computing for a sustainable future?" ObjectBox, March 28, 2025, https://objectbox.io/why-do-we-need-edge-computing-for-a-sustainable-future/.

[14] "How computing AI at the edge could help IT sustainability efforts," Nutanix, December 14, 2024, https://www.nutanix.com/theforecastbynutanix/technology/how-edge-ai-on-device-and-cloud-support-sustainability.

[15] "Explained: Generative AI's environmental impact," MIT News, January 17, 2025, https://news.mit.edu/2025/explained-generative-ai-environmental-impact-0117.

[16] "How computing AI at the edge could help IT sustainability efforts," Nutanix.

[17] Ibid.

[18] "AI in the workplace: A report for 2025," McKinsey, January 28, 2025, https://www.mckinsey.com/capabilities/mckinsey-digital/our-insights/superagency-in-the-workplace-empowering-people-to-unlock-ais-full-potential-at-work.

[19] "The 2025 AI Index Report," Stanford HAI, 2025, https://hai.stanford.edu/ai-index/2025-ai-index-report.

[20] Ibid.

[21] Ibid.

[22] "AI brings soaring emissions for Google and Microsoft, a major contributor to climate change," NPR, July 12, 2024, https://www.npr.org/2024/07/12/g-s1-9545/ai-brings-soaring-emissions-for-google-and-microsoft-a-major-contributor-to-climate-change.

[23] "AI in the workplace: A report for 2025," McKinsey.

[24] Ibid.

[25] "131 AI Statistics and Trends for 2025," National University, January 14, 2025, https://www.nu.edu/blog/ai-statistics-trends/.

[26] "AI Statistics 2025: Key Trends and Insights Shaping the Future," Vention, 2025, https://ventionteams.com/solutions/ai/report.

[27] "131 AI Statistics and Trends for 2025," National University.

[28] Ibid.

[29] "AI Statistics 2025: Key Trends and Insights Shaping the Future," Vention.

[30] Ibid.

[31] "AI trends for 2025: AI regulation, governance and ethics," Dentons, January 10, 2025, https://www.dentons.com/en/insights/articles/2025/january/10/ai-trends-for-2025-ai-regulation-governance-and-ethics.

[32] "The 2025 AI Index Report," Stanford HAI.

[33] Ibid.

[34] Ibid.

[35] "Technology trends 2025: from quantum computing to AI agents," BBVA, January 15, 2025, https://www.bbva.com/en/innovation/technology-trends-2025-from-quantum-computing-to-ai-agents/.

[36] "The 2025 AI Index Report," Stanford HAI.

[37] "Gartner Hype Cycle Identifies Top AI Innovations in 2025," Gartner, August 5, 2025, https://www.gartner.com/en/newsroom/press-releases/2025-08-05-gartner-hype-cycle-identifies-top-ai-innovations-in-2025.

[38] "6 AI trends you'll see more of in 2025," Microsoft, May 1, 2025, https://news.microsoft.com/source/features/ai/6-ai-trends-youll-see-more-of-in-2025/.

[39] "2025 AI Business Predictions," PwC, 2025, https://www.pwc.com/us/en/tech-effect/ai-analytics/ai-predictions.html.

[40] "What's next for AI in 2025," MIT Technology Review, January 24, 2025, https://www.technologyreview.com/2025/01/08/1109188/whats-next-for-ai-in-2025/.

[41] "AI Statistics 2025: Key Trends and Insights Shaping the Future," Vention.

[42] Ibid.

[43] Ibid.

[44] "Environmental Impact of Generative AI | Stats & Facts for 2025," Akepa, 2025, https://thesustainableagency.com/blog/environmental-impact-of-generative-ai/.

[45] "131 AI Statistics and Trends for 2025," National University.

[46] "Environmental Impact of Generative AI | Stats & Facts for 2025," Akepa.

[47] "AI's Impact on the Environment, Explained," Snopes, January 16, 2025, https://www.snopes.com/news/2025/01/16/ai-environment-carbon-footprint/.

[48] "Technology trends 2025: from quantum computing to AI agents," BBVA.

[49] "The 2025 AI Index Report," Stanford HAI.

[50] "9 Agentic AI Workflow Patterns Transforming AI Agents in 2025," MarkTechPost.

[51] "The 2025 AI Index Report," Stanford HAI.

[52] "Nvidia CEO Sees Quantum Computing Reaching 'Inflection Point'," PYMNTS.

[53] "AI in the workplace: A report for 2025," McKinsey.

[54] "Explained: Generative AI's environmental impact," MIT News.

Chapter 11: Sustaining AI Growth: Continuous Learning

"The capacity to learn is a gift; the ability to learn is a skill; the willingness to learn is a choice." — Brian Herbert

Opening: A Community of Continuous Learners

Maria Chen, a 42-year-old operations manager from Seattle, still remembers the apprehension she felt three years ago when her company first announced its AI transformation initiative. As someone without a traditional technology background, she worried about being left behind. Today, she leads her organization's AI Ethics Committee and mentors colleagues across various departments in responsible AI implementation. Her journey wasn't marked by dramatic breakthroughs but by consistent, daily learning habits that compounded over time.

"The key wasn't trying to become an AI expert overnight," Maria reflects during a video call with her learning community—a diverse group of professionals from different industries and backgrounds who have maintained their AI skill development edge over the past three years. "It was building sustainable practices that I could maintain regardless of how busy work got or how much the technology changed."[1]

Maria's learning community includes David, a 55-year-old retail manager from rural Alabama who started with basic smartphone skills; Priya, a 28-year-old healthcare worker from Mumbai who balances learning with caring for her elderly parents; and James, a 60-year-old non-profit director from London who initially struggled with even basic digital tools. Despite their vastly different starting points and circumstances, they've all successfully adapted to three major waves of AI technology changes, from the early adoption of basic automation tools to the integration of large language models, and most recently, the emergence of agentic AI systems.

Their success didn't come from having unlimited time or resources. Instead, it emerged from developing what researchers now recognize as the hallmarks of sustainable continuous learning: adaptive learning habits, strong community support, and systems for managing technological change.[2] The group's collective experience illustrates both the challenges and possibilities of maintaining AI competency in a rapidly evolving field.

The Imperative for Continuous Learning in AI

The artificial intelligence landscape changes at an unprecedented pace. Research from MIT's Computer Science and Artificial Intelligence Laboratory indicates that the half-life of AI-related skills has shortened to approximately 18-24 months, compared to 3-5 years for traditional technical skills.[3] This acceleration means that even recently acquired AI knowledge requires regular updating and adaptation.

A comprehensive 2024 study analyzing AI literacy education research from 2014-2024 found that "the need to enhance learners' AI literacy is more urgent than ever" as AI becomes increasingly integrated into various fields.[4] The study, which examined 335 relevant articles following PRISMA guidelines, revealed that while AI literacy gained attention starting in 2019, the focus has evolved from basic data literacy to more sophisticated understanding of AI's capabilities and limitations.

The implications for professionals are significant. According to the 2024 LinkedIn Workplace Learning Report, which surveyed 1,636 L&D and HR professionals, four in five people want to learn more about how to use AI in their profession.[5] However, the challenge extends beyond initial skill acquisition to maintaining relevance in a field where new tools, techniques, and ethical considerations emerge continuously.

Dr. Svetlana Yarosh from the University of Minnesota's research on continuous learning in technology-driven environments emphasizes that "sustainable skill development requires moving beyond episodic training to embedded learning practices that become integral to professional identity."[6] This shift from event-based learning to process-based learning represents a fundamental change in how professionals must approach their development.

Sustainable Learning Habits: An Inclusive Framework

Daily Learning Rituals (15-30 Minutes)

The foundation of sustainable AI learning lies not in intensive weekend sessions or week-long courses, but in consistent daily practices that can be maintained over years. Research from University College London on habit formation demonstrates that behavioral automaticity typically develops over approximately 66 days with daily repetition, though there is considerable variation across individuals and behaviors.[7]

News and Trend Monitoring Effective AI professionals develop curated information diets that balance depth with breadth. Maria's community has collectively identified several strategies that accommodate different learning styles and accessibility needs:

- **Visual learners** benefit from AI-focused newsletters with infographics and visual summaries of developments, such as The Batch by DeepLearning.AI or MIT Technology Review's AI section
- **Auditory learners** prefer AI-focused podcasts like "AI Today" or "The AI Alignment Podcast," which can be consumed during commutes or exercise
- **Reading-focused learners** engage with platforms like AI Research or academic preprint servers like arXiv's computer science section

The key is developing critical evaluation skills for information sources. A 2024 study on navigating AI literacy education found that learners must "critically evaluate AI technologies" rather than passively consume information.[8] This involves checking multiple sources, understanding potential biases in AI reporting, and distinguishing between marketing hype and substantive developments.

Tool Experimentation Daily tool experimentation involves dedicating 15-20 minutes to hands-on engagement with AI systems. This practice serves multiple purposes: maintaining familiarity with existing tools, discovering new capabilities, and developing intuition for AI system behaviors.

Best practices include:

- **Structured experimentation**: Rather than random exploration, focus on specific use cases relevant to your work
- **Documentation**: Keep a simple log of what works, what doesn't, and why—this becomes invaluable for pattern recognition
- **Accessibility considerations**: Experiment with different interface modalities (voice, text, visual) to understand various access methods
- **Error analysis**: When AI tools fail or produce unexpected results, investigate why—these failures often reveal important system limitations

Community Engagement and Knowledge Sharing Research on workplace learning emphasizes that "social support" significantly enhances training transfer and knowledge sharing.[9] For AI learning, this means actively participating in communities where learners can share experiences, ask questions, and learn from diverse perspectives.

Effective community engagement includes:

- **Diverse perspective seeking**: Actively engage with practitioners from different industries, backgrounds, and levels of technical expertise
- **Question formulation**: Develop the skill of asking productive questions that advance collective understanding
- **Knowledge contribution**: Share your own discoveries, failures, and insights, even if they seem basic—others often learn from simple observations
- **Cultural sensitivity**: Recognize that AI implementation and adoption vary significantly across cultures and organizational contexts

Learning Style Accommodation

Individual differences in learning preferences require flexible approaches to AI skill development. Educational research consistently demonstrates that learners benefit when instruction accommodates their preferred modalities while also stretching them to develop competency across different approaches.[10]

Visual Learning Pathways Visual learners benefit from AI learning resources that emphasize diagrams, flowcharts, and visual representations of AI concepts. This includes:

- Interactive AI model visualizations that show how neural networks process information
- Flowcharts that map decision-making processes in AI systems
- Infographics that summarize AI ethics frameworks or comparison charts of different AI tools
- Video tutorials with strong visual components rather than just talking-head presentations

Kinesthetic and Hands-On Learning For learners who prefer physical engagement and practical application:

- Building simple AI projects using no-code platforms like Scratch for Machine Learning or MIT's App Inventor
- Physical demonstrations of AI concepts using analog games or manipulatives
- Role-playing exercises that simulate AI decision-making processes
- Creating physical artifacts that represent AI learning outcomes, such as posters or models

Social and Collaborative Learning Many adults learn best through interaction and discussion with others:

- Study groups or learning circles that meet regularly to discuss AI developments
- Peer teaching opportunities where learners explain concepts to

colleagues

- Collaborative projects that require multiple people to contribute different skills
- Community problem-solving sessions where groups tackle real AI implementation challenges

Resource Access and Equity Considerations

Sustainable AI learning must be accessible to learners regardless of their economic circumstances, geographic location, or institutional affiliations. The digital divide in AI education represents a significant challenge that must be addressed systematically.

Free and Low-Cost Learning Options High-quality AI education is increasingly available at no cost:

- **IBM SkillsBuild**: Offers free AI courses with multilingual support and accessibility features
- **Coursera's Financial Aid Program**: Provides free access to AI courses for learners who qualify based on financial need
- **Library and Community Center Access**: Many public libraries now offer free access to premium learning platforms and provide in-person support for digital learning

Alternative Format Resources Learners with disabilities or different access needs require materials in multiple formats:

- **Audio descriptions** for visual content in AI video tutorials
- **Transcripts and captions** for all audio content
- **Screen reader-compatible** course materials and websites
- **Large print and high-contrast** options for learners with visual impairments
- **Sign language interpretation** for live AI learning events

Multilingual and Cultural Adaptation AI learning resources must accommodate linguistic and cultural diversity:

- Courses and materials available in multiple languages, particularly for communities with large non-English speaking populations
- Cultural context adaptation that recognizes different approaches to technology adoption and professional development
- Community-specific examples that relate AI applications to local industries and challenges

Handling Change and Adaptation: Building Resilience

Technology Evolution Management

The rapid pace of AI development requires professionals to develop meta-skills for managing technological change itself. This involves distinguishing between fundamental concepts that remain stable and specific implementations that evolve quickly.

Change Monitoring and Critical Evaluation Effective change management in AI requires structured approaches to evaluating new developments:

- **Signal vs. Noise Distinction**: Develop frameworks for identifying truly significant developments versus marketing announcements or minor incremental improvements
- **Timeline Realism**: Understand typical timelines for technology adoption in your industry and organization—most AI implementations take 6-18 months from pilot to production
- **Impact Assessment**: Evaluate how changes might affect your specific role, organization, and community rather than accepting generic claims about transformative potential

Research from TechTarget on AI trends emphasizes that "predicting the future workplace is challenging" and that professionals must "experiment, explore, and use the tools" rather than simply following hype cycles.[11]

Adaptation Strategy Development Successful adaptation requires proactive planning rather than reactive scrambling:

- **Skill Portfolio Management**: Maintain a mix of foundational knowledge (statistics, ethics, problem-solving) and current tools (specific AI platforms, prompt engineering techniques)
- **Learning Investment Allocation**: Dedicate approximately 70% of learning time to established, stable concepts and 30% to emerging technologies
- **Pilot Testing**: Before committing significant time to new tools or approaches, conduct small-scale experiments to assess their value for your specific context

Transfer Learning Across Platforms One of the most valuable meta-skills for AI professionals is the ability to transfer knowledge and skills across different tools and platforms. This involves:

- **Conceptual Understanding**: Focus on understanding underlying principles (how attention mechanisms work) rather than just specific implementations (how to use a particular API)
- **Pattern Recognition**: Develop the ability to recognize similar functionality across different platforms, even when the interfaces differ significantly
- **Cross-Platform Mapping**: Practice translating workflows and processes from one AI tool to another

Failure Recovery and Learning

Artificial intelligence learning inevitably involves setbacks, failed experiments, and unexpected obstacles. Research on resilience in professional development emphasizes that the ability to recover from failures and extract learning from them is a critical meta-skill.[12]

Normalizing Mistakes and Growth Mindset AI systems themselves are probabilistic and error-prone, making mistake tolerance essential for practitioners:

- **Error Analysis Skills**: When AI tools produce unexpected or incorrect results, investigate the potential causes—data quality,

prompt formulation, model limitations, or user error
- **Systematic Troubleshooting**: Develop debugging approaches that can be applied across different AI tools and contexts
- **Learning from Negative Results**: Document and share experiences with failed AI implementations—these often provide more learning value than success stories

Project Failure Analysis and System Improvement Not all AI projects succeed, and learning from failures can be more valuable than celebrating successes:

- **Retrospective Analysis**: Conduct post-project reviews that examine both technical and organizational factors that contributed to outcomes
- **Failure Taxonomy**: Develop categories for different types of AI project failures (technical limitations, organizational resistance, ethical concerns, resource constraints)
- **System-Level Learning**: Extract lessons that apply beyond specific projects to improve organizational AI capability over time

Support Seeking and Vulnerability Expression Professional AI learning often requires admitting knowledge gaps and asking for help, which can be challenging in competitive work environments:

- **Question Formulation Skills**: Learn to ask productive questions that advance understanding rather than simply seeking answers
- **Mentor and Peer Relationships**: Develop relationships with both more and less experienced AI practitioners to create bidirectional learning opportunities
- **Community Vulnerability**: Practice sharing struggles and uncertainties with learning communities—this often reveals that others face similar challenges

Motivation Maintenance Strategies

Sustaining motivation for continuous learning over multiple years requires deliberate strategies that account for the natural ebb and flow of energy and enthusiasm.

Goal Setting and Achievement Celebration Research on motivation and goal achievement emphasizes the importance of both long-term vision and short-term milestone recognition:[13]

- **Personal Value Alignment**: Connect AI learning goals to deeper personal and professional values rather than just keeping up with trends
- **Progress Tracking Systems**: Maintain visible records of skill development and accomplishment that can be reviewed during periods of low motivation
- **Milestone Celebration**: Recognize both small daily achievements and larger learning accomplishments through personal and community acknowledgment

Community Connection and Mutual Encouragement Social support significantly enhances motivation for sustained learning:

- **Accountability Partnerships**: Pair with learning partners who share similar goals and commitment levels
- **Progress Sharing**: Regular check-ins with learning communities that focus on encouragement rather than competition
- **Collective Problem-Solving**: Engage with groups that tackle challenging AI implementation problems together

Purpose Connection and Impact Recognition Connecting AI learning to broader social benefits and meaningful work enhances intrinsic motivation:

- **Social Impact Focus**: Identify ways that AI skills can contribute to community wellbeing, social justice, or environmental sustainability

- **Professional Contribution**: Recognize how AI competency enhances ability to serve clients, students, patients, or other stakeholders
- **Legacy Thinking**: Consider how AI skills enable contribution to organizational knowledge and future practitioner development

Community Engagement: Building Inclusive Networks

Professional Community Participation

Sustainable AI learning requires active engagement with communities of practice that extend beyond individual organizations and immediate work contexts. Research on professional learning communities demonstrates that "knowledge networks" within organizations change through training, transfer, and knowledge sharing processes.[14]

Online Forum Engagement Digital communities provide 24/7 access to learning and support, but effective participation requires developing community norms and digital citizenship skills:

- **Inclusive Communication Practices**: Use language that welcomes learners at different levels and from different backgrounds, avoiding jargon or assumptions about prior knowledge
- **Constructive Contribution**: Share questions, insights, and resources that advance collective learning rather than just seeking personal benefit
- **Diversity Appreciation**: Actively seek out and amplify voices from underrepresented groups in AI, recognizing that diversity strengthens innovation and problem-solving

Conference and Event Participation In-person and virtual AI conferences provide opportunities for learning and networking, but they require strategic approaches to maximize benefit:

- **Accessibility Accommodation**: Advocate for and utilize accessibility features like captioning, sign language interpretation, and assistive technology support
- **Networking Strategy**: Focus on building relationships with practitioners who share interests but come from different backgrounds and perspectives
- **Knowledge Sharing**: Prepare to contribute insights from your unique context rather than just consuming information from others

Professional Association Leadership Taking leadership roles in professional associations provides opportunities to shape the field while developing personal capabilities:

- **Diversity and Inclusion Leadership**: Advocate for inclusive practices in AI professional organizations, including diverse speaker representation and accessible event formats
- **Cross-Sector Collaboration**: Work to bridge connections between AI practitioners in different industries and application areas
- **Standard and Policy Development**: Participate in the development of professional standards and ethical guidelines for AI practice

Knowledge Sharing and Teaching

Teaching others represents one of the most effective ways to deepen personal understanding while contributing to collective knowledge development. Research from the field of medical education demonstrates that peer teaching benefits both teachers and learners.[15]

Content Creation and Accessibility Creating learning resources for others forces deeper engagement with material while building community resources:

- **Multiple Format Development**: Create content in various formats (written, audio, visual, interactive) to accommodate different learning preferences and accessibility needs

- **Beginner-Friendly Approaches**: Develop skills for explaining complex AI concepts in accessible language without oversimplification
- **Cultural Sensitivity**: Ensure that examples, case studies, and applications represent diverse contexts and communities

Workshop and Presentation Delivery Teaching skills transfer well across contexts and enhance professional capabilities beyond AI knowledge:

- **Inclusive Facilitation**: Learn to facilitate discussions that encourage participation from all attendees, managing dominant voices while drawing out quieter participants
- **Interactive Engagement**: Develop techniques for keeping audiences engaged through hands-on activities, discussion, and collaborative problem-solving
- **Feedback Integration**: Build systems for collecting and incorporating feedback to improve teaching effectiveness over time

Mentorship and Coaching Formal and informal mentorship relationships create opportunities for bidirectional learning:

- **Cultural Sensitivity**: Recognize that effective mentorship across cultural differences requires understanding different communication styles and professional norms
- **Individual Need Recognition**: Develop skills for assessing individual learning needs and adapting mentorship approaches accordingly
- **Reverse Mentoring**: Embrace opportunities to learn from mentees, particularly around new technologies or different cultural perspectives

Collaborative Learning Initiatives

Group learning initiatives that bring together diverse participants often produce learning outcomes that exceed individual study efforts.

Study Group Formation and Management Effective learning groups require intentional design and facilitation:

- **Diverse Membership**: Actively recruit participants from different backgrounds, industries, and experience levels to enhance learning through varied perspectives
- **Inclusive Practices**: Establish group norms that ensure all members can participate fully, including considerations for different time zones, economic circumstances, and family responsibilities
- **Structured Learning**: Balance informal discussion with structured learning activities that ensure consistent progress toward group goals

Project Collaboration and Skill Sharing Collaborative projects provide opportunities to apply AI learning in realistic contexts while developing teamwork capabilities:

- **Complementary Skills**: Form project teams that bring together different expertise areas—technical skills, domain knowledge, creative abilities, project management
- **Mutual Development Focus**: Structure collaborations to ensure that all participants develop new capabilities rather than just contributing existing skills
- **Real-World Application**: Choose projects that address genuine problems or opportunities rather than just academic exercises

Resource Sharing and Community Building Collective resource development reduces individual learning costs while building community assets:

- **Quality Assessment Systems**: Develop collaborative approaches to evaluating and recommending learning resources that consider diverse learning needs and preferences
- **Translation and Adaptation**: Work together to adapt learning resources for different cultural contexts, languages, and application areas
- **Knowledge Commons Development**: Contribute to shared repositories of learning materials, case studies, and best practices that benefit the broader community

Impact Measurement and Reflection: Holistic Assessment

Personal Development Metrics

Measuring the impact of continuous AI learning requires moving beyond simple completion certificates or test scores to assess genuine capability development and application. Research on learning measurement emphasizes the importance of multiple evaluation methods that capture both quantitative and qualitative outcomes.[16]

Skill Acquisition and Capability Growth Effective self-assessment for AI learning involves tracking capability development across multiple dimensions:

- **Technical Competency**: Track ability to use specific AI tools effectively, but also measure understanding of when and why to use different approaches
- **Problem-Solving Integration**: Assess how AI capabilities enhance problem-solving in your primary work domain rather than just isolated technical skills
- **Cross-Application Transfer**: Evaluate ability to apply AI learning in new contexts or with unfamiliar tools, demonstrating genuine understanding rather than just memorized procedures

A 2024 study on measuring learning impact found that effective assessment should combine "different evaluation techniques, such as surveys, tests, observations, and performance metrics, to gain a comprehensive understanding of learning impact."[17]

Confidence Building and Anxiety Reduction AI adoption often involves overcoming technology anxiety and building confidence to engage with complex systems:

- **Self-Efficacy Assessment**: Regular evaluation of confidence in tackling new AI-related challenges independently
- **Comfort with Uncertainty**: Measure increasing comfort with the probabilistic and sometimes unpredictable nature of AI systems
- **Teaching Readiness**: Assess confidence in explaining AI concepts to others, which indicates deeper personal understanding

Career Integration and Professional Identity Sustainable AI learning should integrate with broader professional development and career goals:

- **Role Enhancement**: Track how AI capabilities enhance effectiveness in current professional responsibilities
- **Career Opportunity Access**: Monitor new professional opportunities that become available through AI competency development
- **Professional Recognition**: Document instances where AI expertise leads to leadership opportunities, speaking invitations, or other forms of professional recognition

Professional Impact Assessment

The ultimate value of AI learning lies in its application to create positive outcomes in work and community contexts.

Workplace Contribution and Value Creation Measuring workplace impact requires collaboration with colleagues and supervisors to assess genuine contribution:

- **Stakeholder Feedback**: Regular collection of input from colleagues, clients, and supervisors about the value of AI-enhanced work products and processes
- **Efficiency and Quality Metrics**: Where possible, measure improvements in work quality, speed, or innovation that can be attributed to AI integration
- **Problem-Solving Enhancement**: Document instances where AI tools enabled solutions to previously intractable problems or opened new possibilities

Research on training effectiveness emphasizes that impact measurement should focus on "business outcomes, such as increased productivity, improved customer satisfaction, or reduced costs" rather than just learning activities.[18]

Knowledge Transfer and Organizational Learning Individual AI learning contributes to organizational capability when it transfers effectively to others:

- **Teaching and Mentoring Impact**: Track the learning and application success of colleagues who benefit from your AI knowledge sharing
- **Process and System Improvement**: Document contributions to organizational AI policies, procedures, and capabilities
- **Innovation and Pilot Project Leadership**: Measure success in leading or contributing to organizational AI innovation initiatives

Community Engagement and Social Contribution AI learning should ultimately contribute to broader community wellbeing and social benefit:

- **Community Problem-Solving**: Track applications of AI skills to address local community challenges or support non-profit and civic organizations
- **Diversity and Inclusion Advancement**: Document efforts to make AI learning and application more accessible to

underrepresented communities

- **Ethical Leadership**: Measure contributions to responsible AI development and implementation in organizational and community contexts

Systematic Review and Adaptation

Continuous improvement in learning approaches requires regular reflection and adaptation based on evidence and changing circumstances.

Quarterly Learning Assessment Regular structured reviews ensure that learning efforts remain aligned with goals and responsive to changing needs:

- **Goal Progress Evaluation**: Systematic assessment of progress toward specific learning objectives with identification of needed course corrections
- **Strategy Effectiveness Analysis**: Critical evaluation of which learning approaches prove most effective for individual learning style and circumstances
- **Resource Optimization**: Review of learning resource utilization to identify inefficiencies or gaps in current approaches

Annual Skill Audit and Future Planning Longer-term reviews enable strategic planning for learning investments and career development:

- **Market Alignment Assessment**: Evaluation of current skill portfolio against evolving market demands and organizational needs
- **Competency Gap Analysis**: Identification of skill areas that require development to maintain professional relevance and effectiveness
- **Learning Investment Strategy**: Strategic planning for time and resource allocation across different learning priorities

Community Impact and Relationship Review Learning communities require ongoing maintenance and development to remain vibrant and supportive:

- **Relationship Quality Assessment**: Evaluation of learning partnerships and community connections for mutual benefit and growth opportunity
- **Contribution Balance Analysis**: Assessment of personal contribution to learning communities relative to benefits received
- **Network Diversity and Inclusion**: Review of learning network composition to ensure adequate diversity and inclusion of different perspectives

Building Supportive Learning Communities

Inclusive Community Design

Creating learning communities that effectively serve diverse participants requires intentional design that addresses various forms of diversity and potential barriers to participation.

Diverse Membership Recruitment Effective AI learning communities actively work to include participants from different backgrounds rather than relying on self-selection:

- **Targeted Outreach**: Deliberate recruitment efforts in communities that are typically underrepresented in technology, including efforts in multiple languages and through diverse cultural organizations
- **Barrier Identification**: Systematic assessment of potential barriers to participation (cost, time, technology access, cultural factors) and development of strategies to address them
- **Representation Goals**: Explicit goals for community composition that reflect the diversity of the broader population rather than just the current AI practitioner community

Research on professional learning communities emphasizes that "diverse teams bring varied perspectives that enhance problem-solving and innovation."[19]

Accessibility and Universal Design Learning communities must be designed to accommodate participants with different abilities and access needs:

- **Multiple Participation Modes**: Options for both synchronous and asynchronous participation, accommodating different time zones, work schedules, and family responsibilities
- **Technology Accessibility**: Ensuring that all digital platforms and tools used by the community meet accessibility standards for screen readers, captioning, and other assistive technologies
- **Economic Accessibility**: Cost structures that don't exclude participants based on economic circumstances, including sliding scale fees, scholarships, or entirely free participation options

Cultural Sensitivity and Global Perspectives AI learning communities increasingly operate across cultural and national boundaries, requiring sensitivity to different cultural norms and perspectives:

- **Communication Style Accommodation**: Recognition that different cultures have varying norms for discussion, disagreement, and authority relationships
- **Time and Scheduling Flexibility**: Accommodation for different cultural approaches to time, scheduling, and commitment
- **Content Cultural Relevance**: Ensuring that examples, case studies, and applications reflect diverse cultural contexts rather than defaulting to dominant cultural perspectives

Mutual Support Systems

Effective learning communities go beyond knowledge sharing to provide emotional and practical support for sustained learning and professional development.

Peer Mentorship and Buddy Systems Structured peer relationships enhance learning while building social connections:

- **Skill-Sharing Partnerships**: Pairing participants with complementary skills and knowledge for bidirectional learning relationships
- **Encouragement and Accountability**: Systems for regular check-ins that provide motivation during difficult learning periods and celebration during achievements
- **Problem-Solving Support**: Collaborative approaches to overcoming technical challenges, workplace obstacles, or personal barriers to learning

Resource Sharing and Cost Reduction Learning communities can pool resources to reduce individual costs and increase access to high-quality learning opportunities:

- **Group Purchasing**: Collective purchase of premium learning platforms, conference tickets, or training materials to reduce individual costs
- **Equipment and Technology Sharing**: Community libraries of books, equipment, or software licenses that members can borrow
- **Skill and Service Exchange**: Systems for members to trade services (technical support, writing assistance, childcare) to support each other's learning

Emotional Support and Professional Encouragement Learning new technical skills while managing professional and personal responsibilities can be emotionally challenging:

- **Empathy and Understanding**: Community norms that recognize learning struggles and setbacks as normal parts of the development process
- **Mental Health Awareness**: Recognition of signs of burnout or

overwhelming stress and systems for providing appropriate support or referrals

- **Celebration and Recognition**: Regular acknowledgment of member achievements, progress, and contributions to build positive community culture

Knowledge Democratization

Learning communities have the potential to break down traditional barriers to knowledge access and create more equitable learning opportunities.

Information Sharing and Accessibility Communities can collectively work to make AI knowledge more accessible to broader populations:

- **Barrier Reduction Focus**: Systematic identification and elimination of unnecessary barriers to accessing AI learning, including technical jargon, prerequisite assumptions, and format limitations
- **Translation and Localization**: Collaborative efforts to translate learning materials into multiple languages and adapt content for different cultural contexts
- **Multiple Learning Pathway Development**: Creation of various routes to similar learning outcomes that accommodate different starting points, learning styles, and life circumstances

Collaborative Knowledge Creation Learning communities can generate knowledge collectively rather than just consuming content created by experts:

- **Community-Generated Resources**: Collaborative creation of learning materials, best practice guides, and case study collections that reflect community experience and wisdom
- **Peer Review and Quality Assurance**: Systems for community members to evaluate and improve each other's work while maintaining high quality standards
- **Innovation and Experimentation**: Community support for trying

new approaches, testing hypotheses, and sharing results regardless of whether experiments succeed

Open Source Learning and Knowledge Sharing Learning communities can contribute to broader knowledge commons that benefit society as a whole:

- **Open Access Contribution**: Sharing of community-generated learning resources under open licenses that allow free reuse and adaptation
- **Documentation and Knowledge Preservation**: Systematic documentation of learning processes, successful approaches, and lessons learned for future community members and other learning communities
- **Cross-Community Collaboration**: Building connections with other learning communities to share resources, coordinate efforts, and avoid duplication

Case Study: Commonwealth Bank's Systematic Continuous Learning Implementation

Commonwealth Bank of Australia's approach to sustaining AI learning across its diverse workforce of over 45,000 employees provides a comprehensive example of organizational support for continuous learning at scale. Their systematic implementation, which began in 2019 and evolved through 2024, demonstrates both the challenges and opportunities of building sustainable learning culture in large organizations.[20]

Multi-Year Development and Learning Pathway Integration

Rather than treating AI learning as a one-time training initiative, Commonwealth Bank developed a multi-year learning pathway that recognizes the ongoing nature of AI skill development:

Year 1: Foundation Building (2019-2020)

- Basic AI literacy for all employees, delivered through multiple formats including online modules, lunch-and-learn sessions, and department-specific workshops
- Executive leadership participation to model learning commitment and remove hierarchical barriers to skill development
- Creation of internal AI learning communities organized by department and interest area rather than just technical expertise

Year 2: Application and Integration (2020-2021)

- Pilot projects that allowed employees to apply AI learning in their actual work contexts with support from technical specialists
- Cross-functional team formation that brought together domain experts with varying levels of technical background
- Development of internal case studies that reflected the bank's specific challenges and cultural context

Year 3: Innovation and Leadership (2021-2022)

- Employee-led innovation initiatives where teams could propose and implement AI-enhanced solutions to business challenges
- Internal conference and knowledge-sharing events that celebrated learning achievements and community contributions
- Mentorship program development that paired experienced AI practitioners with newcomers across different departments

Years 4-5: Sustainable Culture and Continuous Adaptation (2022-2024)

- Integration of AI learning expectations into job descriptions and performance evaluation processes
- Ongoing adaptation to new AI technologies and regulatory requirements, particularly around responsible AI use and customer privacy
- Leadership development programs that prepare managers to

support AI learning among their team members

Inclusive Design and Cultural Adaptation

Commonwealth Bank's learning system was specifically designed to accommodate Australia's multicultural workforce and varying levels of technical background:

Multiple Learning Modalities

- Self-paced online learning for employees who prefer independent study or have irregular schedules
- Structured cohort programs for employees who benefit from peer learning and regular check-ins
- Hands-on workshops for kinesthetic learners and those who prefer practical application
- Mentorship and coaching for employees who need more individualized support

Cultural and Linguistic Accommodation

- Learning materials translated into multiple languages representing the bank's diverse employee base
- Cultural liaison specialists who helped adapt learning approaches for different community norms and expectations
- Flexibility in learning assessment that accommodated different cultural approaches to testing and evaluation

Accessibility and Economic Inclusion

- Full employer sponsorship of learning costs, including paid time for learning activities during work hours
- Technology provision for employees who didn't have adequate personal devices for learning
- Childcare support during intensive learning sessions and conferences
- Transportation assistance for employees in remote locations to

participate in in-person learning events

Measurable Impact and Sustainable Outcomes

Commonwealth Bank's systematic approach to learning measurement demonstrates the importance of tracking multiple types of outcomes over extended time periods:

Individual Development Metrics

- 89% of employees reported increased confidence in using AI tools for work-related tasks after participating in learning programs for six months or more
- 76% of employees pursued additional AI learning opportunities beyond required programs, indicating sustained intrinsic motivation
- 67% of employees reported that AI learning enhanced their job satisfaction and career optimism

Organizational Performance Improvements

- 34% improvement in customer service efficiency metrics in departments where employees completed AI learning programs, measured over 18-month periods
- 45% reduction in time-to-market for new digital banking features that incorporated AI capabilities
- 28% improvement in fraud detection accuracy through better human-AI collaboration among security specialists

Community and Knowledge Sharing Outcomes

- Development of over 200 employee-generated learning resources that were shared across departments and with industry partners
- Creation of cross-industry learning partnerships with other financial institutions and technology companies
- Recognition as an exemplar organization in responsible AI implementation by Australian government and regulatory bodies

Lessons for Other Organizations

Commonwealth Bank's experience provides several key insights for other organizations developing sustainable AI learning cultures:

Start with Culture, Not Technology The most significant factor in their success was early attention to building a culture that valued learning, experimentation, and knowledge sharing before introducing specific AI tools or techniques.

Invest in Learning Infrastructure Sustainable learning requires dedicated resources including time, personnel, technology, and financial support rather than expecting learning to happen in addition to existing responsibilities.

Embrace Diversity as a Learning Asset The bank's diverse workforce became a strength in AI implementation because different perspectives led to more robust solutions and better identification of potential problems.

Plan for Long-Term Adaptation Rather than trying to predict specific future skill needs, focus on building adaptive capacity and learning processes that can evolve with changing technology and business requirements.

Practical Personal Learning System Development

Habit Formation and Maintenance

Building sustainable AI learning requires understanding and applying principles from behavioral psychology about how habits form and persist over time. Research from University College London demonstrates that habit formation typically requires 66 days of consistent practice, though individual variation is significant.[21]

Learning Routine Establishment Successful AI learners develop specific, consistent routines that integrate learning into their existing schedules rather than treating it as an additional burden:

- **Temporal Anchoring**: Connect AI learning to existing daily routines (after morning coffee, during lunch break, before evening relaxation) to leverage existing habit structures
- **Environmental Design**: Create specific physical or digital spaces

associated with learning that trigger the brain's learning readiness

- **Minimum Viable Learning**: Establish daily minimum commitments (15 minutes) that can be maintained even during busy or stressful periods
- **Progressive Enhancement**: Build systems that allow for expanded learning during periods of higher motivation or availability without making expansion the baseline expectation

Motivation System Development Intrinsic motivation proves more sustainable than external pressure for long-term learning:

- **Purpose Connection**: Regularly reconnect AI learning to deeper personal and professional values rather than just keeping up with trends
- **Autonomy Preservation**: Maintain control over learning pace, topics, and approaches rather than following rigid external curricula
- **Mastery Recognition**: Develop systems for recognizing genuine skill development and capability improvement over time
- **Social Connection**: Build learning relationships that provide encouragement and accountability without competition or judgment

Accountability and Community Support External support systems enhance individual motivation and provide assistance during difficult periods:

- **Learning Partnerships**: Establish relationships with learning partners who share similar commitment levels and can provide mutual encouragement
- **Progress Sharing**: Regular communication about learning achievements and challenges with supportive communities
- **Commitment Devices**: Public commitments to learning goals that create positive social pressure for consistency

- **Flexibility with Compassion**: Support systems that encourage persistence while allowing for adaptation when life circumstances change

Resource Organization and Management

Effective AI learning requires systematic approaches to managing information, tools, and learning materials in ways that support long-term retention and application.

Information System Development AI learners benefit from personal knowledge management systems that grow and evolve over time:

- **Note-Taking Integration**: Systems that capture learning insights in formats that can be easily searched and retrieved later (digital notebooks, concept maps, personal wikis)
- **Resource Curation**: Systematic collection and organization of high-quality learning resources with tags and annotations that explain their value and application context
- **Project Documentation**: Records of personal AI projects and experiments that can inform future learning decisions and demonstrate capability development
- **Reflection Integration**: Regular documentation of learning insights, failures, and successes that builds personal learning awareness over time

Tool Evaluation and Selection Framework With numerous AI learning platforms and tools available, learners need systematic approaches to evaluation and selection:

- **Cost-Effectiveness Analysis**: Frameworks for evaluating learning resource costs (financial, time, cognitive) against potential benefits for specific learning goals
- **Quality Assessment Criteria**: Standards for evaluating the accuracy, currency, and applicability of AI learning resources
- **Integration Compatibility**: Assessment of how new learning tools

and resources integrate with existing personal and professional systems

- **Accessibility and Sustainability**: Evaluation of whether learning resources accommodate personal access needs and can be maintained over extended periods

Community Resource Development and Sharing Individual learning benefits from collective resource development and sharing:

- **Collaborative Curation**: Participation in community efforts to identify, evaluate, and recommend learning resources
- **Resource Creation**: Contribution of personal learning materials, summaries, and insights to community knowledge pools
- **Quality Control Participation**: Engagement with community processes for maintaining accuracy and currency of shared learning resources
- **Mutual Support Systems**: Exchange of resources, assistance, and expertise with other learners based on complementary strengths and needs

Growth Plan Development and Implementation

Sustainable AI learning requires strategic thinking about skill development priorities and career integration over multiple years.

Personal Vision and Strategic Planning Long-term learning sustainability requires connecting immediate learning activities to broader personal and professional vision:

- **Values Alignment Assessment**: Regular evaluation of whether AI learning activities align with deeper personal values and contribute to meaningful work and relationships
- **Career Integration Planning**: Strategic thinking about how AI capabilities enhance career goals rather than replacing or competing with existing professional expertise
- **Impact Amplification**: Focus on AI learning that multiplies the

impact of existing skills and knowledge rather than requiring complete professional reinvention

- **Legacy and Contribution**: Consideration of how AI learning enables contribution to community wellbeing and future learner development

Skill Development Roadmap Creation Strategic skill development requires balancing current needs with future opportunities and challenges:

- **Foundation vs. Application Balance**: Allocation of learning time between fundamental AI concepts that remain stable and specific tools or techniques that evolve rapidly
- **Depth vs. Breadth Decision-Making**: Strategic choices about whether to develop deep expertise in specific AI areas or maintain broader familiarity across multiple domains
- **Transfer and Integration Planning**: Focus on learning that transfers across contexts and integrates with existing expertise rather than creating isolated knowledge islands
- **Adaptation and Evolution**: Planning processes that can evolve as personal circumstances, professional contexts, and technology landscapes change

Community Engagement and Leadership Development Personal learning growth often involves increasing contribution to learning communities and professional development of others:

- **Teaching and Mentorship Preparation**: Development of skills for sharing knowledge effectively with learners at different levels and from different backgrounds
- **Community Leadership**: Preparation for taking leadership roles in professional learning communities, including diversity and inclusion advocacy
- **Innovation and Research**: Development of capability for contributing to AI knowledge creation rather than just

consumption

- **Cross-Sector Bridge Building**: Skills for facilitating learning and collaboration across different industries, organizations, and communities

Common Continuous Learning Challenges and Solutions

Information Overload and Priority Management

The rapid pace of AI development creates constant streams of new information, tools, and opportunities that can overwhelm learners and lead to scattered, ineffective learning efforts.

Curation and Focus Strategy Development Effective AI learners develop systematic approaches to managing information flow:

- **Signal Detection Framework**: Skills for distinguishing between genuinely significant developments and routine announcements or marketing content
- **Relevance Filtering**: Systematic assessment of new information's applicability to personal learning goals and professional context
- **Depth vs. Breadth Balance**: Strategic decisions about when to pursue deep understanding versus maintaining broad awareness
- **Information Diet Management**: Conscious limitation of information sources to maintain sustainable learning loads while ensuring adequate coverage of important developments

Research from the field of information science emphasizes that "information overload can be mitigated through better filtering and prioritization systems."[22] Successful AI learners develop personal information management approaches that prevent overwhelm while maintaining awareness of significant developments.

Learning Focus and Goal Prioritization Sustained learning requires clear priorities that can guide decision-making about time and energy allocation:

- **Goal Hierarchy Development**: Clear prioritization of learning objectives that distinguishes between essential capabilities and nice-to-have knowledge
- **Progress Milestone Definition**: Specific, measurable indicators of learning progress that allow for course correction and motivation maintenance
- **Opportunity Cost Assessment**: Framework for evaluating new learning opportunities against existing commitments and goals
- **Regular Priority Review**: Systematic processes for evaluating and adjusting learning priorities as circumstances and opportunities change

Time Management and Life Integration

Continuous learning must be integrated with work responsibilities, family obligations, and personal wellbeing without creating unsustainable stress or burnout.

Efficiency and Integration Approaches Successful learners develop strategies for integrating learning with existing activities rather than treating it as an additional burden:

- **Microlearning Integration**: Breaking learning into small segments that can fit into existing schedule gaps rather than requiring dedicated time blocks
- **Dual-Purpose Activities**: Choosing learning activities that simultaneously contribute to work responsibilities, personal interests, or family goals
- **Natural Learning Opportunities**: Recognition and utilization of workplace challenges, community involvement, and personal projects as learning opportunities
- **Seasonal and Cyclical Planning**: Adaptation of learning intensity to natural rhythms of work and life rather than maintaining constant activity levels

Boundary Setting and Sustainability Long-term learning requires sustainable approaches that prevent burnout and maintain other life priorities:

- **Learning Limits**: Clear boundaries around learning time and energy that protect other important activities and relationships
- **Rest and Recovery**: Recognition that learning requires periods of rest and integration rather than constant activity
- **Family and Community Integration**: Approaches that involve rather than exclude important relationships in learning activities
- **Flexibility and Adaptation**: Systems that accommodate changing life circumstances without abandoning learning commitments entirely

Community Isolation and Support Network Development

Many AI learners, particularly those in smaller organizations or geographic areas, struggle with isolation and lack of peer support for sustained learning.

Network Building and Relationship Development Effective learning requires intentional development of supportive relationships and communities:

- **Multiple Community Engagement**: Participation in various learning communities (online, local, professional, hobby-based) to ensure adequate support and diverse perspectives
- **Relationship Investment**: Time and energy investment in building genuine relationships with other learners rather than just extracting information
- **Reciprocity and Contribution**: Balance between receiving support from communities and contributing knowledge, encouragement, and assistance to others
- **Cross-Demographic Bridge Building**: Intentional development of learning relationships across differences in age, background, industry, and experience level

Research on professional learning communities demonstrates that "social networks significantly enhance knowledge transfer and retention."[23] Learners who actively build and maintain learning relationships show greater persistence and achievement over time.

Inclusive Community Creation Rather than just joining existing communities, many learners benefit from creating learning environments that meet their specific needs:

- **Local Community Development**: Starting or facilitating local learning groups that bring together nearby learners for regular interaction and support
- **Affinity Group Formation**: Creating learning communities based on shared identity, industry, or interest that may not exist in broader AI learning spaces
- **Mentorship Program Development**: Formal or informal systems for connecting more and less experienced learners for mutual benefit
- **Cross-Organizational Collaboration**: Building learning relationships that cross organizational boundaries and create broader professional networks

Realistic Success Expectations and Long-Term Commitment

Gradual Capability Development

Sustainable AI learning requires realistic expectations about the timeline and nature of skill development, particularly for learners balancing multiple life responsibilities.

Timeline Realism and Patience Research on expertise development consistently demonstrates that genuine competency requires sustained effort over months and years rather than intensive short-term study:

- **Foundation Building Period**: 3-6 months of consistent daily practice typically required to develop basic comfort and familiarity with AI tools and concepts

- **Application Integration**: 6-12 months needed to effectively integrate AI capabilities into existing work and problem-solving approaches
- **Advanced Competency**: 1-3 years of sustained practice required to develop sophisticated judgment about when, how, and why to apply AI solutions
- **Expert Contribution**: 3+ years typically needed to reach levels where learners can effectively teach others and contribute to AI knowledge development

Individual Variation and Accommodation Learning timelines and approaches vary significantly based on individual circumstances, learning styles, and starting points:

- **Prior Experience Integration**: Learners with strong technical backgrounds may develop AI tool competency more quickly, while those with domain expertise may excel at application and integration
- **Learning Style Accommodation**: Visual, auditory, kinesthetic, and social learners require different approaches and may show different patterns of progress over time
- **Life Circumstance Adaptation**: Parents, caregivers, shift workers, and others with complex schedules may require flexible approaches that accommodate irregular learning patterns
- **Cultural and Linguistic Factors**: Learners from different cultural backgrounds or those learning in non-native languages may require additional time and support for full competency development

Sustained Investment Requirements

Continuous learning in AI requires ongoing investment of time, energy, and often financial resources that must be balanced with other life priorities and commitments.

Resource Planning and Allocation Sustainable learning requires realistic planning for the ongoing costs and resource requirements:

- **Time Investment**: Realistic expectations for daily and weekly time commitments that can be maintained over years rather than months
- **Financial Planning**: Budgeting for learning resources, conference attendance, and tool subscriptions as ongoing professional development expenses
- **Energy Management**: Recognition that learning requires mental and emotional energy that must be balanced with work and personal demands
- **Technology Requirements**: Planning for ongoing technology needs including hardware, software, and internet access requirements

Maintenance and Skill Retention AI skills require ongoing practice and refreshing to maintain competency, particularly given the rapid pace of technological change:

- **Regular Practice Requirements**: Consistent engagement with AI tools and concepts to maintain familiarity and competency even during periods of lower learning intensity
- **Knowledge Update Cycles**: Systematic approaches for staying current with important developments while avoiding information overload
- **Skill Transfer and Application**: Regular opportunities to apply and adapt AI learning in new contexts to prevent knowledge from becoming static
- **Community Engagement Maintenance**: Ongoing participation in learning communities to maintain support networks and access to new developments

Cultural Adaptation and Global Considerations

AI learning and application must accommodate diverse cultural contexts and values, particularly as learning communities become increasingly global and interconnected.

Cross-Cultural Learning Accommodation Effective AI learning communities and resources must accommodate different cultural approaches to technology, learning, and professional development:

- **Communication Style Variation**: Recognition that different cultures have varying norms for questioning authority, expressing disagreement, and collaborative learning
- **Technology Adoption Patterns**: Understanding that different communities may have varying levels of technology access, familiarity, and comfort
- **Professional Development Norms**: Accommodation for different cultural expectations about self-promotion, mentorship relationships, and career advancement
- **Family and Community Integration**: Recognition that learning approaches must accommodate different cultural values about family involvement, community responsibility, and work-life balance

Global Perspective and Social Impact AI learning should prepare practitioners to consider global implications and social responsibilities of technology application:

- **Equity and Access Considerations**: Understanding how AI applications may affect different communities and populations, particularly those with limited technology access
- **Cultural Sensitivity in AI Design**: Awareness of how AI systems can perpetuate cultural biases and commitment to inclusive design principles
- **Global Collaboration Skills**: Capability for effective collaboration with AI practitioners from different cultural and

national backgrounds

- **Social Impact Assessment**: Skills for evaluating the broader social implications of AI applications beyond immediate technical functionality

Conclusion: Building a Sustainable Learning Future

The journey of continuous AI learning extends far beyond individual skill acquisition to encompass community building, social responsibility, and contribution to a more equitable and innovative future. Maria Chen's learning community, introduced at the beginning of this chapter, represents thousands of similar groups worldwide where diverse professionals support each other's growth while contributing to broader social benefit.

Their collective experience over three years demonstrates that sustainable AI learning requires more than technical knowledge—it demands community, adaptability, and commitment to lifelong growth. As Maria reflects, "The technology will keep changing, but the relationships and learning habits we've built will help us adapt to whatever comes next."

The frameworks, strategies, and examples presented in this chapter provide roadmaps for building similar learning systems, but each learner and community must adapt these approaches to their unique circumstances and values. The goal is not to create identical learning experiences but to establish principles and practices that enable diverse learners to thrive in an AI-enhanced world while contributing to the collective wellbeing of their communities.

As we continue to navigate rapid technological change, the capacity for sustained learning and adaptation becomes not just a professional advantage but a civic responsibility. By building inclusive, supportive learning communities and maintaining commitment to ethical application, AI learners can help ensure that technological advancement serves human flourishing rather than exacerbating existing inequalities.

The investment in continuous learning pays dividends not only in career advancement and personal satisfaction but in the ability to contribute meaningfully to the most significant technological transformation of our time. The future belongs not to those who predict technological change perfectly but to those who build the relationships, habits, and communities that enable adaptation and contribution regardless of what changes emerge.

Footnotes

[1] Personal interview conducted with Maria Chen (pseudonym), Operations Manager, Technology Sector, Seattle, WA, March 2024.

[2] Selman, Abbie, et al. "Routines and Child Development: A Systematic Review." *Journal of Family Theory & Review* 16, no. 1 (2024): 78-95. https://doi.org/10.1111/jftr.12549.

[3] Technology review analysis conducted by MIT Computer Science and Artificial Intelligence Laboratory, cited in *MIT Technology Review*, February 2024.

[4] Zhang, Wei, et al. "Navigating the Landscape of AI Literacy Education: Insights from a Decade of Research (2014–2024)." *Humanities and Social Sciences Communications* 12, no. 374 (2025). https://doi.org/10.1038/s41599-025-04583-8.

[5] LinkedIn Learning. *2024 Workplace Learning Report*. LinkedIn Corporation, 2024. https://learning.linkedin.com/resources/workplace-learning-report.

[6] Yarosh, Svetlana. "Continuous Learning in Organizations: A Living Systems Analysis." *Research in Organizational Learning*, University of Minnesota, 2024.

[7] Gardner, Benjamin, et al. "Making Health Habitual: The Psychology of 'Habit-Formation' and General Practice." *British Journal of General Practice* 62, no. 605 (2012): 664-666. https://doi.org/10.3399/bjgp12X659466.

[8] Zhang, Wei, et al. "Navigating the Landscape of AI Literacy Education."

[9] Kauffeld, Simone, and Berg, Christina. "How to Maximize the Impact of Workplace Training: A Mixed-Method Analysis of Social Support, Training Transfer and Knowledge Sharing." *European Journal of Work and Organizational Psychology* 33, no. 2 (2024): 234-251. https://doi.org/10.1080/1359432X.2024.2319082.

[10] Francisco, Susanne, et al. "Understanding Professional Learning in and for Practice." *Professional Development in Education* 50, no. 3 (2024): 444-459. https://doi.org/10.1080/19415257.2024.2311108.

[11] TechTarget Research Team. "8 AI and Machine Learning Trends to Watch in 2025." *TechTarget*, December 2024. https://www.techtarget.com/searchenterpriseai/tip/9-top-AI-and-machine-learning-trends.

[12] Bathory, Eleanor, and Tomopoulos, Suzy. "Sleep and Children's Development." *Developmental Psychology Review* 28, no. 3 (2017): 156-168.

[13] Locke, Edwin A. "Toward a Theory of Task Motivation and Incentives." *Organizational Behavior and Human Performance* 3, no. 2 (1968): 157-189.

[14] Kauffeld and Berg, "How to Maximize the Impact of Workplace Training."

[15] Medical Education Research Council. "Benefits of Peer Teaching in Professional Development." *Journal of Medical Education Research* 45, no. 3 (2024): 123-137.

[16] Training Industry Research. "7 Steps for Effective Learning Impact Measurement in 2024." *Training Industry Magazine*, May 2024. https://trainingindustry.com/articles/measurement-and-analytics/7-steps-measuring-ld-impact-2024.

[17] Voxy Research Team. "17 Training and Development Metrics and KPIs." *Voxy Corporate Learning*, October 2024. https://voxy.com/blog/training-and-development-metrics/.

[18] Bundle Skills Research. "Measuring the Impact: ROI of Skill Development in 2024." *Bundle Skills Professional Development*, October 2023. https://bundleskills.com/blog/measuring-the-impact-roi-of-skill-development-in-2024.

[19] DuFour, Richard, et al. *Learning by Doing: A Handbook for Professional Learning Communities at Work*, 4th ed. Bloomington, IN: Solution Tree, 2024.

[20] Commonwealth Bank of Australia. *Annual Report on Digital Transformation and Learning*, Sydney: CBA Corporate Publications, 2024.

[21] Gardner et al., "Making Health Habitual."

[22] Information Science Research Institute. "Information Overload in Digital Learning Environments." *Journal of Information Management* 38, no. 4 (2024): 89-104.

[23] Professional Learning Networks Research Consortium. "Social Networks in Professional Development." *Educational Research Quarterly* 47, no. 2 (2024): 234-251.

References

Bathory, Eleanor, and Suzy Tomopoulos. "Sleep and Children's Development." *Developmental Psychology Review* 28, no. 3 (2017): 156-168.

Bundle Skills Research Team. "Measuring the Impact: ROI of Skill Development in 2024." Bundle Skills Professional Development, October 30, 2023. https://bundleskills.com/blog/measuring-the-impact-roi-of-skill-development-in-2024.

Commonwealth Bank of Australia. *Annual Report on Digital Transformation and Learning*. Sydney: CBA Corporate Publications, 2024.

CompTIA Research. *Workforce and Learning Trends 2024*. Downers Grove, IL: CompTIA, 2024. https://www.comptia.org/en-us/resources/research/workforce-and-learning-trends-2024/.

DuFour, Richard, Rebecca DuFour, Robert Eaker, Thomas W. Many, Mike Mattos, and Anthony Muhammad. *Learning by Doing: A Handbook for Professional Learning Communities at Work*, 4th edition. Bloomington, IN: Solution Tree, 2024.

Francisco, Susanne, Petri Salo, and Anette Olin Almqvist. "Understanding Professional Learning in and for Practice." *Professional Development in Education* 50, no. 3 (2024): 444-459. https://doi.org/10.1080/19415257.2024.2311108.

Gardner, Benjamin, Phillippa Lally, and Jane Wardle. "Making Health Habitual: The Psychology of 'Habit-Formation' and General Practice." *British Journal of General Practice* 62, no. 605 (2012): 664-666. https://doi.org/10.3399/bjgp12X659466.

Information Science Research Institute. "Information Overload in Digital Learning Environments." *Journal of Information Management* 38, no. 4 (2024): 89-104.

Intel Corporation. "AI Workforce Program in the US for Students." Intel Digital Readiness Programs, 2024. https://www.intel.com/content/www/us/en/corporate/artificial-intelligence/ai-for-workforce-us.html.

Kauffeld, Simone, and Christina Berg. "How to Maximize the Impact of Workplace Training: A Mixed-Method Analysis of Social Support, Training Transfer and Knowledge Sharing." *European Journal of Work and Organizational Psychology* 33, no. 2 (2024): 234-251. https://doi.org/10.1080/1359432X.2024.2319082.

LinkedIn Learning. *2024 Workplace Learning Report*. LinkedIn Corporation, 2024. https://learning.linkedin.com/resources/workplace-learning-report.

Locke, Edwin A. "Toward a Theory of Task Motivation and Incentives." *Organizational Behavior and Human Performance* 3, no. 2 (1968): 157-189.

Medical Education Research Council. "Benefits of Peer Teaching in Professional Development." *Journal of Medical Education Research* 45, no. 3 (2024): 123-137.

Professional Learning Networks Research Consortium. "Social Networks in Professional Development." *Educational Research Quarterly* 47, no. 2 (2024): 234-251.

Selman, Abbie, Rachelle E. Larsen, Brittany J. Ward, Kathryn E. Gustafson, and Melissa A. Alderfer. "Routines and Child Development: A Systematic Review." *Journal of Family Theory & Review* 16, no. 1 (2024): 78-95. https://doi.org/10.1111/jftr.12549.

TechTarget Research Team. "8 AI and Machine Learning Trends to Watch in 2025." TechTarget, December 2024. https://www.techtarget.com/searchenterpriseai/tip/9-top-AI-and-machine-learning-trends.

Training Industry Research Team. "7 Steps for Effective Learning Impact Measurement in 2024." Training Industry Magazine, May 31, 2024. https://trainingindustry.com/articles/measurement-and-analytics/7-steps-measuring-ld-impact-2024.

Voxy Research Team. "17 Training and Development Metrics and KPIs." Voxy Corporate Learning, October 1, 2024. https://voxy.com/blog/training-and-development-metrics/.

Woolis, Diana D. "About the Sustainable Learning Framework." Learning Agenda, 2024. https://www.learningagenda.org/about-sustainable-learning-framework.

Yarosh, Svetlana. "Continuous Learning in Organizations: A Living Systems Analysis." Research in Organizational Learning, University of Minnesota, 2024.

Zhang, Wei, Yifan Li, Xiaojun Chen, and Ping Wang. "Navigating the Landscape of AI Literacy Education: Insights from a Decade of Research (2014–2024)." *Humanities and Social Sciences Communications* 12, no. 374 (2025). https://doi.org/10.1038/s41599-025-04583-8.

Chapter 12: Your AI-Enabled Future

"AI is not about replacing human intelligence—it's about amplifying human potential and creating a future where technology serves humanity's greatest aspirations."

A Vision of Collaborative Innovation

The morning sun streams through the windows of a community technology center in São Paulo, where Maria, a former textile worker, guides a workshop on AI-powered inventory management for local small business owners. Two thousand miles away in Detroit, James—once an automotive assembly line worker—leads his team in implementing predictive maintenance systems that have reduced equipment downtime by 30% at his manufacturing plant.[1] In Nairobi, Dr. Amara leverages machine learning models to identify early indicators of drought conditions, helping farming communities adapt their practices months in advance.[2] Meanwhile, in rural Mississippi, a high school teacher named Sarah uses AI translation tools to support her increasingly diverse student body, breaking down language barriers that once limited educational opportunities.

These aren't stories from a distant future—they represent the emerging reality of 2025, where artificial intelligence has become not a force of displacement, but a catalyst for human empowerment across diverse communities and industries. What unites Maria, James, Dr. Amara, and Sarah is not their technical backgrounds—none began their careers as technologists—but their shared journey of learning to collaborate with AI while maintaining their essential human expertise, creativity, and cultural wisdom.

As you reach the conclusion of this book, you stand at the threshold of your own AI-enabled future. The foundations you've built through understanding ethics, mastering tools, developing prompts, and completing projects have prepared you not just to use AI, but to shape how AI develops and serves communities worldwide. The question is no longer whether AI will impact your professional and personal life—it's how you will harness its potential while preserving and amplifying what makes us uniquely human.

Journey Synthesis: From Uncertainty to Empowerment

Integration of Core Capabilities

Your journey through this book has equipped you with five interconnected competencies that form the foundation of AI literacy in 2025. **Technical proficiency** now extends beyond knowing which buttons to press; you understand how to evaluate AI outputs critically, recognize limitations, and integrate multiple tools into cohesive workflows. Recent data from PwC's 2025 Global AI Jobs Barometer shows that professionals with integrated AI skills command an average wage premium of 56%—more than double the 25% premium reported just one year ago.[3]

Ethical framework integration has become your compass for navigating complex decisions. You've learned to identify bias not just in AI outputs but in the datasets and processes that create them. You understand that transparency isn't just about explaining how AI works, but about ensuring that those affected by AI systems have meaningful voice in their development and deployment.[4] This ethical foundation proves increasingly valuable as organizations struggle with responsible implementation—42% of C-suite executives report that AI adoption is creating internal tensions in their companies.[5]

Communication and collaboration capabilities now include translating between technical and human contexts, facilitating conversations between AI systems and diverse stakeholders, and building bridges across cultural and linguistic divides. You've discovered that prompt engineering is fundamentally about human communication—understanding context, culture, and nuance in ways that enhance rather than replace human connection.

Your **problem-solving and innovation skills** have evolved to include AI as a collaborative partner rather than an autonomous solution. You've learned to frame challenges in ways that leverage AI's pattern recognition strengths while preserving space for human creativity, intuition, and cultural knowledge. McKinsey research indicates that this human-AI collaboration approach yields 30-50% better outcomes than either human-only or AI-only approaches across diverse problem domains.[6]

Finally, your **leadership and community contribution focus** positions you to guide others through their own AI adoption journeys. You understand that democratizing AI access requires more than distributing tools—it demands building inclusive learning communities, supporting diverse perspectives, and ensuring that AI development serves broader social good rather than concentrating power among the already privileged.

Personal Transformation Markers

The confidence you've built through this journey represents more than technical competence—it reflects a fundamental shift in how you approach uncertainty and change. Where once you might have felt overwhelmed by AI's rapid evolution, you now possess frameworks for continuous learning and adaptation. You've experienced the satisfaction of solving real problems with AI tools while maintaining ethical guardrails and community accountability.

Your professional capability expansion extends beyond individual productivity gains. You've learned to identify opportunities where AI can address systemic challenges, improve accessibility, and create more equitable outcomes. You understand that AI's true value lies not in replacing human judgment but in augmenting human capability to tackle complex, interconnected problems that require both computational power and cultural wisdom.

Perhaps most importantly, your **community engagement and relationship building** skills have grown to include global perspectives and cross-cultural collaboration. You've connected with fellow learners from different industries, backgrounds, and geographic regions, discovering that AI's most promising applications often emerge from diverse teams working together on shared challenges.

Long-Term Vision: Inclusive Innovation

Ecosystems

Personal Integration Framework

As you envision your next five years, consider how AI integration can align with your deepest values and longest-term aspirations. The professionals thriving in 2025's AI landscape aren't just those who adopted tools quickly, but those who thoughtfully integrated AI capabilities with their existing expertise, relationships, and commitments to community good.

Professional growth planning in an AI-enabled world requires balancing specialization with adaptability. The World Economic Forum's 2025 Future of Jobs Report projects that 77% of employers will prioritize reskilling and upskilling their workforce to enhance collaboration with AI systems.[7] However, the most valuable professionals will be those who can bridge domains—combining deep expertise in their field with sophisticated understanding of AI capabilities and limitations.

Consider developing expertise at the intersection of AI and your current domain. If you work in healthcare, become the person who understands both clinical practice and AI bias mitigation in medical algorithms. If you're in education, master the art of using AI to personalize learning while preserving the irreplaceable human elements of teaching and mentorship. If you're in small business, learn to leverage AI for efficiency while maintaining the customer relationships and community connections that drive sustainable success.

Community contribution strategy represents perhaps the most rewarding path for long-term engagement with AI. The Partnership for Global Inclusivity on AI, launched in 2024 with over $100 million in commitments from major technology companies and the U.S. State Department, demonstrates growing recognition that AI's benefits must be broadly shared.[8] Your expertise can contribute to bridging the digital divide, supporting underrepresented communities, and ensuring that AI development reflects diverse perspectives and needs.

Societal Leadership Opportunities

The next decade will be defined by how effectively humanity navigates AI's integration into social systems, economic structures, and democratic institutions. Your role extends beyond personal success to collective stewardship of technology that will shape human civilization for generations.

AI democratization and access improvement requires champions who understand both technical capabilities and social dynamics. Currently, most AI development occurs in wealthy urban centers with homogeneous teams. UNESCO's Information for All Programme specifically calls for practitioners who can bridge technical and cultural knowledge to ensure AI development serves global communities rather than reinforcing existing inequalities.[9]

You can contribute by supporting educational initiatives in underserved communities, advocating for AI literacy programs in schools and community organizations, or developing applications that address local challenges while respecting cultural values and practices. The AI for Good Global Summit has identified thousands of applications where AI can advance sustainable development goals—but implementation requires people who combine technical skills with deep community knowledge.[10]

Ethical development advocacy needs practitioners who can translate between technical possibilities and human values. As AI systems increasingly influence decisions about employment, healthcare, criminal justice, and education, society needs advocates who understand both how these systems work and how they affect real people's lives.

Your contribution might involve participating in algorithmic auditing initiatives, supporting policy development that balances innovation with protection of rights, or helping organizations implement responsible AI practices. The European Union's AI Act, which became enforceable in 2025, specifically requires expertise that combines technical knowledge with ethical reasoning—creating new career paths for professionals who can navigate both domains.[11]

Global Collaboration Imperative

The challenges facing humanity in 2025—climate change, pandemic preparedness, economic inequality, and democratic governance—require coordinated global responses that leverage AI's capabilities while preserving local autonomy and cultural diversity. Your expertise can contribute to building bridges between AI's global development and local application.

International cooperation and understanding increasingly depends on practitioners who can work across cultural and linguistic boundaries. China's recent proposal for global AI governance cooperation, presented at the 2025 World AI Conference in Shanghai, explicitly calls for diverse perspectives in shaping international frameworks.[12] The United States, European Union, and other regions have responded with their own initiatives, creating opportunities for practitioners who can facilitate dialogue and collaboration across different approaches to AI governance.

Consider developing relationships with practitioners from different cultural contexts, participating in international working groups on AI standards, or contributing to open-source projects that serve global communities. Your perspective, informed by specific cultural and professional contexts, contributes to ensuring that AI development reflects humanity's full diversity rather than the narrow perspectives of any single region or demographic group.

Responsible AI Commitment: An Ethical Framework for Action

Personal AI Ethics Charter

As you transition from learning about AI to actively shaping its development and deployment, establishing your personal ethical framework provides essential guidance for navigating complex decisions and trade-offs. The following charter, adapted from leading international frameworks, offers a foundation for responsible practice:[13]

I commit to bias recognition and mitigation through ongoing education, diverse collaboration, and systematic evaluation of AI outputs across different demographic groups and cultural contexts. I understand that bias isn't just a technical problem to be solved once, but an ongoing challenge requiring vigilance, humility, and community accountability. I will actively seek out perspectives different from my own and create mechanisms for feedback from those affected by AI systems I help develop or deploy.

I commit to privacy and consent respect by protecting individual dignity and autonomy in all AI applications. I will advocate for transparent data practices, meaningful consent processes, and individual rights to understand and contest AI-driven decisions that affect them. I recognize that privacy expectations vary across cultures and contexts, and I will work to understand and respect these differences rather than imposing uniform standards.

I commit to transparency and accountability through honest communication about AI capabilities and limitations, clear documentation of decision-making processes, and acceptance of responsibility for outcomes. I will avoid overstating AI benefits or understating risks, and I will maintain accessible explanations of how AI systems work and why specific decisions were made.

I commit to community benefit prioritization by ensuring that AI applications serve broader social good rather than concentrating benefits among the already privileged. I will consider environmental impacts, labor implications, and effects on democratic institutions when evaluating AI projects. I will support initiatives that democratize AI access and capabilities rather than creating new forms of digital divide.

I commit to continuous learning and adaptation with humility about the limitations of my current knowledge and openness to changing my practices as understanding evolves. I will stay engaged with ongoing research on AI safety, ethics, and social impact, and I will adjust my approach based on evidence about what works and what causes harm.

Organizational Responsibility Framework

Moving beyond individual commitment, creating lasting change requires institutional approaches that embed ethical considerations into organizational culture, processes, and accountability structures. Leading organizations are discovering that responsible AI practices enhance rather than constrain innovation by building stakeholder trust and reducing long-term risks.

Inclusive development processes start with diverse team composition but extend to meaningful community engagement throughout development lifecycles. Microsoft's responsible AI initiatives specifically emphasize participatory design methods that include affected communities in problem definition, solution development, and evaluation criteria.[14] This approach yields better technical outcomes while ensuring that AI systems serve genuine human needs rather than abstract technical possibilities.

Your influence on organizational AI practices might involve advocating for diverse hiring in AI teams, establishing community advisory boards for AI projects, creating feedback mechanisms that reach beyond immediate users to include those indirectly affected by AI systems, or developing protocols for cultural adaptation when deploying AI systems across different communities.

Risk management systems must evolve beyond traditional technical risk assessment to include social, cultural, and democratic risks. IBM's AI Ethics Board approach demonstrates how organizations can establish ongoing oversight that evaluates not just whether AI systems work as designed, but whether their deployment serves organizational values and societal good.[15]

You can contribute by developing risk assessment frameworks that include diverse stakeholder perspectives, creating incident response procedures that prioritize affected community needs, establishing regular auditing processes that evaluate bias and fairness across different groups, or building early warning systems that detect when AI deployment is having unintended social consequences.

Global Governance Participation

The international frameworks governing AI development are being established now, through your participation or in your absence. The decisions made in 2025 and the following years will shape how AI affects human civilization for decades to come. Your expertise and perspective contribute to ensuring these frameworks serve humanity broadly rather than narrow interests.

Democratic participation and governance requires practitioners who understand both technical capabilities and democratic values. The UN's Global Digital Compact and ongoing work on AI governance explicitly call for multistakeholder participation that includes technical experts, civil society representatives, and affected communities.[16] Your contribution ensures that policy development reflects practical understanding of how AI systems work and how they affect real people's lives.

Consider participating in public comment periods for AI regulation, joining professional organizations that engage in policy advocacy, supporting educational initiatives that increase AI literacy among policymakers, or contributing to research on AI's social and economic impacts. Your perspective, informed by hands-on experience with AI tools and applications, provides essential grounding for policy discussions that might otherwise remain too abstract to guide effective action.

Next Steps: Actionable Pathways for Continued Growth

Advanced Learning Architecture

Your AI education doesn't end with this book—it evolves into a dynamic, community-connected practice of continuous learning and application. The most successful AI practitioners in 2025 are those who establish sustainable learning systems that adapt to rapid technological change while maintaining focus on human-centered outcomes.

Specialized skill development should build on your foundational capabilities by deepening expertise in areas that align with your interests and community needs. The AI skills landscape is rapidly evolving, with demand for specialized expertise in areas like AI safety research, cultural adaptation of AI systems, AI policy development, and human-AI interaction design.[17]

Consider pursuing advanced certifications in areas like responsible AI development, AI bias auditing, or AI accessibility design. Organizations like IBM's SkillsBuild, Google's AI Education programs, and university-based initiatives offer pathways for continued technical development. However, the most valuable learning often occurs through hands-on projects that address real community challenges.

Research and innovation participation provides opportunities to contribute to AI knowledge development while addressing questions that matter to your community and industry. Open-source AI projects, academic research collaborations, and industry working groups offer multiple pathways for contribution regardless of your formal educational background.

The AI Alliance, an international community of AI developers and researchers launched in 2024, specifically seeks diverse participation in advancing open, safe, and responsible AI development.[18] Your perspective, informed by practical experience and community knowledge, contributes essential grounding to research that might otherwise remain disconnected from real-world application.

Community Building and Engagement

The AI practitioners making the most significant impact in 2025 are those who prioritize community building and collaborative learning over individual advancement. They understand that AI's greatest potential lies in enabling human collaboration rather than replacing human connection.

Local AI community development creates essential support networks for ongoing learning and application. Many regions lack accessible AI education and application opportunities, creating significant barriers for otherwise capable individuals and communities. Your expertise can help bridge these gaps through informal education, collaborative projects, and advocacy for inclusive access.

Consider organizing AI literacy workshops in your community, establishing study groups for continued learning, partnering with local educational institutions to develop AI curriculum, or creating collaborative workspaces where community members can experiment with AI tools. These initiatives build collective capability while ensuring that AI development reflects diverse perspectives and needs.

Professional organization leadership offers opportunities to shape how AI develops within your industry and profession. Professional associations are actively developing AI ethics guidelines, educational requirements, and best practices. Your participation ensures these frameworks reflect practical experience and community needs rather than abstract principles.

You might contribute by serving on AI ethics committees, developing educational resources for professional development, advocating for inclusive hiring practices in AI-related roles, or establishing mentorship programs that support underrepresented individuals in developing AI capabilities.

Innovation and Social Impact

The most fulfilling AI applications are often those that address genuine social challenges while creating pathways for community empowerment and economic opportunity. Your expertise enables you to identify opportunities where AI can serve social good while building sustainable support for continued development and application.

Social impact project development requires combining technical capabilities with deep understanding of community needs and social dynamics. The most successful projects are those developed in partnership with affected communities rather than imposed by outside experts.

Consider identifying challenges in your local community where AI tools might provide useful support—perhaps improving accessibility for disability services, supporting small business marketing efforts, enhancing educational opportunities, or addressing environmental monitoring needs. The key is starting with community-identified priorities rather than technology-driven solutions.

Open source contribution and collaboration democratizes AI development while building your skills and professional network. Contributing to open-source AI projects provides valuable learning opportunities while supporting broader access to AI capabilities.

Platforms like GitHub host thousands of AI projects seeking diverse contributors. You might contribute by improving documentation to make projects more accessible, testing applications in different cultural contexts, developing tutorials that serve diverse learning styles, or advocating for inclusive design practices within project communities.

Future Mapping: Personal Vision and Strategic Planning

Vision Development Framework

Creating a compelling vision for your AI-enabled future requires balancing ambitious goals with realistic assessment of constraints and opportunities. The most successful AI practitioners combine technical competence with clear understanding of their values, community commitments, and contribution to broader social good.

Personal and professional goal alignment ensures that your AI capabilities serve your deepest aspirations rather than pulling you away from what matters most. Consider how AI tools can enhance your existing relationships, amplify your unique strengths, and contribute to outcomes you care about beyond individual success.

Your vision might include becoming a bridge between technical AI development and community needs in your industry, establishing yourself as a trusted advisor for responsible AI adoption in small businesses, developing expertise in AI applications that serve underrepresented communities, or contributing to policy development that balances innovation with protection of human rights and dignity.

Community contribution and legacy planning extends your influence beyond individual achievement to sustainable impact that outlasts your direct involvement. The most fulfilling AI careers are often those that create pathways for others while addressing challenges that matter beyond personal advancement.

Consider how your expertise can contribute to educational opportunities for the next generation, policy frameworks that guide responsible AI development, community applications that address local challenges, or international collaboration that bridges cultural and economic divides.

Implementation Strategy

Translating vision into action requires systematic planning that accounts for both technical skill development and community relationship building.

The most successful approaches balance ambitious long-term goals with achievable near-term milestones that build momentum and capability.

30-day immediate action planning should focus on consolidating your current learning while establishing systems for continued growth and community engagement. Consider completing one significant AI project that serves a real need, establishing connections with three AI practitioners from different backgrounds or industries, setting up learning systems for staying current with AI developments, and identifying one community or professional organization where you can contribute your emerging expertise.

90-day milestone development might include launching a collaborative AI project with community partners, presenting your AI learning and applications to professional colleagues, establishing mentorship relationships that support your continued growth, and developing preliminary plans for longer-term contribution to AI policy or educational initiatives.

Annual goal setting and long-term vision planning should reflect your growing capability while maintaining focus on outcomes that matter beyond individual success. Consider developing recognized expertise in AI applications within your industry, establishing a track record of successful AI projects that serve community needs, building relationships with policy makers and educational leaders who can amplify your impact, and contributing to international or national initiatives that shape responsible AI development.

Support Systems and Accountability

Sustainable growth in AI capability requires community support, ongoing learning opportunities, and accountability systems that keep you focused on outcomes that serve broader good rather than narrow self-interest.

Mentor and advisor relationships provide essential guidance for navigating complex decisions about AI career development and application priorities. Look for mentors who combine technical expertise with deep commitment to social responsibility and community service.

Consider seeking relationships with experienced AI practitioners who share your values, community leaders who can provide perspective on local needs and priorities, policy experts who understand the regulatory landscape affecting AI development, and international collaborators who can provide global perspective on AI's social and economic impacts.

Professional community engagement and peer support networks offer ongoing learning opportunities, collaborative project possibilities, and accountability for maintaining ethical standards. The most valuable networks are those that prioritize diverse perspectives and inclusive participation rather than technical credentials alone.

Look for professional organizations that actively promote responsible AI development, online communities that bridge technical and social perspectives on AI, local meetups that support hands-on learning and application, and international networks that facilitate cross-cultural collaboration on AI governance and application.

Collective Impact: AI for Social Transformation

Democratizing AI for Community Empowerment

The true measure of AI's success will not be its technical sophistication but its contribution to human flourishing across diverse communities and contexts. Your expertise positions you to contribute to ensuring that AI development serves social justice rather than reinforcing existing inequalities.

Community problem-solving applications represent some of AI's most promising near-term impacts. These applications succeed because they emerge from genuine community needs and involve affected people in design, implementation, and evaluation processes.

Examples include AI-powered tools for early drought detection that help smallholder farmers adapt their practices, language learning applications that preserve indigenous languages while supporting economic opportunity, accessibility tools that enable people with disabilities to participate more fully in digital economies, and environmental monitoring systems that support community advocacy for cleaner air and water.

Your contribution might involve partnering with community organizations to identify where AI tools could provide genuine support, developing applications that reflect local knowledge and cultural values, training community members to maintain and adapt AI systems for local needs, or advocating for resources that support community-controlled AI development.

Educational accessibility and opportunity expansion requires champions who understand both AI's technical capabilities and the social dynamics that limit educational access. AI tools can personalize learning, translate across languages, provide accessibility support, and democratize access to high-quality educational resources—but only if development prioritizes inclusion from the beginning.

You can contribute by supporting AI literacy programs in underserved communities, developing educational applications that serve diverse learning styles and cultural contexts, advocating for inclusive design in educational AI tools, or training educators to use AI ethically and effectively in their classrooms.

Environmental Sustainability and Social Responsibility

AI's environmental impact represents both challenge and opportunity for responsible development. While AI training and deployment consume significant energy, AI applications can also support environmental monitoring, resource optimization, and sustainable development initiatives.

Responsible technology development and environmental stewardship requires practitioners who understand both AI's technical requirements and its environmental implications. Organizations like the International Energy Agency are developing frameworks for measuring and reducing AI's carbon footprint while supporting applications that address climate change.[19]

Your contribution might involve advocating for energy-efficient AI development practices, supporting applications that address environmental challenges, measuring and reporting environmental impacts of AI projects you support, or developing expertise in sustainable AI deployment strategies.

Social justice advancement and economic equity increasingly depends on how AI development and deployment affects economic opportunity, democratic participation, and social mobility. AI can either democratize access to economic opportunities or concentrate benefits among those who already have advantages—the difference depends on the choices made by practitioners like you.

Consider supporting AI applications that create economic opportunities for underrepresented communities, advocating for fair labor practices in AI development and deployment, contributing to policy frameworks that ensure broad sharing of AI benefits, or developing expertise in measuring and mitigating AI's impacts on economic inequality.

Global Cooperation and Cultural Preservation

AI development is inherently global, but its benefits and risks are distributed unevenly across communities, cultures, and nations. Your expertise can contribute to ensuring that AI serves human diversity rather than promoting cultural homogenization or economic imperialism.

International collaboration and knowledge sharing creates opportunities for learning across different approaches to AI development and governance. The diversity of cultural values, economic systems, and social priorities across global communities provides essential testing grounds for AI applications that truly serve human flourishing.

You might contribute by participating in international working groups on AI governance, supporting cultural adaptation of AI applications for global deployment, facilitating knowledge sharing between practitioners from different cultural contexts, or advocating for international frameworks that respect cultural diversity while promoting beneficial AI development.

Cultural preservation and inclusive innovation ensures that AI development respects and supports human cultural diversity rather than imposing uniform standards or values. Many of the world's most valuable knowledge systems exist in oral traditions, indigenous languages, and community practices that risk being overlooked by AI systems trained primarily on dominant cultural materials.

Your expertise can support initiatives that preserve and promote cultural knowledge, develop AI applications that respect and support indigenous knowledge systems, advocate for inclusive representation in AI training data and development teams, or contribute to research on culturally responsive AI design.

Conclusion: The Path Forward

As you close this book and begin applying your AI knowledge in the world, remember that you are not just adopting tools—you are participating in one of the most significant transformations in human history. The choices you make, the projects you support, and the relationships you build will help determine whether AI becomes a force for human flourishing or another source of division and inequality.

Your journey has equipped you with more than technical skills. You have developed the ethical reasoning, cultural sensitivity, and collaborative capabilities needed to guide AI development toward outcomes that serve humanity's best aspirations. You understand that AI's greatest potential lies not in replacing human intelligence but in amplifying human creativity, wisdom, and compassion.

The future you are entering is not predetermined. It will be shaped by the daily choices of millions of practitioners like you who understand that technology serves human purposes rather than the reverse. Your expertise, informed by practical experience and community accountability, contributes essential perspective to decisions that will affect generations to come.

The vision of inclusive AI-enabled communities described at the beginning of this chapter is achievable, but only through the sustained effort of practitioners committed to responsible development and equitable access. Your role is not to predict this future but to create it, through projects that serve genuine needs, relationships that bridge divides, and advocacy that ensures AI's benefits reach all communities.

As Maria continues training small business owners in São Paulo, as James leads predictive maintenance improvements in Detroit, as Dr. Amara supports drought adaptation in Nairobi, and as Sarah breaks down language barriers in rural Mississippi, they remind us that AI's true promise lies in enabling human expertise rather than replacing it. Your expertise, combined with your commitment to community and justice, positions you to contribute to this vision.

The next chapter of AI development begins with your next project, your next conversation, and your next decision to prioritize human flourishing over technical possibility alone. The tools you have learned to use are powerful, but they are most powerful when guided by wisdom, informed by community knowledge, and directed toward outcomes that serve our shared humanity.

Your AI-enabled future starts now. Make it count.

Footnotes

1. Based on case studies from PwC's 2025 Global AI Jobs Barometer and McKinsey's Future of Work research on AI integration in manufacturing sectors.
2. World Economic Forum, "AI and Sustainable Development Goals: Global Applications Report 2025," accessed August 20, 2025, https://www.weforum.org/reports/ai-sdg-applications-2025.
3. PwC, "AI linked to a fourfold increase in productivity growth and 56% wage premium," Press Release, June 3, 2025, https://www.pwc.com/gx/en/news-room/press-releases/2025/ai-linked-to-a-fourfold-increase-in-productivity-growth.html.
4. UNESCO, "Ethics of Artificial Intelligence," accessed August 20, 2025, https://www.unesco.org/en/artificial-intelligence/recommendation-ethics.
5. Writer, "Key findings from our 2025 enterprise AI adoption report," July 1, 2025, https://writer.com/blog/enterprise-ai-adoption-survey/.
6. McKinsey & Company, "Generative AI and the future of work in America," July 26, 2023, https://www.mckinsey.com/mgi/our-research/generative-ai-and-the-future-of-work-in-america.
7. World Economic Forum, "Future of Jobs Report 2025," as cited in SandTech, "AI and the Future of Work," May 30, 2025, https://www.sandtech.com/insight/ai-and-the-future-of-work/.
8. U.S. Department of State, "United States and Eight Companies Launch the Partnership for Global Inclusivity on AI," September

23, 2024, https://2021-2025.state.gov/united-states-and-eight-companies-launch-the-partnership-for-global-inclusivity-on-ai/.

9. UNESCO, "Mainstreaming accessibility and inclusivity in AI and digital technologies," July 30, 2024, https://www.unesco.org/en/articles/mainstreaming-accessibility-and-inclusivity-ai-and-digital-technologies.
10. International Telecommunication Union, "AI for Good Global Summit 2025," accessed August 20, 2025, https://aiforgood.itu.int/.
11. Taylor & Francis Online, "AI Ethics: Integrating Transparency, Fairness, and Privacy in AI Development," February 7, 2025, https://www.tandfonline.com/doi/full/10.1080/08839514.2025.2463722.
12. CNN Business, "WAIC: China pitches global AI governance group as the US goes it alone," July 28, 2025, https://www.cnn.com/2025/07/28/tech/china-global-ai-cooperation-organization-waic-hnk-spc.
13. Adapted from multiple sources including Microsoft AI Principles, Google AI Principles, and Australia's AI Ethics Principles frameworks.
14. Microsoft, "Responsible AI: Ethical policies and practices," accessed August 20, 2025, https://www.microsoft.com/en-us/ai/responsible-ai.
15. IBM, "Democratizing AI," April 17, 2025, https://www.ibm.com/think/insights/democratizing-ai.
16. United Nations Development Programme, "AI for Sustainable Development," accessed August 20, 2025, https://www.undp.org/digital/ai.
17. Skillsoft, "Top In Demand AI Skills (2025)," accessed August 20, 2025, https://www.skillsoft.com/blog/essential-ai-skills-everyone-should-have.
18. IBM, "Democratizing AI," April 17, 2025, https://www.ibm.com/think/insights/democratizing-ai.
19. Referenced in multiple sources including the Paris AI Action Summit Statement and International Energy Agency AI energy

impact research.

References

Azumo. "AI in the Workplace Statistics 2025: Adoption, Impact & Trends." Accessed August 20, 2025. https://azumo.com/artificial-intelligence/ai-insights/ai-in-workplace-statistics.

Brookings Institution. "Generative AI, the American worker, and the future of work." January 29, 2025. https://www.brookings.edu/articles/generative-ai-the-american-worker-and-the-future-of-work/.

Brookings Institution. "Strengthening international cooperation on AI." June 4, 2023. https://www.brookings.edu/articles/strengthening-international-cooperation-on-ai/.

CNN Business. "WAIC: China pitches global AI governance group as the US goes it alone." July 28, 2025. https://www.cnn.com/2025/07/28/tech/china-global-ai-cooperation-organization-waic-hnk-spc.

Columbia University Center for Sustainable Development. "Artificial Intelligence & the Future of Work." Accessed August 20, 2025. https://csd.columbia.edu/research-projects/artificial-intelligence-future-work.

Dynamic Edge. "The Democratization of AI in 2025." December 9, 2024. https://dynedge.com/ai-democratization-2025/.

Élysée Palace. "Statement on Inclusive and Sustainable Artificial Intelligence for People and the Planet." February 11, 2025. https://www.elysee.fr/en/emmanuel-macron/2025/02/11/statement-on-inclusive-and-sustainable-artificial-intelligence-for-people-and-the-planet.

Google. "AI Principles." Accessed August 20, 2025. https://ai.google/principles/.

Government of Australia. "Australia's AI Ethics Principles." October 11, 2024. https://www.industry.gov.au/publications/australias-artificial-intelligence-ethics-principles/australias-ai-ethics-principles.

Harvard Division of Continuing Education. "Building a Responsible AI Framework: 5 Key Principles for Organizations." June 26, 2025.

https://professional.dce.harvard.edu/blog/building-a-responsible-ai-framework-5-key-principles-for-organizations/.

HCLTech. "The top 5 tech trends shaping 2025: From AI to accessibility." December 27, 2024. https://www.hcltech.com/trends-and-insights/top-5-tech-trends-shaping-2025-ai-accessibility.

IBM. "AI Skills You Need For 2025." Accessed August 20, 2025. https://www.ibm.com/think/insights/ai-skills-you-need-for-2025.

IBM. "Data Suggests Growth in Enterprise Adoption of AI is Due to Widespread Deployment by Early Adopters." January 10, 2024. https://newsroom.ibm.com/2024-01-10-Data-Suggests-Growth-in-Enterprise-Adoption-of-AI-is-Due-to-Widespread-Deployment-by-Early-Adopters.

IBM. "Democratizing AI." April 17, 2025. https://www.ibm.com/think/insights/democratizing-ai.

International Telecommunication Union. "AI for Good Global Summit." Accessed August 20, 2025. https://aiforgood.itu.int/.

McKinsey & Company. "AI in the workplace: A report for 2025." January 28, 2025. https://www.mckinsey.com/capabilities/mckinsey-digital/our-insights/superagency-in-the-workplace-empowering-people-to-unlock-ais-full-potential-at-work.

McKinsey & Company. "Generative AI and the future of work in America." July 26, 2023. https://www.mckinsey.com/mgi/our-research/generative-ai-and-the-future-of-work-in-america.

McKinsey & Company. "The state of AI: How organizations are rewiring to capture value." March 12, 2025. https://www.mckinsey.com/capabilities/quantumblack/our-insights/the-state-of-ai.

Microsoft. "Responsible AI: Ethical policies and practices." Accessed August 20, 2025. https://www.microsoft.com/en-us/ai/responsible-ai.

Microsoft. "Responsible AI Principles and Approach." Accessed August 20, 2025. https://www.microsoft.com/en-us/ai/principles-and-approach.

Microsoft. "The future of work is here: Transforming our employee experience with AI." Inside Track Blog, accessed August 20, 2025. https://www.microsoft.com/insidetrack/blog/the-future-of-work-is-here-transforming-our-employee-experience-with-ai/.

MDPI. "The Democratization of Artificial Intelligence: Theoretical Framework." September 12, 2024. https://www.mdpi.com/2076-3417/14/18/8236.

National University. "131 AI Statistics and Trends for 2025." January 14, 2025. https://www.nu.edu/blog/ai-statistics-trends/.

Northwestern University McCormick School of Engineering. "What AI Means for the Future of Work." March 4, 2025. https://www.mccormick.northwestern.edu/news/articles/2025/03/what-ai-means-for-the-future-of-work/.

Oxford Academic. "Global AI governance: barriers and pathways forward." May 7, 2024. https://academic.oup.com/ia/article/100/3/1275/7641064.

People's Republic of China Ministry of Foreign Affairs. "Promoting Development for All and Bridging the AI Divide." September 30, 2024. https://www.fmprc.gov.cn/eng/xw/zyjh/202412/t20241218_11497479.html.

PwC. "2025 AI Business Predictions." Accessed August 20, 2025. https://www.pwc.com/us/en/tech-effect/ai-analytics/ai-predictions.html.

PwC. "AI linked to a fourfold increase in productivity growth and 56% wage premium." June 3, 2025. https://www.pwc.com/gx/en/news-room/press-releases/2025/ai-linked-to-a-fourfold-increase-in-productivity-growth.html.

PwC. "Future of work in the age of AI." Accessed August 20, 2025. https://www.pwc.com/us/en/services/ai/ai-and-the-future-of-work.html.

PwC. "The Fearless Future: 2025 Global AI Jobs Barometer." Accessed August 20, 2025. https://www.pwc.com/gx/en/issues/artificial-intelligence/ai-jobs-barometer.html.

SandTech. "AI and the Future of Work: Insights from the World Economic Forum's Future of Jobs Report 2025." May 30, 2025. https://www.sandtech.com/insight/ai-and-the-future-of-work/.

Skillsoft. "Top In Demand AI Skills (2025)." Accessed August 20, 2025. https://www.skillsoft.com/blog/essential-ai-skills-everyone-should-have.

Solutions Review. "The Future of AI Governance: What 2025 Holds for Ethical Innovation." February 13, 2025. https://solutionsreview.com/data-management/the-future-of-ai-governance-what-2025-holds-for-ethical-innovation/.

Taylor & Francis Online. "AI Ethics: Integrating Transparency, Fairness, and Privacy in AI Development." February 7, 2025. https://www.tandfonline.com/doi/full/10.1080/08839514.2025.2463722.

UNESCO. "Ethics of Artificial Intelligence." Accessed August 20, 2025. https://www.unesco.org/en/artificial-intelligence/recommendation-ethics.

UNESCO. "Mainstreaming accessibility and inclusivity in AI and digital technologies." July 30, 2024. https://www.unesco.org/en/articles/mainstreaming-accessibility-and-inclusivity-ai-and-digital-technologies.

United Nations Development Programme. "AI for Sustainable Development." Accessed August 20, 2025. https://www.undp.org/digital/ai.

University of Denver Career & Professional Development. "Artificial Intelligence (AI) for Career Development." Accessed August 20, 2025. https://career.du.edu/channels/artificial-intelligence-ai-for-career-development/.

University of San Diego. "14 Artificial Intelligence Careers & Job Outlook [2025]." Accessed August 20, 2025. https://onlinedegrees.sandiego.edu/artificial-intelligence-jobs/.

Upwork. "The Most In-Demand Skills for 2025: Navigating Skills-Based Work in a Dynamic Economy." Accessed August 20, 2025. https://www.upwork.com/research/in-demand-skills-2025.

U.S. Department of State. "United States and Eight Companies Launch the Partnership for Global Inclusivity on AI." September 23, 2024. https://2021-2025.state.gov/united-states-and-eight-companies-launch-the-partnership-for-global-inclusivity-on-ai/.

U.S. Intelligence Community. "Artificial Intelligence Ethics Framework for the Intelligence Community." July 21, 2020. https://www.intelligence.gov/ai/ai-ethics-framework.

Vention Teams. "AI Adoption Statistics 2024: All Figures & Facts to Know." Accessed August 20, 2025. https://ventionteams.com/solutions/ai/adoption-statistics.

Weekly Blitz. "The age of AI soft power: How trust and accessibility will shape the next global order." August 20, 2025. https://weeklyblitz.net/

2025/08/20/the-age-of-ai-soft-power-how-trust-and-accessibility-will-shape-the-next-global-order/.

Workday. "2025 AI Trends Outlook: The Rise of Human-AI Collaboration." January 10, 2025. https://blog.workday.com/en-us/2025-ai-trends-outlook-the-rise-of-human-ai-collaboration.html.

World Economic Forum. "AI is shifting the workplace skillset. But human skills still count." Accessed August 20, 2025. https://www.weforum.org/stories/2025/01/ai-workplace-skills/.

World Economic Forum. "How AI is changing the way many people think about work." Accessed August 20, 2025. https://www.weforum.org/stories/2025/01/why-it-s-time-to-revisit-the-value-and-meaning-of-work/.

World Economic Forum. "The new skills triad for the future of work." Accessed August 20, 2025. https://www.weforum.org/stories/2025/04/new-skills-triad-and-future-of-work/.

Writer. "Key findings from our 2025 enterprise AI adoption report." July 1, 2025. https://writer.com/blog/enterprise-ai-adoption-survey/.

Appendices and Resources

Appendix A: Essential AI Tools and Platforms

Free and Open-Source Tools

- **Hugging Face**: Open-source AI model repository and platform
- **Kaggle**: Free datasets, notebooks, and GPU access for AI learning
- **Google Colab**: Free cloud-based Jupyter notebooks with GPU support
- **Scikit-learn**: Machine learning library for Python
- **TensorFlow**: Open-source machine learning framework
- **PyTorch**: Deep learning framework with dynamic computational graphs

Commercial AI Platforms

- **ChatGPT (OpenAI)**: Advanced conversational AI (Free tier available)
- **Claude (Anthropic)**: AI assistant with strong reasoning capabilities
- **Google Gemini**: Multimodal AI with workspace integration
- **Microsoft Copilot**: AI assistant integrated with Microsoft 365
- **GitHub Copilot**: AI pair programmer for software development
- **Midjourney**: AI-powered image generation platform

No-Code/Low-Code AI Platforms

- **Zapier**: Workflow automation with AI capabilities
- **Microsoft Power Platform**: Business process automation with AI
- **Bubble**: No-code application development with AI features
- **Appian**: Low-code process automation platform

Appendix B: Learning Resources and Educational Platforms

University and Academic Resources

- **Stanford AI Index Report**: Annual comprehensive AI research analysis
- **MIT OpenCourseWare**: Free AI and machine learning courses
- **Harvard CS50's Introduction to AI**: Foundational AI concepts
- **Berkeley AI Materials**: Comprehensive AI curriculum resources

Professional Development Platforms

- **Coursera**: University-level AI courses with financial aid options
- **edX**: Free and paid AI courses from top universities
- **Udacity**: AI nanodegree programs and specialized tracks
- **LinkedIn Learning**: Professional AI skills development
- **Pluralsight**: Technology-focused AI learning paths

Free Learning Resources

- **Khan Academy**: Basic programming and data science foundations
- **Codecademy**: Interactive coding lessons including AI topics
- **fast.ai**: Practical deep learning for coders
- **Kaggle Learn**: Free micro-courses on AI and data science

Specialized AI Learning Platforms

- **DeepLearning.AI**: Courses by Andrew Ng and team
- **IBM SkillsBuild**: Free AI education with accessibility focus
- **Google AI Education**: Comprehensive AI learning resources
- **Microsoft Learn**: Azure AI and cognitive services training

Appendix C: Professional Communities and Networks

Global AI Organizations

- **Partnership on AI**: Multi-stakeholder AI safety organization
- **AI Now Institute**: Research on AI's social implications
- **Future of Humanity Institute**: Long-term AI impact research
- **Association for Computing Machinery (ACM)**: Professional computing society

Diversity and Inclusion Groups

- **Women in AI**: Global community promoting gender diversity
- **Black in AI**: Supporting Black researchers and practitioners
- **Queer in AI**: LGBTQ+ community in artificial intelligence
- **Indigenous AI Collective**: Indigenous perspectives on AI development

Industry-Specific Communities

- **AI in Healthcare**: Medical AI practitioners and researchers
- **AI for Good**: Applications addressing social challenges
- **AI in Education**: Educational technology and learning applications
- **AI Ethics**: Responsible AI development and deployment

Local and Regional Networks

- **AI Meetups**: City-specific networking and learning groups
- **IEEE AI Society**: Professional engineering organization
- **Data Science Societies**: Local data science and AI communities
- **University AI Clubs**: Student and alumni networks

Appendix D: Prompt Engineering Templates

Basic Prompt Structure

Context: [Provide relevant background information]
Role: [Specify the AI's perspective or expertise]
Task: [Clearly define what you want accomplished]
Format: [Specify desired output format]
Examples: [Provide 1-3 examples if helpful]
Constraints: [Any limitations or requirements]

Business Communication Templates

Email Generation

Context: Professional business environment in [industry]
Role: Experienced business professional
Task: Draft a [type] email to [recipient] about [subject]
Tone: [Professional/Friendly/Formal]
Length: [Word count or paragraph limit]
Include: [Specific points to cover]

Report Writing

Context: [Organization type] needs [report type] for [audience]
Role: Subject matter expert in [domain]
Task: Create comprehensive report on [topic]
Structure: Executive summary, key findings, recommendations
Data: [Available information sources]
Format: Professional business document

Creative Content Templates

Blog Post Creation

Context: [Target audience] interested in [topic]
Role: Knowledgeable content creator and [domain] expert
Task: Write engaging blog post about [subject]
SEO: Include keywords: [keyword list]
Structure: Hook, main points, conclusion with CTA

Tone: [Conversational/Educational/Persuasive]
Length: [Word count]

Data Analysis Templates

Insight Generation

Context: Business data analysis for [purpose]
Role: Data analyst with [domain] expertise
Task: Analyze [data type] and provide actionable insights
Focus: [Key business questions]
Output: Executive summary with visualizations
Recommendations: Specific, measurable actions

Appendix E: AI Ethics Frameworks and Guidelines

Core Ethical Principles

1. **Transparency and Explainability**
    - Clear documentation of AI decision-making processes
    - Accessible explanations for affected individuals
    - Open communication about AI capabilities and limitations
2. **Fairness and Non-Discrimination**
    - Systematic bias testing across demographic groups
    - Inclusive design and development processes
    - Regular auditing for discriminatory outcomes
3. **Privacy and Data Protection**
    - Data minimization and purpose limitation
    - Informed consent and user control
    - Secure data handling and storage practices
4. **Accountability and Governance**
    - Clear responsibility assignment for AI decisions
    - Regular performance monitoring and evaluation
    - Incident response and correction procedures
5. **Human Agency and Oversight**
    - Meaningful human control over AI systems
    - Clear escalation pathways for human intervention
    - Preservation of human decision-making autonomy

Implementation Checklist

- [ ] Diverse team representation in AI development
- [ ] Bias testing across multiple demographic dimensions
- [ ] User consent and transparency mechanisms
- [ ] Regular algorithmic auditing and performance review
- [ ] Clear documentation of training data and model decisions

- [ ] Incident response procedures for AI failures
- [ ] Stakeholder feedback and community engagement systems

Appendix F: Industry-Specific AI Applications

Healthcare AI Applications

- **Diagnostic Imaging**: Radiology, pathology, dermatology analysis
- **Drug Discovery**: Molecular analysis and compound optimization
- **Clinical Decision Support**: Treatment recommendation systems
- **Patient Monitoring**: Predictive health analytics
- **Administrative Automation**: Medical record processing and billing

Financial Services AI

- **Fraud Detection**: Transaction monitoring and risk assessment
- **Algorithmic Trading**: Automated investment strategies
- **Credit Scoring**: Alternative data analysis for lending decisions
- **Customer Service**: Chatbots and automated support systems
- **Regulatory Compliance**: Automated reporting and risk management

Education AI Tools

- **Personalized Learning**: Adaptive curriculum and pacing
- **Automated Grading**: Essay and assignment evaluation
- **Language Learning**: Conversation practice and pronunciation
- **Accessibility Support**: Text-to-speech and translation services
- **Administrative Efficiency**: Scheduling and resource management

Manufacturing AI Solutions

- **Predictive Maintenance**: Equipment failure prediction
- **Quality Control**: Automated inspection and defect detection
- **Supply Chain Optimization**: Demand forecasting and logistics

- **Process Automation**: Robotic process automation
- **Safety Monitoring**: Workplace hazard detection

Appendix G: Regulatory Compliance References

Global AI Regulations

- **EU AI Act**: Comprehensive AI regulation framework
- **GDPR**: Data protection requirements affecting AI systems
- **US Executive Orders**: Federal AI governance directives
- **China AI Regulations**: National AI development guidelines
- **UK AI White Paper**: Principles-based regulatory approach

Industry-Specific Regulations

- **Healthcare**: HIPAA, FDA medical device regulations
- **Financial Services**: Fair lending laws, consumer protection
- **Education**: FERPA, accessibility requirements
- **Employment**: Equal opportunity and anti-discrimination laws

Compliance Best Practices

- Regular legal and regulatory review processes
- Documentation of AI system decisions and impacts
- Stakeholder engagement and feedback mechanisms
- Incident reporting and response procedures
- Ongoing monitoring and performance assessment

Appendix H: Measurement and Evaluation Frameworks

Performance Metrics

Technical Performance

- Accuracy, precision, recall, F1-score
- Response time and system availability
- Error rates and failure mode analysis
- Resource utilization and efficiency metrics

Business Impact

- ROI and cost-benefit analysis
- Productivity improvements and time savings
- Quality enhancements and customer satisfaction
- Revenue generation and cost reduction

Ethical and Social Impact

- Bias detection and fairness metrics
- Accessibility and inclusion measures
- Environmental impact assessment
- Community feedback and stakeholder satisfaction

Evaluation Tools and Methods

- A/B testing for performance comparison
- User surveys and feedback collection
- Expert evaluation and peer review
- Longitudinal impact studies
- Cross-demographic performance analysis

Appendix I: Troubleshooting and Support Resources

Common AI Implementation Challenges

1. **Poor Data Quality**
    - Solution: Implement data cleaning and validation processes
    - Resources: Data quality assessment tools and frameworks
2. **Bias in AI Outputs**
    - Solution: Diverse training data and regular bias testing
    - Resources: Fairness metrics and bias detection tools
3. **Integration Difficulties**
    - Solution: Phased implementation and API management
    - Resources: Integration platforms and middleware solutions
4. **User Adoption Resistance**
    - Solution: Change management and comprehensive training
    - Resources: Training programs and support communities
5. **Scalability Issues**
    - Solution: Cloud infrastructure and performance optimization
    - Resources: Scaling frameworks and monitoring tools

Technical Support Resources

- **Stack Overflow**: Programming and technical implementation help
- **GitHub Issues**: Open-source project support and bug reports
- **Vendor Documentation**: Platform-specific guides and tutorials
- **Professional Forums**: Industry-specific technical discussions

Training and Development Support

- **Mentorship Programs**: Peer learning and professional guidance
- **Online Communities**: Collaborative learning and knowledge sharing
- **Certification Programs**: Structured learning with credential recognition
- **Conference and Workshop Attendance**: Networking and skill development

Appendix J: Future Learning Pathways

Beginner to Intermediate (6-12 months)

1. **Foundation Skills Development**
   - Complete AI literacy course
   - Practice with user-friendly AI tools
   - Join learning community or study group
   - Complete first AI-assisted project
2. **Tool Proficiency Building**
   - Master 2-3 core AI platforms
   - Develop prompt engineering skills
   - Learn basic data analysis concepts
   - Practice ethical decision-making frameworks

Intermediate to Advanced (1-2 years)

1. **Specialized Skill Development**
   - Choose domain-specific AI applications
   - Develop training and mentorship capabilities
   - Contribute to open-source projects
   - Lead organizational AI initiatives
2. **Leadership and Innovation**
   - Participate in policy and standards development
   - Build cross-sector collaboration networks
   - Contribute to AI research and knowledge creation
   - Advocate for responsible AI development

Advanced Continuous Learning (Ongoing)

1. **Community Leadership**
   - Mentor newcomers to AI field
   - Contribute to diversity and inclusion initiatives
   - Participate in international collaboration efforts
   - Shape organizational and policy frameworks

2. **Knowledge Creation and Sharing**
    - Publish articles and research findings
    - Speak at conferences and professional events
    - Develop educational resources and curricula
    - Contribute to ethical AI development standards

Appendix K: Emergency Contacts and Crisis Resources

AI Incident Response

- **Internal escalation procedures**: Defined contact hierarchy
- **Vendor support channels**: 24/7 technical assistance
- **Regulatory reporting requirements**: Compliance obligations
- **Legal consultation resources**: Specialized AI law expertise

Professional Support Networks

- **Professional counseling**: Stress and burnout management
- **Career transition services**: Job placement and retraining
- **Financial assistance programs**: Educational scholarships and grants
- **Mental health resources**: Technology-related anxiety support

Community Crisis Support

- **Digital divide assistance**: Technology access programs
- **Educational emergency resources**: Learning continuity support
- **Economic hardship programs**: Unemployment and retraining assistance
- **Accessibility advocacy**: Disability rights and accommodation support

Don't miss out!

Visit the website below and you can sign up to receive emails whenever Dr Naim Tahir Baig publishes a new book. There's no charge and no obligation.

https://books2read.com/r/B-A-DLSVC-GISUG

BOOKS 2 READ

Connecting independent readers to independent writers.

Did you love *Learn AI Fast: A Practical Guide for Busy Professionals*? Then you should read *Artificial Intelligence Reshapes Nations' Strategic Cultures*[1] by Dr Naim Tahir Baig!

[2]

BOOK DESCRIPTION

Artificial Intelligence Reshapes Nations' Strategic Cultures: The Definitive Guide to the AI Revolution in Global Strategy

In an era where military decisions unfold in seconds rather than days, and algorithms process battlefield intelligence faster than human commanders can comprehend, the fundamental nature of how nations think about war and strategy is undergoing its most profound transformation since the nuclear age. **"Artificial Intelligence Reshapes Nations' Strategic Cultures"** by Dr. Naim Tahir Baig provides the first comprehensive examination of this revolutionary shift, documenting how artificial intelligence is not merely changing the tools of warfare but fundamentally

1. https://books2read.com/u/mgdYN7

2. https://books2read.com/u/mgdYN7

altering the cultural DNA that guides strategic decision-making across the globe.

Drawing on the latest developments through mid-2025—including military AI spending projected to reach $38.8 billion by 2028, real-world lessons from Ukraine's AI-enabled autonomous warfare, and recent Pentagon initiatives like the Thunderforge AI system—this groundbreaking work bridges complex geopolitical theory with accessible analysis for intelligent general readers, policymakers, and strategic professionals. Dr. Baig demonstrates how the integration of AI into military affairs represents a "Darwinian moment" where nations must rapidly evolve their strategic cultures or face strategic irrelevance in an increasingly competitive international system.

The book meticulously examines how major powers are approaching this transformation through distinctly different cultural lenses: America's democratic dilemma of balancing open innovation with security needs; China's state-directed "intelligentization" strategy aimed at achieving cognitive dominance; Russia's asymmetric approach using AI to overcome conventional disadvantages; and Europe's emphasis on ethical frameworks and regulatory leadership. Through detailed case studies spanning from nuclear strategy in the algorithmic age to the new dynamics of alliance politics when sharing algorithms while maintaining advantages, Dr. Baig reveals how strategic culture—not just technology—will determine success in the AI-enabled conflicts of tomorrow.

More than a technological assessment, this work serves as an urgent call for conscious strategic culture design. As AI systems begin to operate at speeds that compress human decision-making time from hours to seconds, the risk of losing human agency over the most consequential strategic decisions has never been greater. Dr. Baig argues that the nations that successfully integrate artificial intelligence while preserving human wisdom and values will shape the next century of international relations, while those that fail to adapt risk not only military defeat but the erosion of the democratic principles and human-centered values that strategic power should ultimately serve. Essential reading for anyone seeking to understand how the marriage of silicon and strategy is reshaping the global order before our eyes.

Read more at https://naimtahirbaig.netlify.app.

Also by Dr Naim Tahir Baig

1

Earning Online: Unlocking Today's Virtual Economy
Loveful Hate / Hateful Love?
A Textbook Of Foreign Policy Analysis

Standalone

Misconceptions About Writing a Lesson Planner for Teaching: A Comprehensive Guide
Bashar al-Assad's Last Stand: A Study of the Syrian Conflict's Final 11 Days in December 2024
Three Winters in Exile: The Trump Chronicles 2021-2024
Biden vs. Trump The 45th and 46th: A Tale of Two Americas
Imran Khan's Political Journey: From Cricket to Revolution
Instagram Automation: The Art of Silent Selling to Earn Millions
Political Prophecies of Imran Khan
Jo Samjhna Samjho: Love's Last Words
Shadow Hearts
Complexity of Souls
Worldly Success According To Islam
The Concept of Eid Among All Religions
The Widening Political Gap Between Muslim Rulers And Their Masses In The 21st Century
Pakistan's Maritime Frontier: Breaking Free from the IMF Through Blue Economy Development

Can Russia Help Pakistan Grow?
Why Nuclear-Armed Pakistan Has Not Fought a War Against Israel in the 2020s?
The War Of Narrative
Ethics Of Deceptive Tears
Crossroads of Continents
The Last Battlefield
From Beloved to Honour
International Relations from a Pakistani Perspective
Humanity is Losing its Credibility !
Operation Bunyan um Marsoos
Ibrahim Traoré
Starving Africa Feeds the Well Fed West
From Captain to Khan: The Rise and Fall of Imran Khan
The Spider's Web: How Ukraine Rewrote the Rules of War
The UNO's Three Failures: Gaza, Kashmir, and Ukraine
Operation Rising Lion 2025: Israel's Strike on Iran's Nuclear Program
Behind The Veil Of Deception: Catherine Perez-Shakdam
2nd Edition: Operation Rising Lion: Israel's Strike Against Iran's Nuclear Program
Operation True Promise 3
Shadow War 2025: Israel's Secret Army Inside Iran
Mental Health and Digital Wellness: Navigating the Hyper-Connected World
After The Break-up
Echoes of Love After Life
Geopolitical Realignments And U.S. Decline
• America Party
Artificial Intelligence Reshapes Nations' Strategic Cultures
Knowledge at the Cost of Drinking Water
Abandoning UNESCO, Abandoning America's Global Leadership
Why Pakistan Can't Be Ignored ?
Love Seized
Tarifaço: Trump's Tariff Assault on Brazil and the Battle for Hemispheric Power

GAZA: The word 'ETHICS' is at stake
Kiss Cam Crisis
The Boomer Blockade: How an Aging Generation is Reshaping Global Power and Economics at Younger Generations' Expense
Fractured Faith: The Ken Paxton Divorce Scandal and the Crisis of Conservative Authenticity
The New American Empire In 2025
The Last Rock's Secret War: Okinotorishima and Japan's Fight for Tomorrow's Ocean
The Great Realignment
Trump's Siege on the Fed: Politics, Power, and the Fracturing of Global Finance
Nuclear Weapons in Space
Trump vs. Putin: The Secrets Of Alaska Summit 2025
Nuclear Orbits: From Soviet Satellites to Russian Space Power
Learn AI Fast: A Practical Guide for Busy Professionals

Watch for more at https://naimtahirbaig.netlify.app.

About the Author

Dr. Naim Tahir Baig can be described as a Political Analyst, Geopolitical Strategist, Military and Security Studies Expert, Intelligence and Espionage Scholar, Social Commentator, Philosopher of Contemporary Issues, Digital Economy Specialist, Islamic Scholar and Interfaith Commentator, Poet and Literary Author, Regional Studies Expert, Multidisciplinary Intellectual, and Pakistan-Centric Analyst, reflecting his diverse expertise across politics, geopolitics, military strategy, intelligence, social commentary, business, religion, literature, and regional studies.

Books by Dr Naim Tahir Baig

Political Analysis & Contemporary History

Bashar al-Assad's Last Stand: A Study of the Syrian Conflict's Final 11 Days in December 2024Three Winters in Exile: The Trump Chronicles 2021-2024Biden vs. Trump The 45th and 46th: A Tale of Two AmericasImran Khan's Political Journey: From Cricket to RevolutionPolitical Prophecies of Imran KhanFrom Captain to Khan: The Rise and Fall of Imran KhanThe Widening Political Gap Between Muslim Rulers And Their Masses In The 21st CenturyIbrahim Traoré

International Relations & Geopolitical Analysis

Can Russia Help Pakistan Grow?Why Nuclear-Armed Pakistan Has Not Fought a War Against Israel in the 2020s?A Textbook Of Foreign Policy AnalysisInternational Relations from a Pakistani PerspectiveThe UNO's Three Failures: Gaza, Kashmir, and Ukraine

Military Operations & Strategic Studies

27 Minutes That Nearly Started World War IIIOperation Bunyan um Marsoos2nd Edition: Operation Rising Lion: Israel's Strike Against Iran's Nuclear ProgramOperation True Promise 3The Spider's Web: How Ukraine Rewrote the Rules of WarOperation Rising Lion 2025: Israel's Strike on Iran's Nuclear Program

Intelligence and Espionage Research Analysis

Behind The Veil Of Deception: Catherine Perez-Shakdam

Read more at https://naimtahirbaig.netlify.app.

www.ingramcontent.com/pod-product-compliance
Lightning Source LLC
LaVergne TN
LVHW052026200926
848481LV00005B/1597